D1132535

PUBLIC LIBRARY

Presented to the
Library
by

PubWest

WITHDRAWN

Lake Oswego Public Library
706 Fourth Street
Lake Oswego, Oregon 97034

57603706

the FIELD GUIDE *to Drinking in* AMERICA: A TRAVELER'S HANDBOOK TO STATE LIQUOR LAWS

BY NIKI GANONG

Overcup Press

Art Direction & Design by Cole Gerst / option-g

ISBN:978-0983491729

Overcup Press, Portland, OR 97206
Overcupbooks.com
© 2015 Overcup Press
All rights reserved. Published 2015

Illustrations © Cole Gerst / option-g

Kurt Vonnegut quote from Breakfast of Champions used by permission of the Trust u/w of Kurt Vonnegut, Jr.

Printed in China.

Disclaimer:
The information presented in The Field Guide to Drinking in America: A Traveler's Guide to State Liquor Laws should not be considered legal advice. Neither the author nor the editors are lawyers. While every effort to was made to ensure the accuracy of statements of fact before going to press, the information presented here is for information and entertainment purposes only.

All intellectual property including, but not limited to, copyrights and trademarks remain the property of their respective holders and are only used for information and entertainment purposes to identify a product and refer to its long-standing and proud association with the state. No endorsement of any type should be implied.

- *Naragansett Brewing* is a trademark of The Naragansett Brewing Company
- *Fee Brothers* is a trademark of Fee Brothers
- *Yuengling* is a registered trademark of D.G. Yuengling & Son Inc.
- *Krueger* is a registered trademark of Krueger Brewing Company
- *VW* trademarks are owned by the Volkswagen Corporation Wolfsburg, GERMANY
- *National Bohemian* and the Natty Bo logo is a registered trademark of Pabst Brewing Company
- *Miller* is a registered trademark of MillerCoors, LLC
- *Brew Thru* is a registered trademark of Branash Enterprises, Inc.
- *Cheerwine* is a registered trademark of Carolina Beverage Corporation
- *Coors* is a registered trademark of MillerCoors, LLC
- *Auburn University Tigers* is a registered trademark of Auburn University
- *University of Alabama Crimson Tide* is a registered trademark of Board of Trustees of the University of Alabama
- *Clyde May's* is a registered trademark of Conecuh Ridge Distillery, Inc.
- *Top of the Hops Beer Festival* is a registered service mark of Red Mountain Entertainment
- *Tabasco* is a registered trademark of the McIlhenny Company
- *Peychauds* is a registered trademark of Sazerac Co., Inc.
- The image of "Jack on the Rocks" is an artist's sketch of the statue of Jack Daniel at the Jack Daniels Distillery in Lynchburg, TN.
- *Budweiser* is a registered trademark of the Anheuser-Busch Company
- *Mountain Valley Spring Water* is a registered trademark of Mountain Valley Spring Company, LLC
- *Rock Town Distillery* is a registered trademark of Rock Town Distillery, Inc.
- *Mountain Dew* is a registered trademark of PepsiCo, Inc.
- *Boscos* is a registered trademark of Roma Pomodori, Inc
- *Stroh's* is a registered trademark of Pabst Brewing Co., LLC
- *Schlitz* is a registered trademark of Pabst Brewing Co., LLC
- *Hamm's* and the Hamm's Bear are registered trademarks of MillerCoors, LLC
- *Rainier* is a registered trademark of Pabst Brewing Co., LLC

The opinions expressed by the bartenders are their own and do not necessarily represent the views of the author or Overcup Press.

Please enjoy alcohol responsibly.

DEDICATION

I am legally drunk with gratitude to the barkeeps, brewers, vintners and distillers for their advice and education on my journeys. And I'd also like to raise a glass to the friends and family who bellied up to the bar and bent their elbows beside me. Finally, here's to you, the tippling traveler. I'll see you at the pub.

INTRODUCTION

Welcome to America! As anyone who has traveled throughout our great nation can tell you, our liquor laws are unpredictable. When Prohibition was repealed, states, counties, and even towns were left to regulate how alcohol was bought and sold within their borders. Ever since, many a surprised traveler has been caught off guard by an unexpectedly early last call, a sad and liquorless Sunday, or the choice of 3.2% beer or nothing at all. Almost everyone has a story about this.

This book began with the simple idea that travelers needed a different type of guidebook to keep them informed about how to buy alcohol while on the road. We all know how things are in our home state because these laws have a large influence on local culture. People in Indiana buy their "Sunday beer" on Saturday, Arkansans aren't puzzled by wet and dry counties, and Coloradans remember which specific chain store holds the liquor license. So, this is for those of us who are just passing through—which is to say, all of us at some point or another.

This book is more than just a collection of laws and regulations; it also tells the story of America through alcohol. From the first New England colonists who literally had to start making alcohol from scratch, to the German immigrants of the Midwest who industrialized brewing in the nineteenth century, to the California vintners who currently produce as much wine as their European rivals, there is a narrative complete with people, places, conflicts, and values, all connected by the thread of alcohol. The states are grouped regionally and arranged from east to west, allowing a rough chronology to emerge. This shows each state's contribution to our national culture, past and present. It also helps explain our ever-changing attitudes toward drinking. We won't make any great claim about what it all means, but there are more than enough facts presented here to support countless conclusions. We hope you find the content of this book useful, fascinating, and fun as you travel throughout America.

--Overcup Press

TABLE OF CONTENTS

QUICK REFERENCE COLOR GUIDE

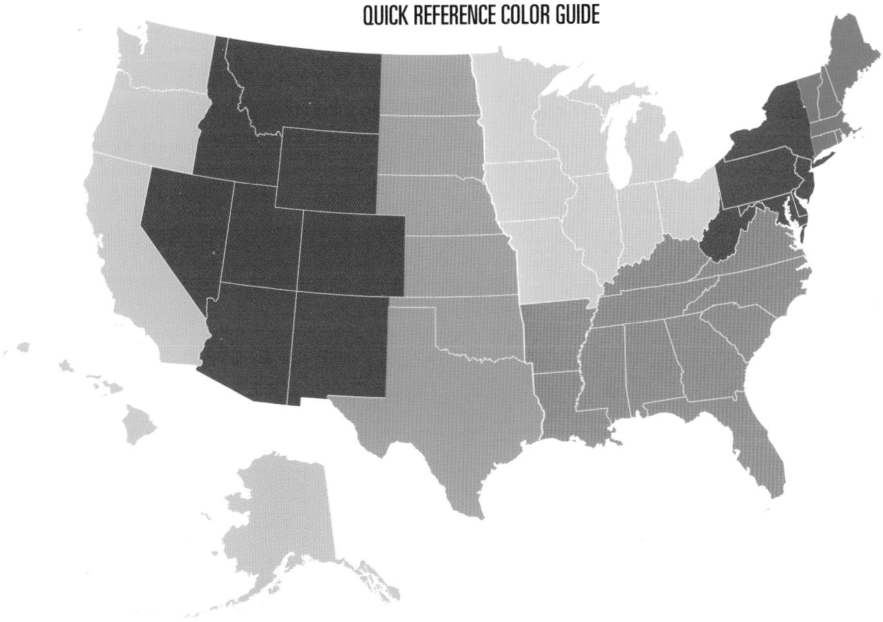

QUICK REFERENCE ICON GUIDE

Growlers: Refillable containers that can be filled from the taps of bars, breweries, and brewpubs.

Bottle Deposit: The state collects a refundable deposit on recyclable containers.

Corkage: Customers are permitted to bring a bottle of wine not purchased at the restaurant. Fees may apply.

Control States (ABC): The state sells some or all alcohol within the state.

Re-corking: Taking home a bottle of unfinished wine.

Smoking ban in bars and restaurants

MAINE

Dirigo
(I Lead)

America's day begins in Maine, and so did the dawn of Prohibition. The nation's noble experiment started unofficially with businessman-turned-eventual-mayor Neal Dow and evolved into what is known as the Maine Law of 1851. As a businessman, the future "Father of Prohibition" sought to eliminate worker's "eleveners" (a mid-morning tipple that was often repeated at 4:00 p.m.). Elected mayor on this platform, Dow instituted The Maine Law, which prohibited alcohol except when used for medicinal, mechanical, or manufacturing purposes. The Maine Law, as well as Mayor Dow's term in office, was not long for this world, however. Rumors spread that a host of hooch was being held in Portland City Hall. In June of 1855, a throng of mainly Irish immigrants stormed the building in what became known as the Portland Rum Riot. When the crowd refused to disperse, Mayor Dow ordered the militia to fire on his own people. One was killed, and seven were injured. Though the law was overturned the following year, the seeds of temperance had been sown, and twelve other states stayed on the wagon. Maine was one of the last states to ratify the repeal of Prohibition, doing so on December 6, 1933, the day after the Twenty-First Amendment was ratified by Congress.

Despite their Prohibition past, Mainers have carved out some unique drinking habits (and habitats). According to *BeerAdvocate* magazine, the best beer bar in the world is located about an hour and a half from Portland, near the White Mountain National Forest. Ebenezer's Pub in wee Lovell has thirty-five rare Belgian taps, over 700 rare and aged bottles, and select few seats. Thankfully, they take reservations for those from away.

Mainers reach for Allen's Coffee Brandy five times more than any other spirit, to the tune of more than $10 million a year in sales. The "Champagne of Maine" has been the state's best-selling spirit for twenty years, and locals are shaking up more than just Sombreros (coffee brandy and cream) with the stuff. Mix Allen's with the state's other ubiquitous beverage, the uniquely-flavored Moxie, and you get a cocktail called a Burnt Trailer (named not necessarily just for its aroma).

So whether you're drinking be-yahs in the ba-ar or martinis in Millinocket, here's to you, you princes of Maine, you kings of New England!

NEAL DOW

"Father of Prohibition"

The Burnt Trailer: Allen's Coffee Brandy mixed with Moxie soda.

MAINE

WHAT'LL IT BE?

Although Maine is a control state, it does not operate its own liquor stores. It licenses the right to sell liquor to agency stores, much like Vermont does. These agency stores can be grocery stores and pharmacies as well as stores that exclusively sell liquor. Beer and wine are available for purchase at grocery stores, convenience stores, and pharmacies. Sunday sale hours in Maine are limited, especially before holidays. Bars and restaurants do not allow the purchase or consumption of alcohol on premises after 1:15 a.m. (2:15 a.m. on January 1).

Maine allows some latitude for local variation in liquor laws. Towns and cities can prohibit the sale of alcohol, and 56 municipalities have done so. This applies to both on- and off-premise sales in some locations and just off-premise sales in others.

QUICK REFERENCE

WHAT YOU CAN DO

- Buy package liquor between 5:00 a.m. and 1:00 a.m. Monday through Saturday and between 9:00 a.m. and 1:00 a.m. on Sundays from a licensed liquor agency.
- Buy beer and wine in most grocery stores, convenience stores, and pharmacies between 5:00 a.m. and 1:00 a.m. Monday through Saturday, and between 9:00 a.m. and 1:00 a.m. on Sunday.
- Order a drink in bars and restaurants between 6:00 a.m. and 1:15 a.m. Monday through Saturday and between 9:00 a.m. and 1:15 a.m. on Sundays.
- Bring your own bottle of wine to a restaurant that does not have a wine license.
- Get your nickel back from bottle and can deposits, and get fifteen cents back for wine and liquor bottles.
- Fill a growler at a brewery.

WHAT YOU CAN'T DO

- Smoke in bars and restaurants. Maine has a statewide smoking ban for enclosed spaces.
- Order a drink in bars and restaurants in the 56 dry towns.
- Bring your own bottle of wine to a restaurant that has a wine license.
- Drink alcohol or be publicly intoxicated in Maine state parks.
- Buy a drink between 1:00 a.m. and 6:00 a.m. Monday through Saturday and between 1:00 a.m. and 9:00 a.m. on Sundays.

Source: Maine Bureau of Alcoholic Beverages & Lottery Operations

Curling clubs in Maine can hold a liquor license.

In the event of riots, hurricanes, and floods, the governor can order liquor stores to stop selling spirits and fortified wine.

Ebenezer's Pub

It's like you died and went to Belgium.

Best Beer Bar In The World
-*BeerAdvocate* magazine

ALL LIQUOR STORES IN MAINE
ARE REQUIRED TO HAVE A MINIMUM OF
100 TYPES OF SPIRITS
IN STOCK AND ON HAND

NED WIGHT
DISTILLER, NEW ENGLAND DISTILLING IN PORTLAND

TIP: "We've come a long way since the days of Neal Dow and early temperance here in Portland. In fact, Portlanders seem so intent to shake off our temperance history that we've swung to the apex on the opposing side. With ten breweries, three distilleries, one kombuchery, and one meadery, there is no shortage of local booze to imbibe, so pace yourself and enjoy all that Portland and Maine has to offer."

NEW HAMPSHIRE

Live Free or Die

They take their liberty seriously in New Hampshire. There's no income tax and no sales tax, no seatbelt laws for adults, no helmet laws, minimal fireworks laws, little handgun legislation, and liquor stores the size of outlet malls line the sides of the highways.

The state's tax-free status extends to its Manchester-Boston Airport, for those who are just passing through. And it seems like quite a few are just passing through (and on their way to buy tax-free booze)! New Hampshire sets ridiculous records when it comes to the selling of alcohol. In terms of per capita sales, they rank #1 in the country overall, #1 in sprits, and #1 in beer. The beer sales alone are two full gallons more than the second-highest state, North Dakota. That's forty-three gallons of beer for every person of drinking age in the state!

New Hampshire's beer records are not confined to the present. In the 1860s, True Jones and his brother Frank both started their respective brewing operations in the state. True brewed ales for millworkers in Manchester, while Frank started his operation in Portsmouth. Within twenty years, True Jones' story faded into history as brother Frank came to be the largest brewer of ales in the country, producing 150,000 barrels a year.

The brewery would not survive Prohibition intact: the equipment was sold off and the name bounced around with various owners until it disappeared for good in 1950. In 1993, the former Frank Jones Brewing factory was purchased at a bankruptcy auction by the state's first, and currently largest, craft brewery, Smuttynose Brewing. That brewery takes its name from Smuttynose Island, located just seven miles off the coasts of Maine and New Hampshire. The island itself has its own storied past as the site of the infamous and brutal Double Axe Murders of 1873. It was the dead of night on Smuttynose Island when three Norwegian women were attacked by an axe-wielding madman. One escaped and survived the frosty March night to name the murderer. The killer's alibi was that he was drinking in Portsmouth at the time of the murders.

When it comes to the selling of alcohol, New Hampshire rules!

Home to the 1873 Double Axe Murders

FYI

There are only four dry communities that remain in New Hampshire, and all of them have populations under 800: Ellsworth (pop. 87); Sharon (pop. 360); Monroe (pop. 759); and Brookfield (pop. 604).

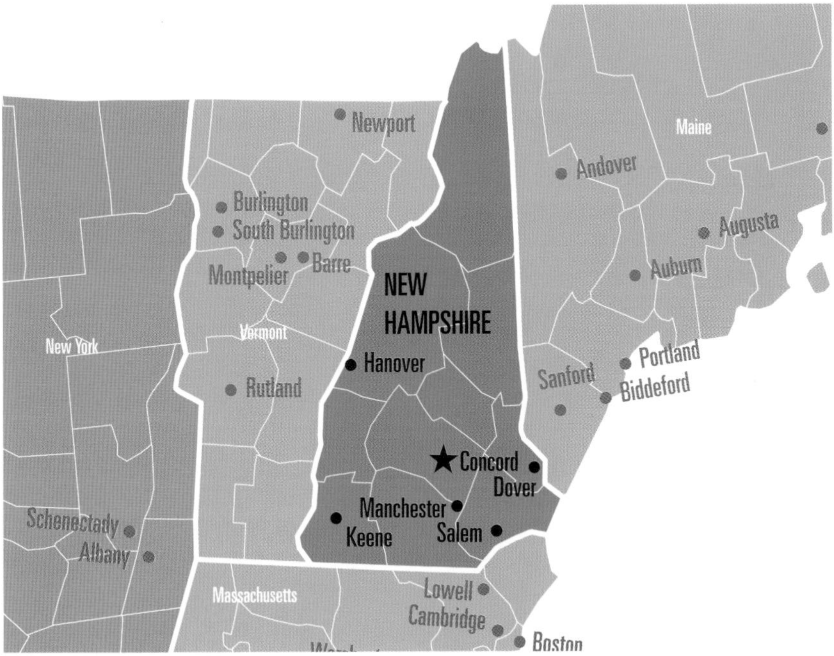

NEW HAMPSHIRE

WHAT'LL IT BE?

New Hampshire is a control state. Package liquor is only sold through state-run liquor outlets, which are closed on Easter, Thanksgiving, and Christmas. Beer and beverages under 6% ABV are not available at the state-run outlets, but are widely available at licensed grocery stores, convenience stores, and pharmacies. Wine is available at state-run outlets as well as licensed grocery stores, convenience stores, and pharmacies. The lack of state liquor taxes draws buyers from nearby states, especially Massachusetts, which is technically illegal but not enforced. Bars and restaurants are allowed to serve alcohol between 6:00 a.m. and 1:00 a.m. every day of the year.

New Hampshire state law allows for local variation in its liquor laws. Towns can vote to limit the operation of state-run outlets or prohibit the sale of alcohol entirely. Some small towns have limited on- and off-premise sales, and Ellsworth, Brookfield, Monroe, and Sharon are completely dry.

QUICK REFERENCE

WHAT YOU CAN DO

- Buy package wine and liquor between 6:00 a.m. and 11:45 p.m. seven days a week from state-run outlets.
- Buy beer and wine in most grocery stores, convenience stores, and pharmacies between 6:00 a.m. and 11:45 p.m. seven days a week.
- Order a drink in bars and restaurants between 6:00 a.m. and 1:00 a.m. seven days a week; some towns allow sales until 2:00 a.m.
- Fill a growler at a brewery.
- Take an unfinished bottle of wine from dinner home.
- Bring your own bottle of wine to a restaurant that has permission from the state to allow corkage. Restaurants are required to charge a corkage fee.

WHAT YOU CAN'T DO

- Smoke in bars and restaurants. New Hampshire has a statewide smoking ban for enclosed spaces.
- Purchase a ready-filled growler at a brewery.
- Order a drink at a bar or restaurant between 1:00 a.m. (2:00 a.m. in some places) and 6:00 a.m.
- Buy alcohol between 11:45 p.m. and 6:00 a.m. for off-premise consumption.
- Buy package alcohol on Easter, Thanksgiving, or Christmas.

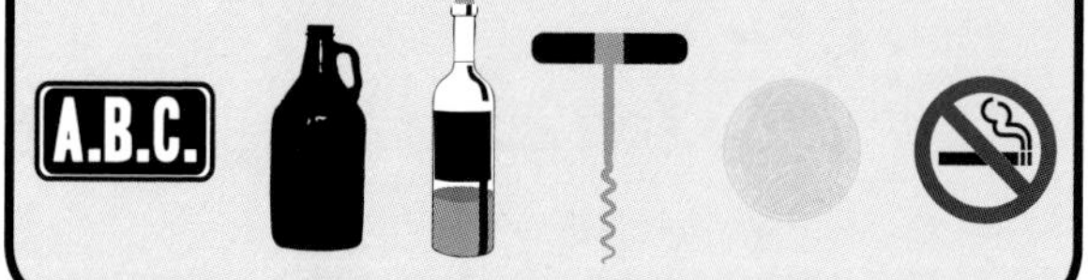

Source: New Hampshire Liquor Commission, Division of Enforcement

ALL BARS IN NEW HAMPSHIRE MUST BE

Portsmouth has a number of breweries: **SMUTTYNOSE, PORTSMOUTH BREWERY, EARTH EAGLE BREWINGS,** and **GREAT RHYTHM.** Nearby, you'll find **RED HOOK BREWERY** in Newington. Further down the coast in North Hampton are **THROWBACK BREWERY** and **SEA HAGG DISTILLERY. BLUE LOBSTER BREWING COMPANY** is in Hampton. Finally, just across the Merrimack River in Massachusetts, is **NEWBURYPORT BREWING COMPANY.**

In what was hailed as a "common-sense measure" by the state legislature, New Hampshire lawmakers passed a bill in 2012 allowing beer to be sold at farmers markets, giving people who like to shop locally the opportunity to pick up beer with their fresh eggs and vegetables.

JAMES IVES
BARTENDER, PINE IN THE HANOVER INN DARTMOUTH, HANOVER

TIP: "New Hampshire is a place where New Hampshire State Liquor & Wine Outlet stores are found at the rest areas along the interstates, as well as in shopping centers throughout the state. As the name implies – great deals are found in these state-controlled stores! "

VERMONT

The Green Mountain State

A notoriously hard-drinking wild man named Ethan Allen, his brother Ira, and his infamous Green Mountain Boys made their base in Bennington, Vermont. Their watering hole/club house was a drinking institution known as the Catamount Tavern, thusly named for the stuffed cougar that was mounted outside. Ethan Allen's drink of choice was a cocktail made from rum cut with hard apple cider, called a Stone Fence. It's with this drink that those Bennington Rioters fortified themselves as they set out to capture the well-armed British at Fort Ticonderoga. The Green Mountain Boys were little more than an enthusiastic ad hoc gang, but history would not record their loss here. They did not defeat the British, though, so much as they walked right through the gates past a sleeping sentry and into textbooks as American heroes.

When today's Americans reach for hard cider, they're probably ordering Vermont's own Woodchuck Cider, the number one cider in the country. Hard cider is a drink that's practically deregulated in the state. It can be produced at home and sold without a liquor license, provided the casks are greater than thirty-two gallons. The Stone Fence is still a popular autumnal cocktail in New England, though you'll more often find it made with whiskey or bourbon and non-alcoholic cider.

A wooden statue of Ceres, the Roman goddess of agriculture and grain crops, stands atop the capitol building in Montpelier, the smallest capital city in the country. Though small in size, Vermont has more craft breweries per capita than any other state in the country. Montpelier's own Three Penny Taproom is a great place to try a sampling of what's brewing in the region. In 2013, Ratebeer.com named Hill Farmstead in Greensboro the Best Brewery in the World, and Burlington's Magic Hat is the state's largest. Beer and wine with less than 17% ABV are available in grocery stores.

More rule roundup: Though the last drink must be served by 2:00 a.m., patrons may linger over it until 2:30. That spirit of hospitality doesn't extend to happy hours, as they are verboten in the state. And forget about having a bucket of Margaritas or a super-sized Long Island Iced Tea here. Drinks may contain no more than four ounces of liquor. Also note that Vermont is one of the very few states that charges a bottle deposit on liquor—15 cents. Beer comes with a 5-cent deposit, but Vermont knows its history (and which side its bread is buttered on). Hard cider is exempt.

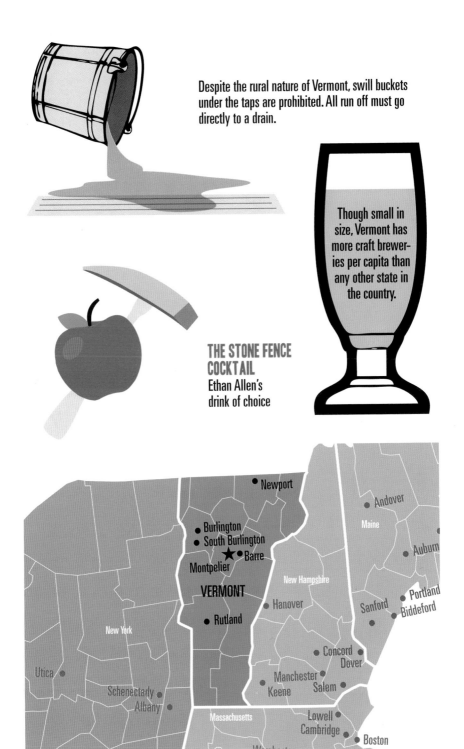

Despite the rural nature of Vermont, swill buckets under the taps are prohibited. All run off must go directly to a drain.

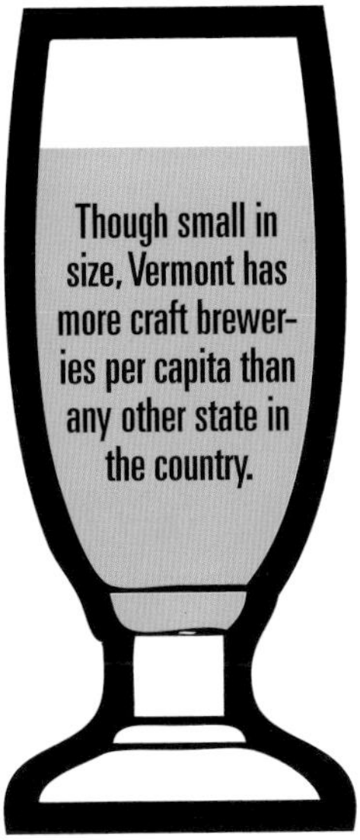

Though small in size, Vermont has more craft breweries per capita than any other state in the country.

THE STONE FENCE COCKTAIL

Ethan Allen's drink of choice

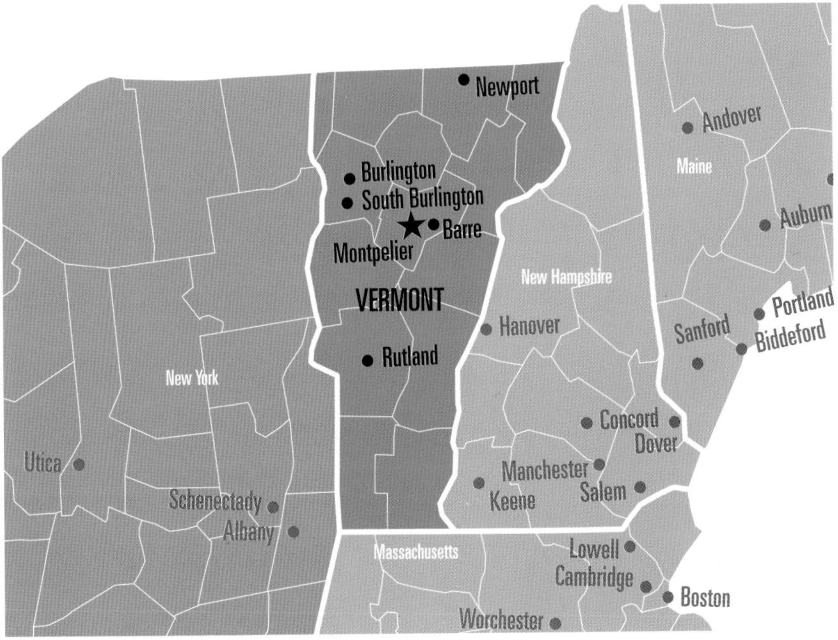

VERMONT

WHAT'LL IT BE?

Although Vermont is a control state, its liquor laws are actually more permissive than those of its neighbors. The state contracts out liquor sales to private agencies, which can be gas stations, grocery stores, convenience stores, and pharmacies in addition to the more familiar liquor stores. There are currently 78 of these agencies throughout the state, and you can spot them by their "Vermont Liquor Outlet" signs. Beer and wine are widely available for purchase at grocery stores, convenience stores, and pharmacies. Alcohol purchase for both on- and off-premise consumption is permitted every day of the year, depending on retailer hours.

Vermont does not allow for a local option. Laws relating to alcohol are consistent statewide.

QUICK REFERENCE

WHAT YOU CAN DO

- Buy package liquor until midnight seven days a week from one of 78 agencies.
- Buy beer and wine in most grocery stores, convenience stores, and pharmacies until midnight seven days a week.
- Order a drink in bars and restaurants until 2:00 a.m. seven days a week.
- Get your nickel back from bottle and can deposits, and get fifteen cents back for liquor bottles.
- Fill a growler at a brewery or at other licensed retailers. Growlers must be labeled with the retailer, product, ABV, and manufacturer.
- Take an unfinished bottle of wine or specialty beer (between 8% and 16% ABV) from dinner home.

WHAT YOU CAN'T DO

- Smoke in bars and restaurants. Vermont has a statewide smoking ban.
- Purchase a second drink if you have not finished your first.
- Participate in a game or contest that encourages excessive drinking.
- Bring your own bottle of wine to a restaurant that has a wine license.
- Buy package liquor anywhere other than a state-licensed agency.
- Buy package alcohol after midnight.
- Order a drink in a bar or restaurant after 2:00 a.m.

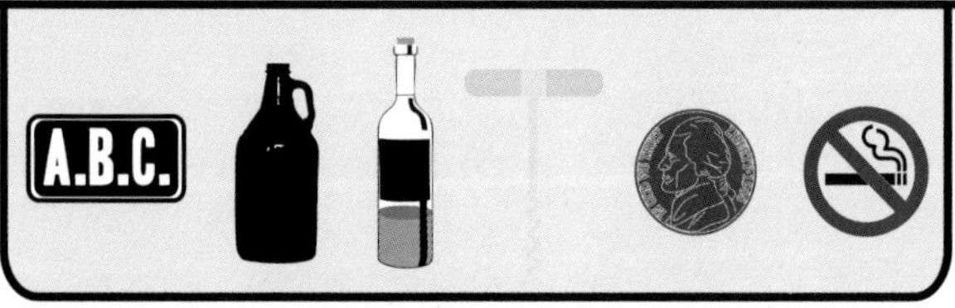

Source: Vermont Department of Liquor Control

It's been said that all Vermonters have a little maple in their blood. It's no wonder then that some are producing maple "sap beers" while others distill maple liqueur.

R.I.P.
BEN & JERRY'S
FLAVOR
GRAVEYARD
INCLUDES
WHITE RUSSIAN
WHICH WAS MADE FOR A DECADE
WITH KAHLUA LIQUEUR.
THE FLAVOR WAS RETIRED WHEN
THE ICE CREAM MAKER FOUND THAT
IT WAS SINGLE-HANDEDLY
DRIVING UP THE PRICE OF KAHLUA.

Look for
LAWSON'S MAPLE NIPPLE (AND TRIPPLE) ALES
and **SAPLING VERMONT MAPLE LIQUEUR**

100%
97%
BEER
50%
0%

VERMONT RECYCLES!

The overall redemption rate for all returnable bottle and cans in Vermont is 85%, one of the highest in the nation. Beer containers specifically have a 97% return rate.

JEFF BAKER
BARTENDER, THE FARMHOUSE TAP & GRILL IN BURLINGTON

TIP: "Don't expect 'happy hours' or 64 oz pitchers of beer in Vermont (as both are illegal). What you can count on is a bounty of locally-brewed craft beers served in proper glassware. Want to do a tasting flight of those beers? Until recently, only breweries could offer flights, but with new legislation on the books in 2014 all bars and restaurants can serve up a flight of up to 32 oz of beer to a patron at a time!"

MASSACHUSETTS

The Bay State

Let's start at the very beginning of America, as it's positively drenched in drinking, and drinking on boats to boot. Hailing from Spain, Christopher Columbus set sail for America with stores of sherry, and the Pilgrims packed more beer than water for their voyage. The Pilgrims had better luck with navigation, however, and landed at Plymouth Rock. They planned to sail on to Virginia, but had run out of beer. At first, the Pilgrims would try brewing beer with anything fermentable they could find in the New World, such as Indian corn, berries, and even pumpkins.

The two basic social institutions of colonial America were the tavern and the church. While not the site of the first church, Massachusetts was the site of the first tavern, opened in 1634 by Samuel Cole. The Massachusetts General Court and the church had a problem with one particular tavern mainstay, however: "the common custom of drinking to one another is a mere useless ceremony, and draweth on the abominable practice of drinking healths." In layman terms, that meant no toasting. It proved impossible to enforce, however, and was repealed six years later.

America's first institution of higher learning, Harvard, was founded in 1636 in Massachusetts. Not long after, a brewery was established on the campus to serve the students, providing not just refreshment, but perhaps also an historical foundation for future brewers. A pair of Harvard classmates and friends opened Harpoon Brewery in 1986, and several founders of what was to become The Boston Beer Company are Harvard alumni as well. But the brewing brains behind Boston Beer is Jim Koch, whose grandfather's recipe is the basis for Sam Adams Boston Lager. Coming from a long line of brewers, it's no surprise that Koch has some advice for keeping your wits about you through a night of beer drinking: yeast. Koch told Aaron Goldfarb of *Esquire* magazine that one teaspoon of dry yeast per beer, mixed in yogurt before drinking, can "mitigate" the effects of alcohol.

Twenty-three percent of people in the Bay State, the most in the country, claim to be of Irish descent. Since 1901, hundreds of thousands of Southies and their brethren have participated in the Boston St. Patrick's parade, inevitably calling in sick the next day with a bad case of the Irish flu. Double fisting in Beantown is known as having Irish handcuffs, and it's also the limit of what a bartender can serve you at one time. Though liquor stores remain open for the St. Pat's, they usually close early. Stock up before Memorial, Thanksgiving, and Christmas Days, and on Sundays before 10:00 a.m., as liquor stores are closed then as well.

Native son Jack Kerouac's life on the road begat a very Bay Stater sentiment to live by: "Why on earth aren't people continually drunk? I want ecstasy of the mind all the time."

THE PILGRIMS landed at Plymouth Rock on December 19, 1620, so the crew of the Mayflower would be able to conserve their ration of beer for the trip home. The English, and thus the Pilgrims, were accustomed to drinking "small beers" as their primary source of hydration, because the water at the end of the Middle Ages was very polluted. Small beers had very little alcohol, but it was enough to kill any harmful bacteria. The Pilgrims' concerns about water quality and dependence on beer for calories made the production of beer one of the first priorities of the colonists. However, the first barley introduced to New England was not suitable for the climate. Brewing supplies and even beer itself continued to be imported from England for many years. Most of the brewing (and beer drinking) done by the colonists was done at home, until the introduction of six-row barley to New York made commercial barley production more viable.

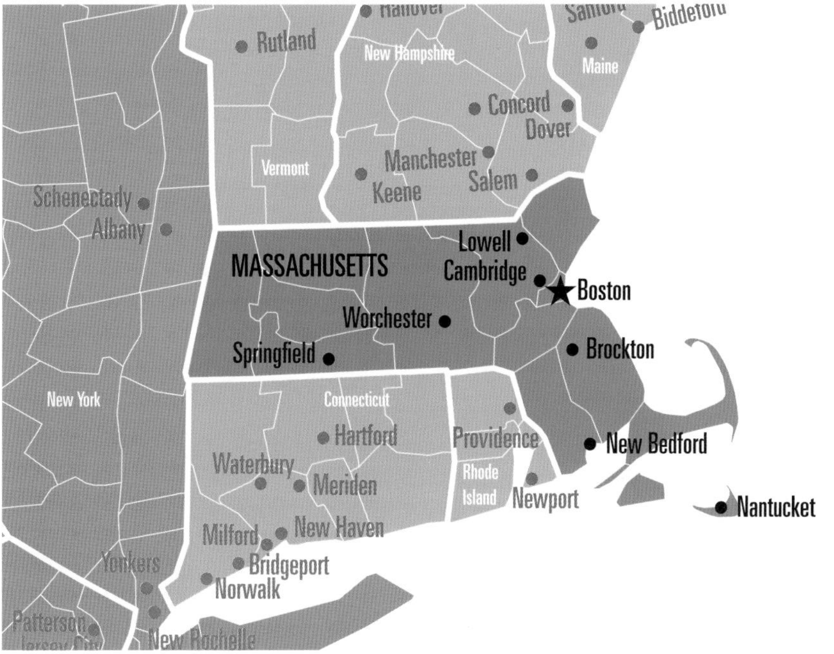

MASSACHUSETTS

WHAT'LL IT BE?

Massachusetts is not a control state for liquor, but it does have a tiered licensing structure for both on- and off-premise sales. This means that some places are able to sell only beer, some only wine, some both beer and wine, and some all forms of alcohol. Licenses to sell alcohol are available on a quota basis; the number of licenses available is based on the latest census. In addition, no one company may operate more than five locations selling alcohol in the entire Commonwealth, with no more than one in a given town or two in a city. As a result, chain stores do not necessarily stock alcohol in all of their locations. Despite these limits, alcohol is widely available for on- and off-premise consumption seven days a week. There is, however, a statewide ban on sales on Election Day, Memorial Day, Thanksgiving, Christmas Day, and the day after Christmas if it is a Sunday. Most localities opt out of the Election Day ban.

Massachusetts law allows for local variation. The commonwealth has no dry counties, but it does have several dry towns. These include the small towns of Alford, Chilmark, Dunstable, Gosnold, Hawley, Montgomery, Mount Washington, and Westhampton.

QUICK REFERENCE

WHAT YOU CAN DO

- Buy package beer, wine, and liquor between 11:00 a.m. and 11:00 p.m. seven days a week from licensed retailers. Local licensing authorities may extend hours to 8:00 a.m. to 2:00 a.m.
- Order a drink in bars and restaurants between 11:00 a.m. and 11:00 p.m. seven days a week. In many locations, establishments serve until 1:00 a.m., and in Boston, you can get a drink until 2:00 a.m.
- Get your nickel back from bottle and can deposits.
- Purchase a growler directly from a brewery with the brewery label on it.

WHAT YOU CAN'T DO

- Order a pitcher of beer or a bottle of wine if you are dining alone.
- Purchase more than two drinks at a time.
- Bring your own bottle of wine to a restaurant that has a wine license.
- Smoke in bars and restaurants, including open-air patios with covered areas. Massachusetts has a statewide smoking ban for enclosed spaces.
- Buy alcohol between 2:00 a.m. and 8:00 a.m. Monday through Saturday, between 1:00 a.m. and 10:00 a.m. on Sundays, and on Memorial Day, Election Day, Thanksgiving, Christmas, or the day after Christmas if it is a Sunday.
- Fill your own growler, as a personal growler will lack the brewery label.

Source: Commonwealth of Massachusetts, Alcoholic Beverages Control Commission

FYI

Massachusetts is home to Belchertown, named after colonial governor Jonathan Belcher.

"The secret of drunkenness is that it insulates us in thought whilst it unites us in feeling."
-Ralph Waldo Emerson, Concord, Massachusetts

JOHNNY APPLESEED

John Chapman, better known as Johnny Appleseed, is the official folk hero of Massachusetts. Hailing from Leominster, Johnny Appleseed lived on the vanguard of the frontier planting apple trees throughout the Midwest. By the time the settlers arrived, the trees were bearing fruit. Despite being too tart to eat, the apples still increased the value of the land by providing a source of fermentable sugar, which was used to create hard cider and applejack. Food writer Michael Pollan has christened Johnny Appleseed "the American Dionysus." He writes that "because American grapes weren't sweet enough to ferment successfully, the apple served as the American grape, cider the American wine."

RUSS DeMARIANO
BARTENDER, THE BRAHMIN AMERICAN CUISINE & COCKTAILS IN BOSTON

TIP: "Boston is the best city in the country to visit and have some wicked drinks! Us Bostonians can make any type of cocktail from anywhere, but we also serve up a nice, cold, local Sam Adams. Be wary and don't ask questions when you are told you can't have your drink on one of our patios without food, or why the bars close at 2:00 am. Look out for the shoe shots if someone offers, and don't ask a bartender to put on the Yankees game unless they're playing the Sox!"

RHODE ISLAND

Hope

In colonial times, the state of Rhode Island was so rife with criminal enterprise and pirating that it earned the nickname Rogue's Island. It was pivotal in the Atlantic Triangular Trade, importing molasses from the Caribbean to be distilled into rum in New England. The profits from the sale of molasses purchased goods which were then sent to Africa in exchange for slaves, who were sent to work the sugar plantations of the Caribbean. In the mid-1760s, the country's smallest state had twenty-two rum distilleries operating within its borders.

It's no surprise then that Prohibition was not popular here. Indeed, Rhode Island was one of two states that refused to ratify the Eighteenth Amendment. Though it was still subject to federal law, with 400 miles of coastline, the Ocean State proved to be one of the wettest during Prohibition. The city of Newport was just 200 nautical miles from Canada, where distillers were only happy to profit from America's "noble experiment." Though they were smuggling mostly Canadian whiskey, the boats were still called rum runners. The Rum Runner II still remains in use for the tourist trade, offering a great way to see the bay.

The last of the Newport distilleries closed more than 150 years ago, but a recent newcomer has arrived, reinvigorating the rum lore of yore. It's called Thomas Tew, after the gallant "pirate of Rhode Island," the third-highest pillaging pirate of all time according to *Forbes* magazine. The bottle even bears what was purportedly Tew's version of the Jolly Roger, an upraised arm brandishing a sword. Liquor prices are a little more affordable for Rhode Islanders since the state recently eliminated the 7% sales tax on spirits and wine, though not for beer.

Brewing since 1877, Narragansett Beer is currently one of the top fifty producing breweries in the country. For the ultimate uber-local experience, seek out two 'Gansett specialty brews: the Autocrat Coffee Milk Stout, which is a beery interpretation of the Official Beverage of the State of Rhode Island and Providence Plantations, and Del's Shandy, made with Del's Frozen Lemonade.

The horror writer H.P. Lovecraft hailed from Providence and though he was a tee-totaller himself, he was well-versed in madness. The mind behind Cthulu wrote that "Almost nobody dances sober, unless they happen to be insane." Roman philosopher Cicero observed the same thing almost 2000 years earlier: *Nemo enim fere saltat sobrius, nisi forte insanit.* Ancient truths still prevail.

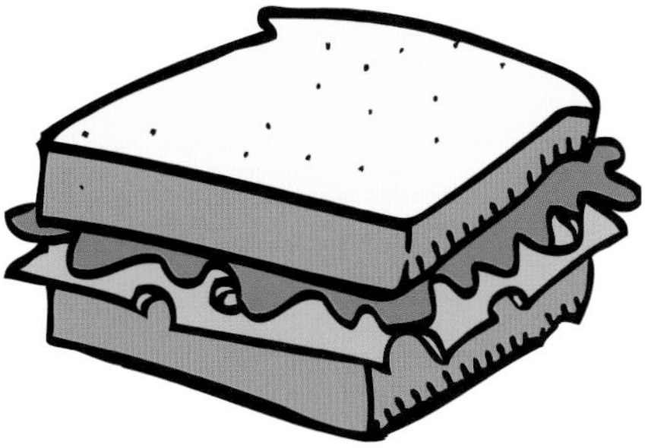

Businesses with a tavern/victualer license must serve food at least at the **"SANDWICH LEVEL."** Snack foods such as chips, pretzels, and "stuffies" are not sufficient. Stuffies, a Rhode Island specialty, are baked stuffed clams on the half shell with breadcrumbs.

DR. SEUSS once did illustrations for Narragansett Beer. In the nineteenth century, his family owned the Kalmbach and Geisel Brewery, known by the locals as the Come Back and Guzzle.

FYI

Knowingly furnishing wood alcohol as a beverage may result in a life sentence.

RHODE ISLAND

WHAT'LL IT BE?

Beer, wine, and liquor are only sold in package stores. While not a control state, Rhode Island considers everything over 3.2% ABW to be alcohol, and alcohol can only be purchased in a package store. These are privately-owned businesses, but they cannot sell anything but alcohol and mixers. Consequently, grocery stores, convenience stores, and pharmacies are not able to hold a retail license. The state also regulates the hours of retail sales: 9:00 a.m. to 10:00 p.m. Monday through Saturday, and 10:00 a.m. to 6:00 pm on Sunday. Bars and restaurants can serve until 1:00 a.m. seven days a week. Sales are allowed 365 days a year.

Rhode Island state law allows for local variation, which is usually exercised by limiting retail hours. The last dry town in the state voted to allow the sale of alcohol in 2011.

QUICK REFERENCE

WHAT YOU CAN DO

- Buy package beer, wine, and liquor between 9:00 a.m. and 10:00 p.m. Monday through Saturday and between 10:00 a.m. and 6:00 p.m. on Sundays from a licensed retailer.
- Order a drink in bars and restaurants between 9:00 a.m. and 1:00 a.m. Monday through Saturday and between noon and 1:00 a.m. on Sundays.
- Order a drink in bars and restaurants until 2:00 a.m. on Fridays and Saturdays in Providence.
- Enjoy discounted drinks if you are a senior citizen or active military and reservists.
- Bring your own bottle of wine to a restaurant that does not have a wine license.
- Fill a growler at a liquor store.

WHAT YOU CAN'T DO

- Smoke in bars and restaurants, including some open-air patios.
- Fill a growler at a brewery or vineyard.
- Bring your own bottle of wine to a restaurant that has a wine license.
- Purchase wine, beer, and liquor at a grocery store, convenience store, or pharmacy.
- Go on an organized, commercial pub-crawl with a large group of people.
- Operate low-speed vehicles or amusement park rides while drunk.
- Buy package beer, wine, and liquor between 10:00 p.m. and 9:00 a.m. Monday through Saturday or after 6:00 p.m. on Sundays.
- Order a drink in bars and restaurants between 1:00 a.m. and 9:00 a.m. Monday through Saturday and between 1:00 a.m. and noon on Sundays.

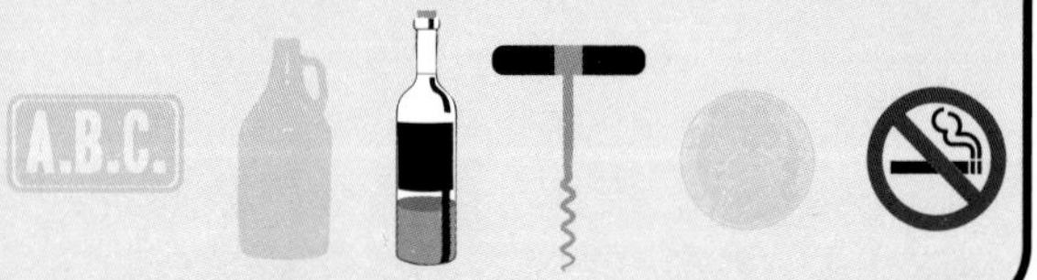

Source: Rhode Island Division of Commercial Licensing and Regulation

Family members or employers of alcoholics (defined as "HABITUALLY INTEMPERATE PERSONS") may give written notice for individual retailers not to serve them. If the retailers ignore the notice, they could be held liable for damages in a civil action.

Established in 1673 and still serving today, **THE WHITE HORSE TAVERN** in Newport is arguably America's oldest bar. The White Horse hosted everyone from colonists to British and Hessian soldiers to pirates and sailors to our founding fathers. It was a quintessential colonial American tavern.

The pirate **THOMAS TEW** was thought to have used this image as his Jolly Roger. It is now used on bottles of Thomas Tew Rum.

SEAN LARKIN
MASTER BREWER AT REVIVAL BREWING/NARAGANSETT BEER IN PROVIDENCE

TIP: "Rhode Island is a hidden gem for beer drinkers. Providence and the surrounding cities of Cranston, Pawtucket, and Warwick have some of the best-known beer bars in the state. If Old World pubs of the Revolutionary period and sailor bars are you thing, Warren, Bristol, and Newport have more than enough. And Newport's rich sailing tradition as well as its retired Revolution-era Naval Bases provide a backdrop for those drawn to the sea."

CONNECTICUT

Qui Transtulit Sustinet
(He Who Transplanted Still Sustains)

America's #1 selling spirit might not have been were it not for the great state of Connecticut. Though vodka is hundreds of years old, its introduction to America is largely due to two entrepreneurs and the Connecticut-based Heublein Company. In the 1920s, Russian expat Rudolf Kunnett wrangled the Smirnoff vodka recipe from Smirnov scion Vladimir and began distilling it in the United States. Five years later, Kunnett sold the brand to the Heublein Company. Vodka was first marketed as "White Whiskey" with "no taste, no smell," and initially it didn't sell well. It was Heublein Company chairman John G. Martin's meeting with Jack Morgan, a Sunset Strip bar owner, that would lead to an explosion in vodka sales. Morgan's Cock & Bull bar had a surplus of ginger beer, which they combined with vodka and a squeeze of lime to concoct a cocktail that is drunk to this day, the Moscow Mule.

You can also thank Connecticut for the Car Bomb (equal parts Irish whiskey and Irish cream poured into a shot glass, then dropped into a pint of Guinness). The St. Patrick's Day staple was invented in 1979 in the state's oldest bar, Billy Wilson's Aging Still in Norwich.

Bridgeport is the birthplace of the dedicated boozer and actor Robert Mitchum. From the Mitchum biography by Lee Server, *Baby I Don't Care*, comes the story of the friendship of the Night of the Hunter actor and Frank Sinatra. Mitchum introduced Sinatra to his surefire hangover remedy, the Ramos Gin Fizz cocktail, a frothy elixir that goes down "like mother's milk." Eternally grateful, Sinatra nicknamed Mitchum "Mother," and for years sent the actor a card on Mother's Day.

Connecticut is second only to Utah in the least amount of beer consumed. Beer is readily available, however, even in grocery stores, though not after 9:00 p.m. or before 8:00 a.m. Those same hours apply to spirits sales and include all major holidays as well as the Monday following any holiday that falls on a Sunday. So, keep an eye on the calendar and plan accordingly.

FYI

Breweries can't give free samples after 8:00 p.m.

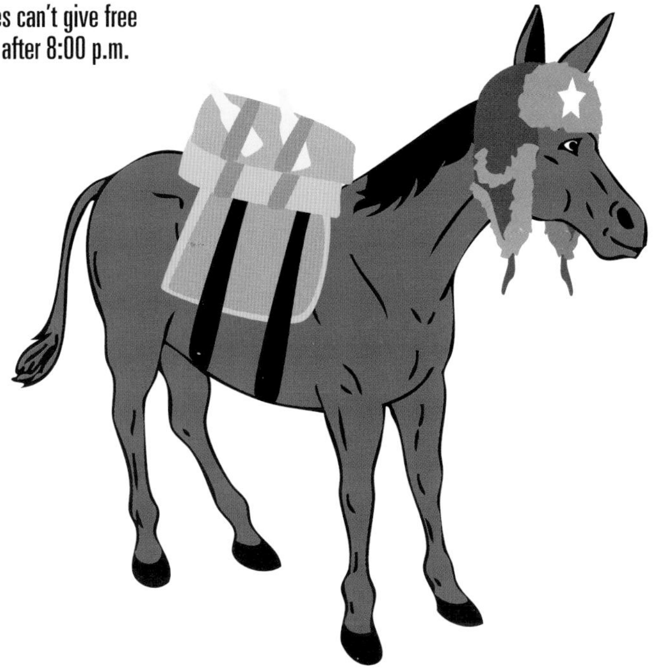

Combine some ginger beer with vodka and a squeeze of lime to make yourself a **MOSCOW MULE**.

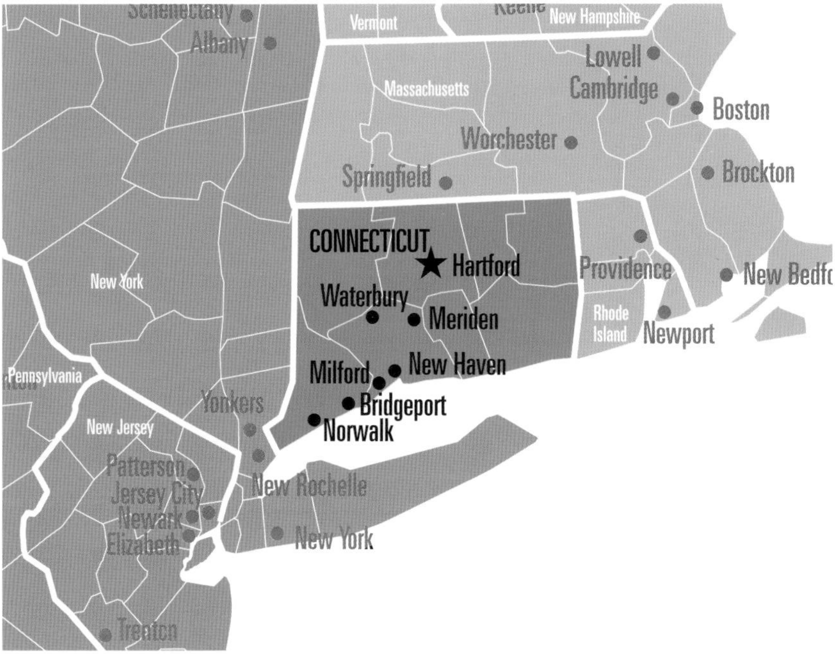

CONNECTICUT

WHAT'LL IT BE?

Liquor licensing in Connecticut is relatively restrictive. The state lifted its ban on Sunday liquor sales in 2012, but off-premise purchasing hours are limited compared to neighboring states. Wine and liquor are only available from retailers with a wine and liquor license; beer, however, is widely available in supermarkets, convenience stores, and pharmacies. Hours of sale for package alcohol are the same, whether it is beer, wine, or liquor. Alcohol is available for on-premise purchase every day of the year, but package alcohol is not available on Thanksgiving, Christmas, or New Year's Day.

Local ordinances can be more restrictive than state law for operating hours, which means towns can further limit the hours alcohol is available for purchase. Towns and counties cannot, however, extend alcohol purchasing hours beyond state limits. Bridgewater (pop. 1,727) is the last remaining dry town in Connecticut.

QUICK REFERENCE

WHAT YOU CAN DO

- Buy package beer, wine, and liquor between 8:00 a.m. and 9:00 p.m. Monday through Saturday and between 10:00 a.m. and 5:00 p.m. on Sundays from retailers with a wine and liquor license.
- Buy beer in most grocery stores, convenience stores, and pharmacies.
- Order a drink in bars and restaurants between 9:00 a.m. and 1:00 a.m. Monday through Thursday, between 9:00 a.m. and 2:00 a.m. on Friday and Saturday, and between 11:00 a.m. and 1:00 a.m. on Sundays.
- Get your nickel back from bottle and can deposits.
- Fill a growler at a brewery.
- Take an unfinished bottle of wine from dinner home.
- Bring your own bottle of wine to a restaurant that does not have a wine license; corkage fees will vary.

WHAT YOU CAN'T DO

- Smoke in bars and restaurants, with the exception of some open-air patios. Connecticut has a statewide smoking ban for enclosed spaces.
- Bring your own bottle of wine to a restaurant that has a wine license.
- Buy package beer, wine, and liquor between 9:00 p.m. and 8:00 a.m. Monday through Saturday and before 10:00 a.m. or after 5:00 p.m. on Sundays.
- Purchase package alcohol on Thanksgiving, Christmas, or New Year's Day.
- Order a drink in bars and restaurants between 1:00 a.m. and 9:00 a.m. Monday through Friday, between 2:00 a.m. and 9:00 a.m. on Saturday, and between 2:00 a.m. and 11:00 a.m. on Sundays.

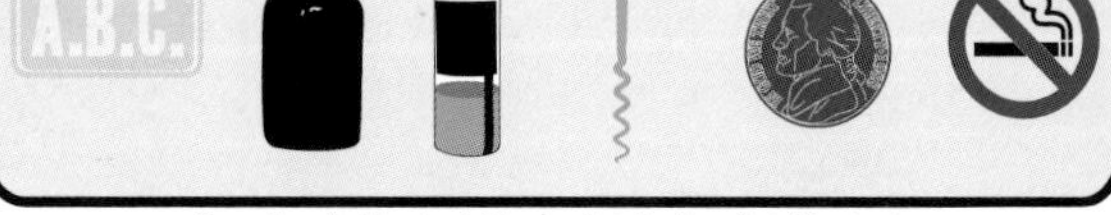

Source: Connecticut Department of Consumer Protection, Liquor Control Department

PLAY SAFE

There are special licenses for bowling establishments and racquetball facilities in Connecticut. Bowling alleys must have ten or more lanes and prohibit drinking in the lanes before 2:00 p.m. Racquetball permits are only issued to places with more than five courts.

Heavenly
VINTAGE RESERVE
PINOT NOIR
PINOT NOIR
because HE didn't turn water into just any wine

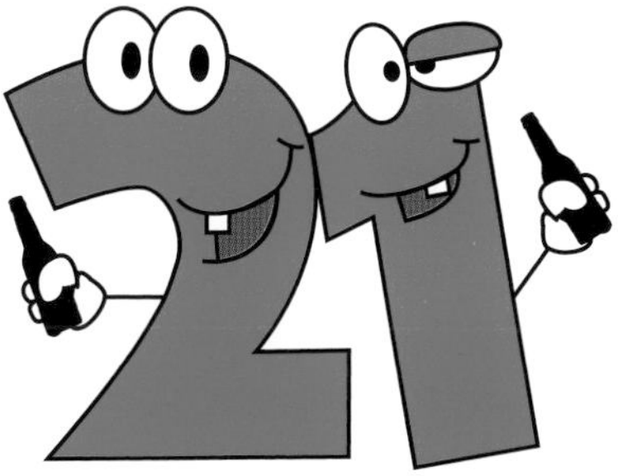

Today, the drinking age in all fifty states is twenty-one because of a federal law that ties compliance to highway funding. However, there was a period from the early 1970s to mid-1980s when thirty states, including Connecticut, lowered their drinking age to eighteen or nineteen. The reason was the Twenty-Sixth Amendment, which lowered the voting age from twenty-one to eighteen. Since this was now the "age of majority" when one is no longer considered a minor, many states adjusted their drinking age limits as well.

Connecticut prohibits the use of Santa Claus and biblical characters in liquor advertising.

GREG GENAIS
BARTENDER, PARALLEL POST IN FAIRFIELD

TIP: "Happy Hour in Connecticut is a big plus as it offers great deals to patrons without much regulation from the state. A bar owner can discount alcohol as he or she sees fit, so a $9 draft is $3 at Parallel Post during Happy Hour. There is no set time for Happy Hour, but they usually begin around 2:00 p.m."

NEW YORK

Excelsior
(Ever Upward)

The Martini, the simple combination of gin and vermouth, is said to have been concocted around the 1880s, and one of its origin stories cites its place of birth as the Turf Club in Manhattan. Curiously, the building that housed the Turf Club later spawned the Manhattan Club (and along with it another myth on the origin of the city's namesake cocktail). The Statue of Liberty, illuminated by the bright lights of the big city, shouldn't be holding a torch aloft—she should be raising a cocktail glass!

Lately, when it comes to drinking in New York, you are likely drinking something from New York. From Brooklyn Gin, to Seneca Lake winery Hermann J. Weimer, to Cooperstown's Ommegang Brewing, loads of libations are being produced in NY, and a lot of that is thanks to legislation being passed in Albany. All have a local-sourcing caveat as well as size limitations in common. As comedian Lewis Black said in a state-sponsored commercial, "if you can grow it, someone in this state will turn it into booze. Because, thank God, New York was founded by businessmen—not Puritans!"

Distilleries with limited production that use 50% of NY-grown ingredients not only earn a greatly reduced license fee through the 2007 Farm Distillery Act, but are also allowed to offer tastings and sell on premises. One of the first distilleries to take advantage of the act is Gardiner's Tuthilltown Spirits, which is now producing world-class whiskies and ryes. Though New York Distilling is based in Williamsburg, it uses upwards of 70,000 pounds of state-grown rye in the production of its spirits. Try their Perry Tot, the first Navy-strength gin to be produced in America at 114 proof. Despite being a stone's throw from the Brooklyn Navy Yard, traditional Navy-strength gins originated with the British Royal Navy. Hudson Valley distillery Hillrock Estates keeps it all in-house, so to speak. They not only produce all the barley and rye needed for their whiskies, they also built their own malt house, something no other distillery has done since Prohibition. New York now leads the nation in small-batch spirits producers.

The 2012 Farm Brewery license allows for a decades-long scaling-up of local ingredients—mostly because demand now outstrips supply. The state's breweries and distilleries use a huge amount of grain, much more than the state currently generates. So for the bill to be successful, more farms need to begin planting wheat, rye, hops, and malt to supply the industry. Long-term solutions don't grow overnight. But the incentive is there, and in time, the acreage will follow. The number of microbreweries in the state has tripled in the few years since the act went into effect.

The whole locavore legislative movement began with the state's 1976 Farm Winery Act. Before this bill, there were just a handful of wineries operating in the state. Now there are more than 300! Though the Finger Lakes region produces 90% of the wine produced in the state, the Hudson Valley, Long Island, and Lake Erie AVA wine trail regions are worth exploring as well.

If all this alcoholic agritourism has tired you out, order in. It's legal across the state for licensed outlets to deliver beer along with food!

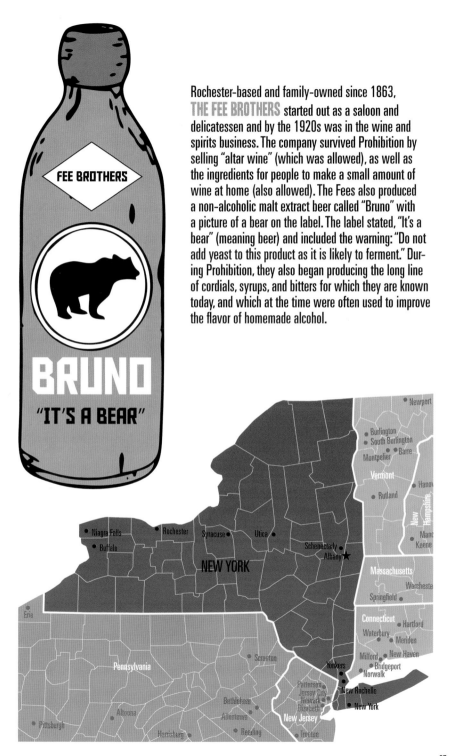

Rochester-based and family-owned since 1863, **THE FEE BROTHERS** started out as a saloon and delicatessen and by the 1920s was in the wine and spirits business. The company survived Prohibition by selling "altar wine" (which was allowed), as well as the ingredients for people to make a small amount of wine at home (also allowed). The Fees also produced a non-alcoholic malt extract beer called "Bruno" with a picture of a bear on the label. The label stated, "It's a bear" (meaning beer) and included the warning: "Do not add yeast to this product as it is likely to ferment." During Prohibition, they also began producing the long line of cordials, syrups, and bitters for which they are known today, and which at the time were often used to improve the flavor of homemade alcohol.

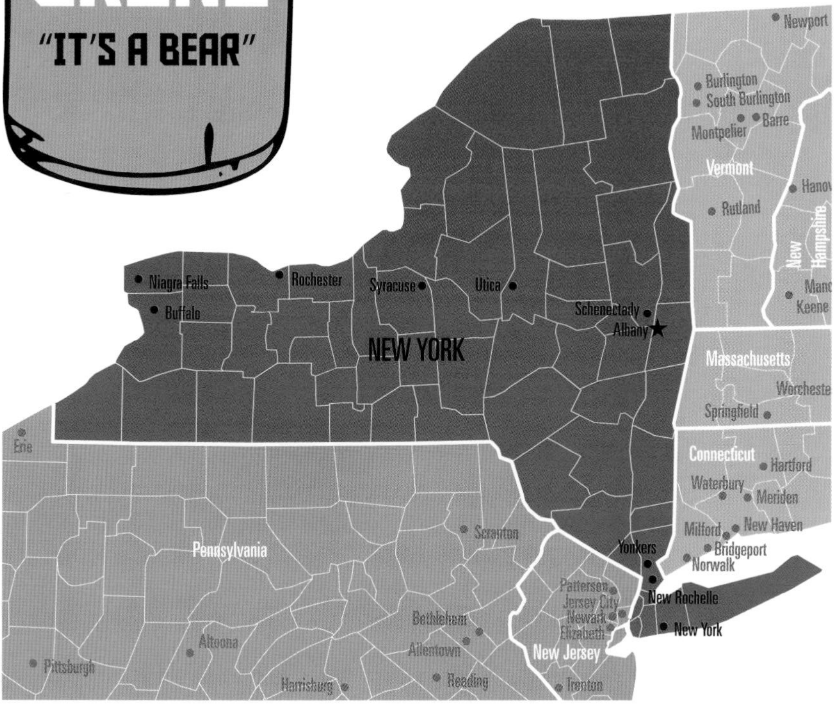

NEW YORK

WHAT'LL IT BE?

Alcohol is easy to find in New York. Wine and liquor are available from liquor stores, which can be open between 8:00 a.m. and midnight Monday through Saturday, with slightly shorter hours on Sundays. Christmas is the only no-sale day for package liquor and wine. Liquor stores don't carry beer, but it is available from grocery stores, convenience stores, and pharmacies between 8:00 a.m. and 3:00 a.m. seven days a week and twenty-four hours a day, seven days a week in New York City. Hours for on-premise consumption are also generous; bars and restaurants can serve drinks from 8:00 a.m. to 4:00 a.m. the following day, with slightly shorter hours on Sunday. Most places outside New York City will close earlier. Customers have thirty minutes to finish their drink after last call.

New York does allow for local variation. There are no dry counties, but towns can limit the hours when alcohol is available, restrict purchasing to either on- or off-premise, and limit the businesses that can possess licenses (usually to hotels or racetracks). Nine small towns upstate are completely dry; Argyle (pop. 3,782) is the largest of these towns.

QUICK REFERENCE

WHAT YOU CAN DO

- Purchase package beer from licensed grocery stores, convenience stores, and pharmacies between 8:00 a.m. and 3:00 a.m. seven days a week, and twenty-four hours a day, seven days a week in New York City.
- Buy package wine and liquor at licensed liquor stores between 8:00 a.m. and midnight Monday through Saturday, and between noon and 9:00 p.m. on Sunday.
- Order a drink in bars and restaurants between 8:00 a.m. and as late as 4:00 a.m. Monday through Saturday in some cities; however, most bars statewide close earlier. Bars don't open until noon on Sunday.
- Get your nickel back from bottle and can deposits.
- Order beer along with a meal for delivery or take-out.
- Enjoy happy hour specials.
- Bring your own bottle of wine to a restaurant.
- Fill a growler at a brewery.

WHAT YOU CAN'T DO

- Purchase package wine and liquor on Christmas.
- Smoke in bars and restaurants.
- Purchase package wine and liquor between midnight and 8:00 a.m. Monday through Saturday, and before noon or after 9:00 p.m. on Sunday.
- Purchase package beer between 3:00 a.m. and 8:00 a.m. outside of New York City.
- Order a drink between 4:00 a.m. and 8:00 a.m. Monday through Saturday, or between 4:00 a.m. and noon on Sunday.

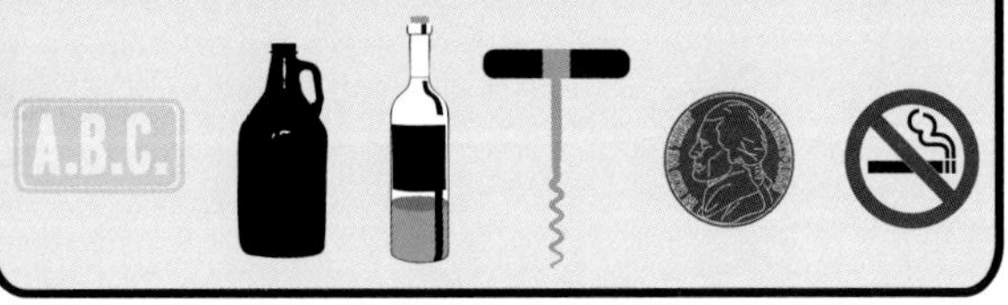

Source: New York State Liquor Authority

New Yorker **FRANKLIN D. ROOSEVELT** ran on an anti-Prohibition platform, calling the noble experiment a "damnable affliction." Within his first thirty days of office, he signed the Cullen-Harrison Act, which permitted the manufacture and sale of 3.2 beer. When he signed the act, the country was in the midst of the Great Depression and Roosevelt said, "I think this would be a good time for a beer." Nine months later, on Dec 5, 1933, the Twenty-First Amendment was ratified and the federal prohibition of alcohol was repealed.

MCSORLEY'S OLD ALE HOUSE at 15 East 7th Street in Manhattan takes its traditions seriously. Opened in 1854 by Irish immigrant John McSorley, they have operated continuously at the same location ever since. They defiantly remained open during Prohibition, serving patrons what they called "near beer." To this day, they only serve two beers: family recipes of pale ale and dark stout. When Prohibition was repealed and many bars began to admit women, McSorley's firmly stuck to their philosophy of "Good Ale, Raw Onions, and No Ladies." This policy continued until 1970, when a court order forced them to admit women. It did not, however, force them to provide women's restrooms, which didn't appear until 1986.

ERIN SERPICO
BARTENDER, DOGWOOD IN BEACON
TIP: ""Please" and "Thank You" go a long way. NYC might have a reputation for being brusque, but manners are a sign of respect, and that can make all the difference when ordering drinks and thus getting good service. Also, just because a bar stays open till 4:00 a.m. does not mean you should be there until 4:00 a.m. Or even close."

PENNSYLVANIA

Virtue, Liberty & Independence

The same people that brought you the DMV control every aspect of drinking in Pennsylvania, from warehousing and distributing liquor and wine to regulating the sale and consumption of beer.

If you want to buy wine or booze, you may do so only at a store owned and operated by the state. And when it comes to the beer here, it seems like the Commonwealth wants you to consume it by the case. There are only two ways to buy beer in Pennsylvania: by the case from a beer distributor, or by the six-pack (at an inflated price) from a bar or restaurant. The term "restaurant" is used loosely. Because of Pennsylvania's kooky liquor laws, supermarkets and gas stations that wish to sell beer to-go must obtain a restaurant license. This isn't just a legal loophole. The restaurant license dictates that they must be able to seat thirty people, and it must be in a segregated area of the establishment. Suds shoppers should be on the lookout for larger gas stations and supermarkets.

The City of Brotherly Love has a few colonial-era spots where you can raise a tankard. Look to the City Tavern (circa 1773) in Rittenhouse Square, the unofficial club house of the Continental Congress. Or visit the city's oldest continuously operating tavern, the 150-year-old McGillan's Olde Ale House. In Pottsville you'll find Yuengling, the oldest (and largest) American-owned brewery in the country, which is still run by the same family that founded it in 1829.

Just thirty-five years earlier, President George Washington and his Secretary of the Treasury Alexander Hamilton took up arms against their fellow countrymen in an effort to collect a young nation's first excise tax—a tax levied against whiskey production. In a time when the spirit was bartered for everything it wasn't used for, this tax enraged the entire nation. But it was the Monongahela rye-making "whiskey boys" of southwestern Pennsylvania that Washington chose to make an example of, leading a militia of over 13,000 men to quash the Whiskey Rebellion. The tax survived for just a few years, quietly overturned when Thomas Jefferson (who called it "odious") took office.

Celebrate distillation emancipation by heading to the South Side of Pittsburgh and any one of its more than 100 bars. Originally, East Carson Street served only to slake the thirst of steel workers from the foundries that once lined the mighty Mon. Pay homage to those hardworking men on whose backs our great nation was built by ordering a real Steel City cocktail, the Boilermaker—a shot and a beer. Make yours an "imp 'n arn" (a shot of Imperial Whiskey chased with an Iron City beer).

In the end, cocktail historian David Wondrich (who was "born on the banks of the Monongahela"—the very river that fed those steel mills and rye stills) knows how effective a belt is at soothing away any lingering anarchistic feelings you yourself might harbor towards the state's alcoholic big brother: "A proper drink at the right time – one mixed with care and skill and served in a true spirit of hospitality – is better than any other made thing at giving us the illusion, at least, that we're getting what we want from life."

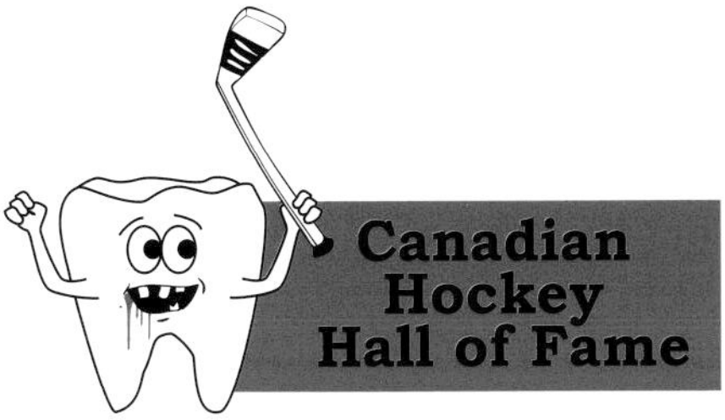

PRESIDENT OBAMA sent two cases of Yuengling beer to Canadian Prime Minister David Harper after losing a friendly wager over the 2010 Olympic gold women's ice hockey match. Harper wagered Molson. The cases of Pennsylvanian beer (from America's oldest brewery) now reside in the Canadian Hockey Hall of Fame in Toronto.

Pittsburgh's **IRON CITY BEER** introduced the world's first pull-tab beer can in 1962, which led to the rapid phaseout of flat-top cans that required a churchkey to open. By 1965, three-quarters of the breweries in America had adopted the new style, and by 1975 the industry had settled on the Sta-Tab design that is common today.

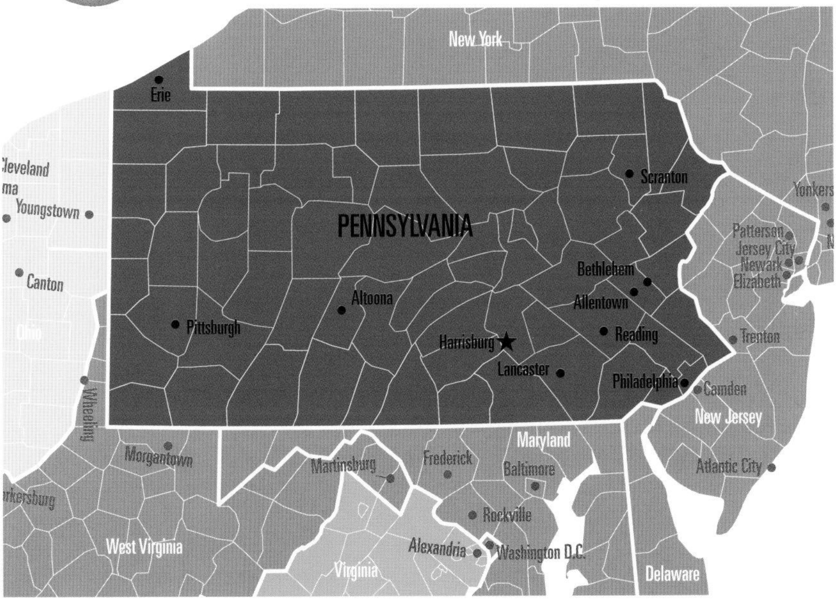

PENNSYLVANIA

WHAT'LL IT BE?

Pennsylvania is a control state for alcohol, and their laws are complicated. Package wine and liquor are only available from state-run liquor stores, which are open between 9:00 a.m. and 10:00 p.m. Monday through Saturday, but are closed on Sundays (unless the store has a Sunday license) and on federal holidays. Beer is not sold at the state stores, but it is available either from distributors or bars; distributors sell beer by the case or keg, while bars sell by the six-pack, growler, or large bottle (more than 22 ounces). Some grocery stores will have a restaurant attached so that they can sell beer, but beer must still be purchased through the restaurant rather than the grocery store. On-premise sales are allowed between 7:00 a.m. and 2:00 a.m. Monday through Saturday, with Sunday hours 11:00 a.m. to 2:30 a.m. by special permit. Restaurants without a Sunday permit can sell alcohol starting at 11:00 a.m. on Super Bowl Sunday, St. Patrick's Day, and New Year's Eve, if the latter two fall on Sundays.

Pennsylvania does allow for local options, both in licensing and taxation. More than 688 small communities (amounting to 12% of the state's population) prohibit all on- and off-premise alcohol sales. Allegheny County has a 7% tax on liquor, so drink prices will be higher in Pittsburgh.

QUICK REFERENCE

WHAT YOU CAN DO

- Purchase package wine or liquor from state liquor stores between 9:00 a.m. and 10:00 p.m. Monday through Saturday, and between 10:00 a.m. and 5:00 p.m. on Sunday if the store has a Sunday license.
- Order a drink at a bar or restaurant between 7:00 a.m. and 2:00 a.m. Monday through Saturday, and between 11:00 a.m. and 2:30 a.m. on Sunday if the establishment has a Sunday permit.
- Enjoy happy hour and drink specials.
- Bring your own bottle of wine to a restaurant.
- Purchase package beer at a distributor, bar, or brewery. Distributors only sell beer by the case, while bars and breweries typically sell six-packs. Bars and breweries can also fill growlers and sell larger bottles.
- Fill a growler at a bar or brewery.

WHAT YOU CAN'T DO

- Purchase package wine or liquor on the following federal holidays: Martin Luther King, Jr., Day, Presidents Day, Easter, Memorial Day, Independence Day, Labor Day, Columbus Day, Veterans Day, Thanksgiving, Christmas, and New Year's Day.
- Smoke in all enclosed bars and restaurants.
- Purchase package beer in a grocery store or liquor store.
- Order a drink at a bar between 2:00 a.m. and 7:00 a.m. Monday through Saturday, or before 11:00 a.m. on Sunday.
- Purchase package wine or liquor between 10:00 p.m. and 9:00 a.m., and before 10:00 a.m. or after 5:00 p.m. on Sundays.

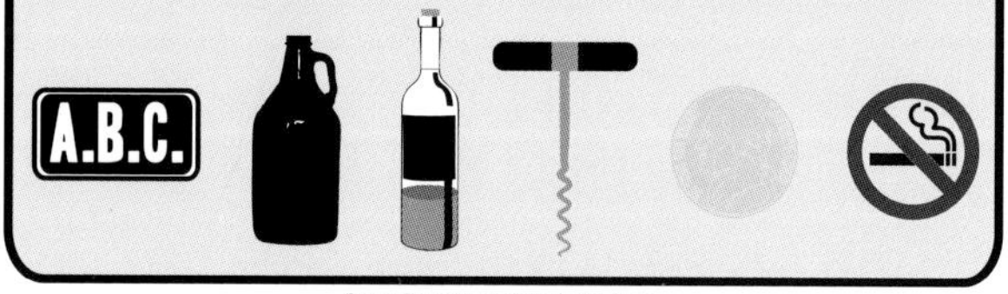

Source: Pennsylvania Liquor Control Board

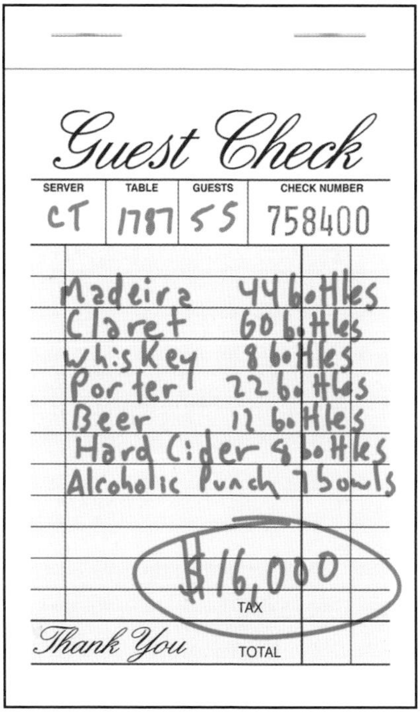

Philadelphia was the site of the **CONSTITUTIONAL CONVENTION** in 1787. As the founding fathers neared the finish line, they set out to celebrate. A bar tab from a farewell party for George Washington at the City Tavern shows that the fifty-five attendees drank fifty-four bottles of Madeira, sixty bottles of Claret, eight bottles of whiskey, twenty-two bottles of porter, twelve bottles of beer, eight bottles of hard cider, and seven bowls of alcoholic punch. In US dollars today, that bar tab would be about **$16,000.**

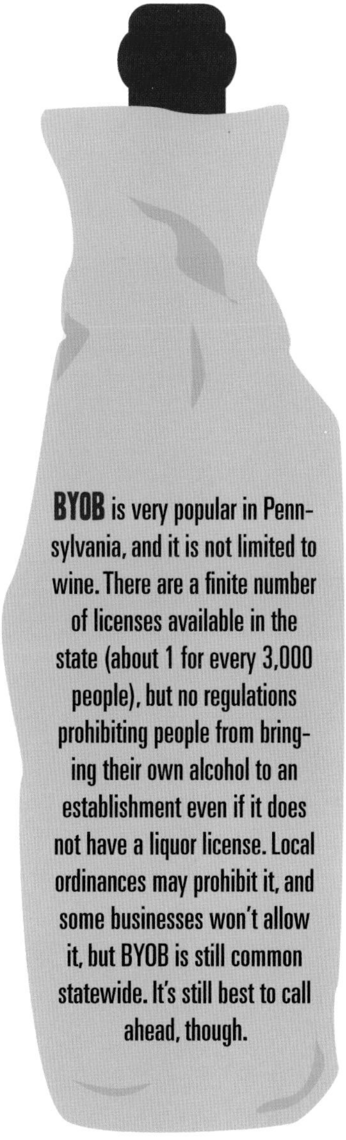

BYOB is very popular in Pennsylvania, and it is not limited to wine. There are a finite number of licenses available in the state (about 1 for every 3,000 people), but no regulations prohibiting people from bringing their own alcohol to an establishment even if it does not have a liquor license. Local ordinances may prohibit it, and some businesses won't allow it, but BYOB is still common statewide. It's still best to call ahead, though.

TIM KWEEDER
WINE DIRECTOR AT PETRUCE ET. AL. IN PHILADELPHIA

TIP: "Welcome to the Quaker State, where the government is the puppet master of the liquor system. Wine and liquor prices are as high as Cheech and Chong. Beer was given the "princess" treatment long ago, and because of that there is no shortage of stellar places for a nifty pint. Ole Brotherly Love is one of the best beer cities in the U.S. of A."

NEW JERSEY

Liberty and Prosperity

As the saying goes, you can't drink all day unless you start in the morning. For a full day's worth of drinking, head to Atlantic City, where there is no last call. Atlantic City is forty-eight blocks of fun: 24/7 drinking, gambling, and shopping, even on its four-mile-long boardwalk. Full-fledged bars and nightclubs spring up on the boardwalk in the summer months, with some pouring 24/7. Built in 1870, the boardwalk was the first of its kind. It was conceived by the aptly named Alexander Boardman, a railroad conductor intent on keeping sand from being tracked in from the beach to the city's trains and hotels.

New Jerseyan weekenders don't go to the "beaches," they go to the "shore." But not every New Jersey shore is a *Jersey Shore*. One need not GTL* with the guidos to drink in just the sun and sand. Indeed, the resort town of Ocean City is totally dry—no establishment sells alcohol there. There are dozens of other centuries-old communities in the state that are dry as well, some of which were founded by religious groups like the Quakers and Methodists.

Founded more than 200 years ago is Laird & Company, the oldest commercial distillery in the country. The company's main firewater is Laird's Applejack, also known as Jersey Lightning. This apple brandy distillate blend is as old as America itself, with records indicating that founding father George Washington requested the recipe.

The twenty-eighth president of the United States, Woodrow Wilson, has a Jersey connection: he was governor of the state before he took office. He also had the unfortunate honor of being the president of Princeton University who was responsible for the ouster of then-freshman Eugene O'Neill. *The Long Day's Journey into Night* playwright is rumored to have been expelled for throwing a beer bottle through President Wilson's window. In *The Iceman Cometh*, O'Neill, a life-long boozehound himself, wrote about three aging alcoholics who drink their days away at Harry Hope's Saloon. The jilted Jimmy Tomorrow, nicknamed for the date on which he would seek his old job back, learned early on that life frightened him when he was sober. So when his girlfriend left him he was happy to have "a good tragic excuse to drink as much as I damn well pleased."

*gym, tan, laundry

If you have been convicted of driving while intoxicated, you cannot apply for personalized license plates in New Jersey

I feel sorry for people who don't drink. When they wake up in the morning, that's as good as they are going to feel all day.
- FRANK SINATRA

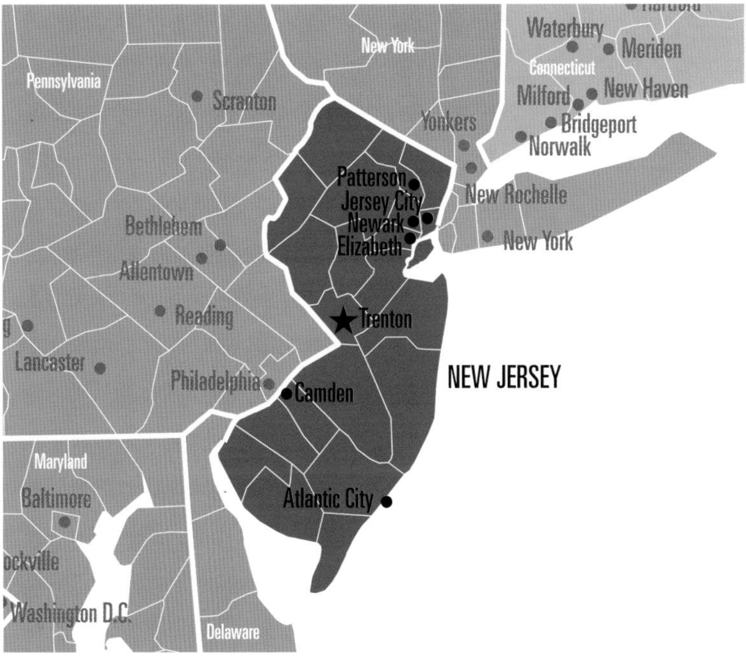

NEW JERSEY

WHAT'LL IT BE?

Alcohol laws in New Jersey differ by municipality. Package beer, wine, and liquor are available from "package" stores between 9:00 a.m. and 10:00 p.m. seven days a week. These package stores may be part of a bar or tavern, but will have a separate entrance. Beer and wine are also available at grocery stores, convenience stores, and pharmacies during hours when bars are open. Companies are not permitted to sell alcohol at more than two locations, so chain stores may not stock alcohol at all of their locations. Hours for on-premise sales and holiday sales vary by town.

New Jersey allows for significant local variation in setting sale hours and controlling retail licenses. Thirty-five small communities in southern New Jersey with Quaker or Methodist histories are completely dry and do not allow on- or off-premise sales, but possession is still allowed. In Atlantic City and Brigantine, on the other hand, alcohol sales are regulated by the Casino Control Commission rather than the Division of Alcohol Beverage Control. These two cities are the only places in the state where on-premise gambling is allowed, and alcohol is available for on- and off-premise purchase twenty-four hours a day.

QUICK REFERENCE

WHAT YOU CAN DO

- Purchase package beer, wine, or liquor from licensed liquor stores, grocery stores, convenience stores, and pharmacies between 9:00 a.m. and 10:00 p.m. seven days a week.
- Bring your own bottle of wine to a restaurant.
- Enjoy happy hour specials.
- Fill a growler at a brewery.

WHAT YOU CAN'T DO

- Gamble at most on-premise establishments, with the exception of casinos in Atlantic City and Brigantine.
- Play crane or claw games in bars, because it's not a game of skill but rather a gambling device.
- Smoke in all enclosed bars and restaurants, including e-cigarettes. Casinos are currently exempt from the smoking ban.
- Purchase package beer, wine, or liquor between 10:00 p.m. and 9:00 a.m. seven days a week.

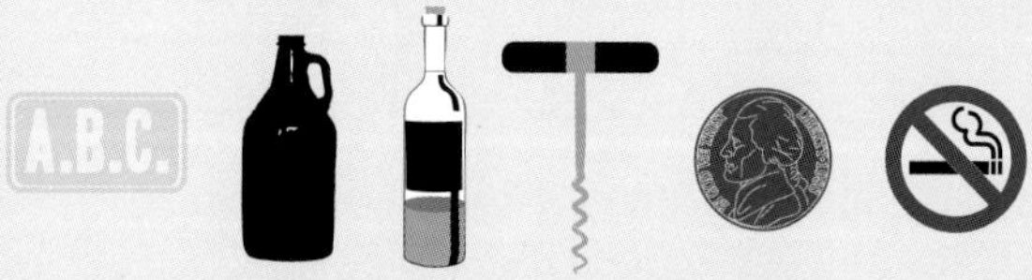

Source: The State of New Jersey Division of Alcoholic Beverage Control

The first American beer sold in a can was made by **NEWARK'S KRUEGER BREWING** in 1935. The American Can Company had been trying to persuade beer makers to can their product since the repeal of Prohibition, but all of the largest breweries were wary of transitioning from bottles. Mid-sized Krueger test-marketed 2,000 cans of its beer in January 1935, and the response was so positive that within three months Krueger was beginning to eat into the market share of the "big three": Anheuser-Busch, Pabst, and Schlitz. Krueger's competitors began canning immediately, and by the end of 1935, over 200 million cans of American beer had been sold, ushering in a new era of American beer drinking.

New Jersey is like a beer barrel, tapped at both ends, with all the live beer running into Philadelphia and New York.

- BEN FRANKLIN

SHANE MARKLEY
BARTENDER, DUSK NIGHTCLUB IN ATLANTIC CITY

TIP: "Atlantic City is one of the few municipalities in New Jersey that allow the sale of alcohol twenty-four hours a day. Drinking in public is not allowed and includes the beach and the boardwalk. This can constitute a heavy fine. One of Atlantic City's close neighbors, Ocean City, New Jersey, is a dry town and has never issued a liquor license, forbids the sale of alcohol, and prohibits BYOB at restaurants."

DELAWARE

Liberty and Independence

About the great state of Delaware, it's been said that any place that you really want to go is just a three-hour drive away! Chances are that you'll find yourself driving the I-95, a twenty-three-mile stretch that's one of the most congested routes in the country. Plan to stop for a snort and do some drinking, Delaware-style. Delaware has no sales tax on anything, including alcohol, making it an attractive shopping destination for neighboring states Pennsylvania, New Jersey, and Maryland. Though drinking while driving is illegal, there are no open container laws in the state, making a passenger's "cargarita" or "cardonnay" perfectly legit.

If you're making beer your travel buddy, take the road to Rehoboth Beach, where Dogfish Head was born. Its owner and founder Sam Calagione, who has written several books and even did a TV series, has almost single-handedly put Delaware on the beer destination map. Dogfish Head produces dozens of beers, including one of the highest alcohol beers ever manufactured: World Wide Stout, an imperial version that reaches 15-20% ABV (the strength of fortified wine)! Thankfully, the Dogfish Head empire now includes a beer-themed inn located within biking distance of the Rehoboth Beach pub, perfect for sleeping off all those pints.

Famous Delawarians include Dr. Oz, who advocates drinking a moderate amount of red wine, and Vice President and former Delaware Senator Joe Biden, who has reportedly never taken a drink in his life. That being said, the 2012 Obama campaign offered beer can cozies emblazoned with Biden's face and the toast, "Cheers Champ." Native son George Thorogood of the (Delaware) Destroyers made famous the order for one bourbon, one scotch, and one beer. But heed not his drinking advice, toasting travelers. Though the song goes, "the clock on the wall say three o'clock," last call for alcohol in Delaware is just one.

In 1753, a man traveling through the Delaware Valley made a list of all the drinks he encountered. Of the forty-eight beverages on the list, only three did not contain alcohol.

The Delaware legislature allowed liquor stores to fill growlers with draft beer in 2013 and the trend is growing. Unlike neighboring Maryland, where you have to purchase the growler in the store, in Delaware you can BYOG (Bring Your Own Growler) again and again and again.

Obama / Biden 2012 campaign memorabilia included a beer cozy with Sober Joe's mug.

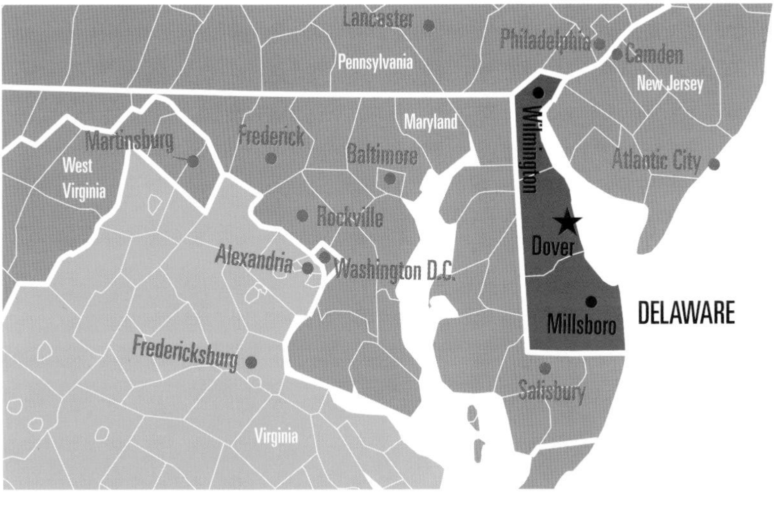

DELAWARE

WHAT'LL IT BE?

Although Delaware is not a control state, package beer, wine, and liquor are only available at liquor stores, tap rooms, and breweries. These are open between 9:00 a.m. and 1:00 a.m. Monday through Saturday, but are closed Thanksgiving, Christmas, and Easter. Sundays are considered holidays and many stores are closed, but those that have a Sunday license can operate between noon and 8:00 p.m. On-premise consumption is permitted between 9:00 a.m. and 1:00 a.m. seven days a week, except for Thanksgiving, Christmas, and Easter.

Delaware does allow for local variation in liquor laws. Towns of more than 50,000 can vote to restrict sale hours, but none appear to have done so. As in New Jersey and Pennsylvania, municipalities with a Methodist or Quaker history are likely to limit significantly the number of liquor licenses operating in the town.

QUICK REFERENCE

WHAT YOU CAN DO

- Purchase package beer, wine, or liquor from a licensed store between 9:00 a.m. and 1:00 a.m. Monday through Saturday, or between noon and 8:00 p.m. on Sunday if the store has a Sunday license.
- Order a drink at a bar or restaurant between 9:00 a.m. and 1:00 a.m. seven days a week.
- Fill a growler at a brewery.

WHAT YOU CAN'T DO

- Purchase package alcohol in grocery stores, convenience stores, or pharmacies.
- Smoke in all enclosed bars and restaurants.
- Buy more than one drink within fifteen minutes of last call.
- Purchase alcohol on Thanksgiving, Christmas, or Easter.
- Order a drink at a bar or restaurant between 1:00 a.m. and 9:00 a.m.
- Purchase package beer, wine, or liquor between 1:00 a.m. and 9:00 a.m. Monday through Saturday, or before noon and after 8:00 p.m. on Sunday.

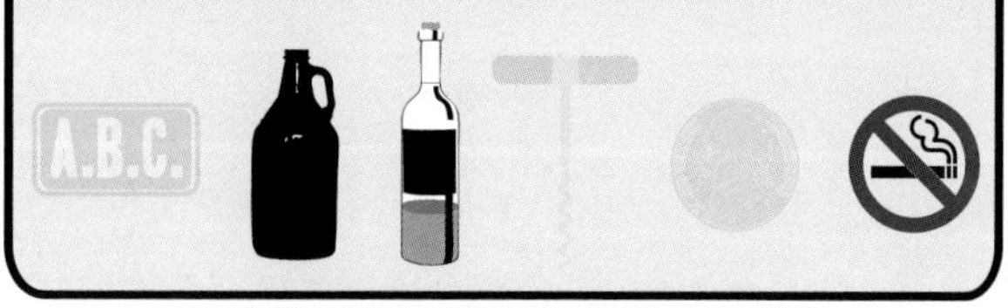

Source: The Office of the Delaware Alcoholic Beverage Control Commissioner (OABCC)

Alcohol is not subject to a sales tax in Delaware, and citizens of neighboring states are often tempted to take advantage of the lower booze prices. Transporting that bottle across state lines, however, can run afoul of laws in other states. Pennsylvania, for example, considers this **BOOTLEGGING** or "border bleed" and, if caught, violators can be subject to fines as high as $10 per bottle or can of beer and $25 per bottle of liquor. State Liquor Control enforcement officials may also confiscate the contraband.

Legend has it that **GEORGE WASHINGTON**, while Commander of the Continental Army, quenched his thirst at the same artesian well that provides the water for Twin Lakes Brewing's beer. Greenville-based Twin Lakes is named after the two spring-fed lakes on their property and has a tasting room in a former tractor barn of the Twin Lakes farm (est. 1826).

CHRISTINE BICHLER
BARTENDER, LULA BRAZIL A BRAZILIAN IN REHOBETH BEACH

TIP: "If you want to be part of the crowd, spend your summers at the beaches and your winters in the city of Wilmington. As a reminder to out of state visitors: liquor stores are one stop shopping in Delaware and the only place to purchase beer, wine, and liquor. Liquor cannot be purchased at any grocery or convenience stores. Liquor stores are open seven days a week now. The Blue Laws were lifted in 2003 for Sunday liquor sales."

MARYLAND

Fatti Maschii, Parole Femine
(Strong Deeds, Gentle Words)

Edgar Allan Poe made his home in Baltimore. His writings feature hallucinogenic visions and delirious verses, but his reputation as a booze-hound and opium addict has been largely exaggerated by history and perpetuated by fans eager to romanticize their hero as a debaucher extraordinaire, much like his French translator Charles Baudelaire. What's not disputed is that he is so closely associated with the city that his former residence is now a museum, the day of his birth is celebrated nearby at his gravesite, and even the city's football team is named after his epic poem. "The Raven" is also the name of a special lager produced by the Baltimore-Washington Beer Works. The city's oldest bar, The Horse You Came In On Saloon (known to locals simply as The Horse) even boasts that they served Poe his last beer. They're still serving beer at The Horse, just as they did before, during, and after Prohibition—they also claim to be the country's oldest continually-operating saloon.

While you ponder weak and weary where to purchase your next beery, here's some advice to keep you from rapping, tapping on that barroom door. Maryland is a local option state districted by counties, though there are no dry counties in the state. There are essentially only a couple of state-wide laws: a closing time of 2:00 a.m., and a recently imposed increase in alcohol taxes. This tax increase, the first in forty years, brings the rate on liquor and beer up to a whopping 9%. In the D.C. metropolitan area, Maryland has the highest taxes on alcohol, so you are likely to pay less in the District itself, followed by Virginia.

Iconic indulger George Herman "Babe" Ruth is from Baltimore, born just blocks away from Camden Yards. The Bambino's alcoholic appetites are as legendary as his batting average. He could pitch, he could hit, and he could put away a dozen hot dogs and the better part of a barrel of beer before a game. He was rumored to have broken a batting slump by pulling an all-nighter.

The Babe was long retired when the United States entered WWII, but it was during that war that baseball stadiums across the country began playing the national anthem before they played ball. Maryland lawyer Francis Scott Key penned the words to "The Star-Spangled Banner" at Chesapeake Bay as he witnessed Ft. McHenry withstand the massive British bombardment. The rousing melody of our national anthem, however, belongs to an old English drinking song. So when you stand and doff your cap, also raise your beer and toast "To the land of the free, and the home of the brave!"

NATIONAL BOHEMIAN beer, or Natty Boh, has been associated with Baltimore since 1885. Even though it is now owned by Pabst and no longer brewed in Maryland, most of the Boh brewed is still consumed in the state. They were the first beer to roll out a six-pack in the 1940s and are the official sponsor of the Orioles.

In 1662, **LORD BALTIMORE** established 300 acres of vineyards to promote alcohol production in colonial America.

An Edgar Allan Poe-inspired beer, "The Raven," is the name of a special lager produced by the **BALTIMORE-WASHINGTON BEER WORKS.**

THE RAVEN

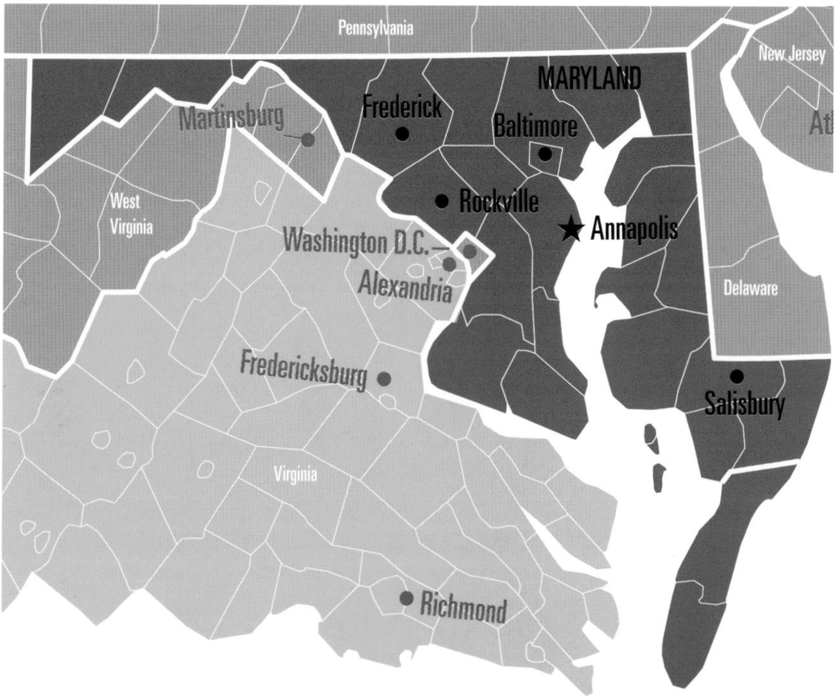

MARYLAND

WHAT'LL IT BE?

Maryland liquor laws are determined at the local level, with each of the 23 counties plus the city of Baltimore weighing in on how alcohol is regulated. In general, package alcohol is available from licensed retailers from 6:00 a.m. until midnight, but some counties may have longer or shorter hours In some places, stores may open as late as 11:00 a.m. and close as early as 6:00 p.m. or as late as 2:00 a.m. On-premise sales are generally allowed from 6:00 a.m. until 2:00 a.m. the following day, again subject to county ordinances. Alcohol sales may be restricted on Sundays, New Year's Day, and Election Day, subject to county laws.

There is significant local variation in liquor laws in Maryland. Counties can curtail sale hours and restrict the days when alcohol is available for purchase, especially on Sundays. Counties can also limit the businesses eligible for different types of on- and off-premises licenses, so retailers will vary county by county. The city of Baltimore, for example, does not allow grocery store package sales, but in a handful of counties, including Talbot and St. Mary's, beer, wine, and liquor are sold in grocery stores.

QUICK REFERENCE

WHAT YOU CAN DO

- Purchase package beer, wine, or liquor from a licensed liquor store between 8:00 a.m. and 2:00 a.m., Monday through Saturday, and between 11:00 a.m. and 6:00 p.m. on Sunday.
- Order a drink at a bar or restaurant between 6:00 a.m. and 2:00 a.m. seven days a week, depending on county ordinances.
- Enjoy happy hour specials.
- Fill a growler at a brewery, brewpub, or liquor store, depending on county ordinances.

WHAT YOU CAN'T DO

- Smoke in all enclosed bars and restaurants.

***It's very difficult to make general statements about what you can't do statewide in Maryland because the laws are determined locally.

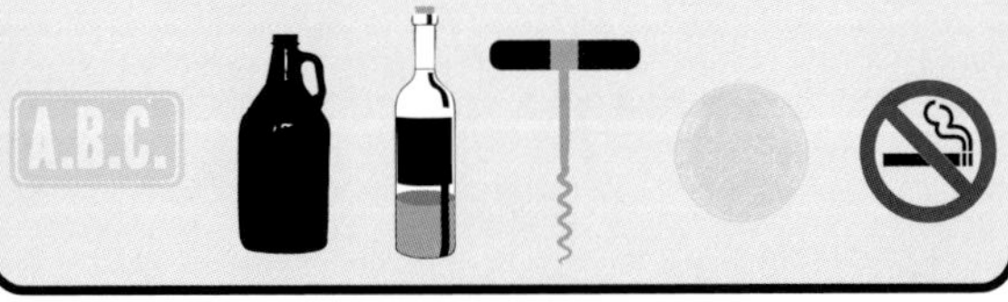

Source: Code of Maryland

While still a colony, Maryland outlawed **PUBLIC DRUNKENNESS** as early as 1638, with a fine of 30 pounds of tobacco. By 1642, this fine had more than tripled, and a third charge of drunkenness led to a three year loss of voting rights.

"NOT DRUNK IS HE WHO FROM THE FLOOR, CAN RISE AGAIN AND STILL DRINK MORE, BUT DRUNK IS HE WHO PROSTRATE LIES, WITHOUT THE POWER TO DRINK OR RISE."

-Maryland resident Justice Askham defending his own sobriety after a display of public drunkenness

In an effort to curb sexual assaults and binge drinking among college students, Maryland recently joined twelve other states in banning **HIGH-PROOF GRAIN ALCOHOL**. The bill was backed by a group of university presidents.

BRENDAN DORR
BARTENDER, B&O AMERICAN BRASSIERE IN BALTIMORE

TIP: "Maryland has a long history of beer and spirits, from American whiskey's humble beginnings of Maryland Style Rye to the German breweries scattered about Baltimore City. Even William Walters, Baltimore's local philanthropic art collector, now the Walters Art Museum, built his fortune on rye whiskey. However, if you are going to drink in Baltimore and feel like a real local, then order a shot of Pikesville Rye and Natty Boh, hon!"

Justitia Omnibus
(Justice to All)

WASHINGTON D.C.

Our nation's capital, bordered by Virginia and engulfed by Maryland, is just sixty-eight square miles large. It is a city without a state, governed by a mayor and a city council, though overseen by Congress. With a single non-voting representative in Congress, the District has all the burdens of statehood without any of the rights. Their license plates read, "Taxation without Representation." The District also went dry nearly three years before the rest of the country, making for sixteen miserable years of Prohibition for Washingtonians. It's enough to drive a Districter to drink!

Bar hopping in Washington, be it in Adams Morgan or Dupont Circle, Foggy Bottom or Georgetown, is terribly simple, thanks to the Metro. It runs until 3:00 a.m. on the weekends, which is also coincidentally when bars close. Last call is 2:00 a.m. on weekdays and 4:00 a.m. on New Year's.

Cabs are plentiful in the District of Cocktails. Smart lushes will remember to pick up their hotel's business card before heading out to paint the town red (or blue). Since there are scores of hotel chains in the city, it will make getting back much easier. At the end of the night, just hand the card to the cabbie and pour yourself into the back seat.

Washington is a city full of Republicans and Democrats, but one thing they have usually agreed on is drinking. President Washington distilled whiskey, Jefferson was an oenophile, and Madison had his own cocktail (A Yard of Flannel, a drink consisting of ale, eggs, sugar, nutmeg, ginger, and rum or brandy). Madison also proposed the creation of an official federal brewery and a "Secretary of Beer." President Obama held the infamous Beer Summit near the White House Rose Garden, and his kitchen also turns out White House Honey Ale home brew.

Since the 1850s, presidents and politicians have indulged in quiet deals over stiff drinks at the Round Robin bar inside the Willard Hotel. Located just one block from the White House, the Willard has been visited by too many politicians, insiders, and writers to list. One of them was the poet Walt Whitman, whose portrait hangs in the Round Robin bar. Whitman even wrote about the establishment, though not too kindly. In disgust over his government's backroom machinations, he roared: "Resolution, manliness, seem to have abandoned Washington.... Sneak, blow, put on airs there in Willard's sumptuous parlors and barrooms...no explanation shall save you."

The official drink of Washington, D.C., as declared by their City Council in 2011, is the RICKEY. It originates from a long-gone dive bar named Shoomaker's. In the 1860s, powerful politicians and journalists would gather in the filth and drink what's been described as "air conditioning in a glass."

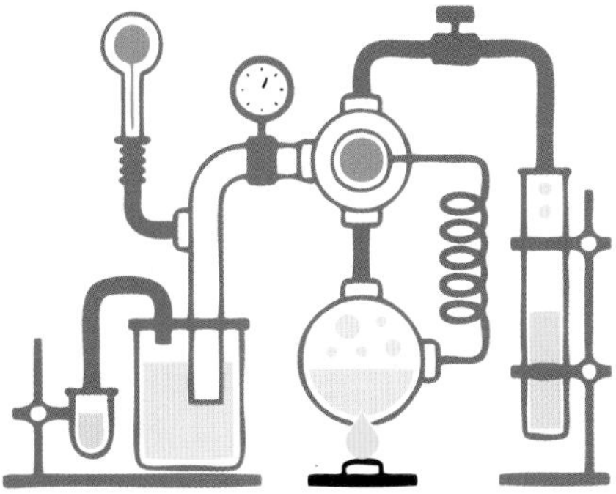

One of the most famous home stills in American history was the prop created for the television show M*A*S*H, which for eleven years was the centerpiece of the Swamp. At the end of production, 20th Century Fox donated the set, including the still, to the Smithsonian Institute. It was on display at the National Museum of American History for a year and a half. When the exhibit ended, the still was packed into a box and is presumably warehoused in DC.

WASHINGTON D.C.

WHAT'LL IT BE?

Washington, D.C., liquor laws are less restrictive than neighboring Maryland's. Package liquor is available from liquor stores, while package beer and wine can be purchased from grocery stores, convenience stores, and pharmacies. Hours of sale for both on- and off-premise consumption are from 8:00 a.m. to 2:00 a.m. Monday through Thursday, from 8:00 a.m. to 3:00 a.m. Friday and Saturday, and from 10:00 a.m. to 2:00 a.m. on Sundays. Alcohol sales are allowed until 4:00 a.m. on days preceding federal holidays and on weekends adjacent to Memorial Day, Labor Day, Independence Day, and New Year's Day. This holiday extension does not apply to Inauguration Week.

Liquor laws are consistent through all the wards of Washington, D.C. Much like states' local option laws, district law permits wards to prohibit the sale of alcohol, but currently none do.

QUICK REFERENCE

WHAT YOU CAN DO

- Purchase package alcohol or order a drink at a bar, restaurant, or brewery between 8:00 a.m. and 2:00 a.m. Monday through Thursday, between 8:00 a.m. and 3:00 a.m. Friday and Saturday, and between 10:00 a.m. and 2:00 a.m. on Sundays.
- Bring your own bottle of wine to a restaurant.
- Enjoy happy hour specials.
- Fill a growler with beer at a brewery or grocery store, or at a brewpub between 7:00 a.m. and midnight.
- Fill a growler or bottle with wine at a wine pub between 7:00 a.m. and midnight.
- Smoke in a restaurant's patio area or other outdoor seating, at the discretion of the establishment.
- Purchase alcohol until 4:00 a.m. on a federal or district holiday, including the Saturdays and Sundays before Labor Day and Memorial Day.

WHAT YOU CAN'T DO

- Smoke in all enclosed bars and restaurants.
- Buy less than six miniature bottles of spirits or wine at a time.
- Purchase a half pint of hard liquor, except for Scotch, Irish whiskey, brandy, or rum.
- Order your next drink before you've finished your last.
- Fill a growler with beer or wine between midnight and 7:00 a.m.
- Purchase alcohol for on- or off-premise consumption between 2:00 a.m. and 8:00 a.m. Monday through Friday, 3:00 a.m. and 8:00 a.m. on Saturday, or 3:00 a.m. and 10:00 a.m. on Sunday.

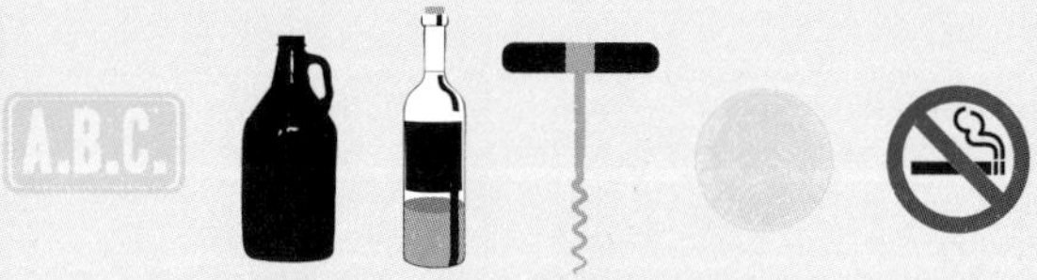

Source: Washington, D.C., Alcoholic Beverage Regulation Administration

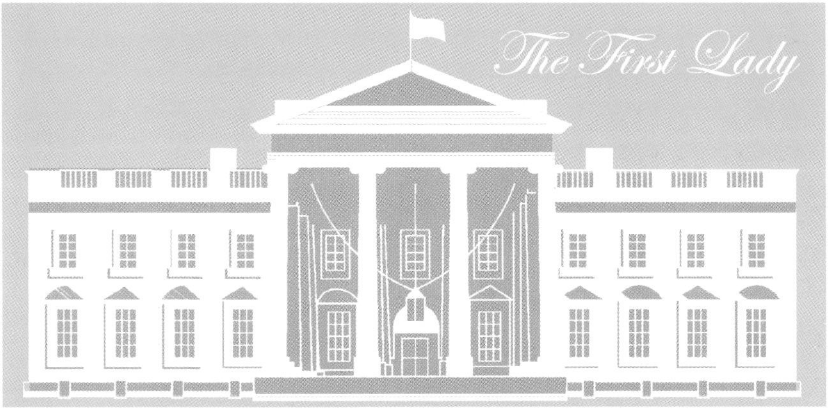

THE NATIONAL FIRST LADIES' LIBRARY has cataloged the favorite alcoholic beverages of several presidential wives and what they preferred to serve (or not serve) guests while living in the White House. Lucy Hayes banned alcoholic beverages, earning her the nickname "Lemonade Lucy"; Sarah Polk served only wine but not hard liquor; Rosalynn Carter only served wine and beer; Frances Cleveland served alcohol to her dinner guests but only drank mineral water herself. They also note that several First Ladies were teetotalers for either religious reasons or because of alcoholism in their family. And Betty Ford courageously went public with her addition to alcohol in 1977, the year after she left the While House, and founded the Betty Ford Center for Addiction Recovery.

There were several First Ladies, however, who enjoyed a regular cocktail including:

JACQUELINE KENNEDY - a traditional Lime Daiquiri
MAMIE EISENHOWER - a fruit Old-Fashioned
BESS TRUMAN - a plain Old-Fashioned
HELEN "NELLIE" TAFT - lager beer and Champagne cocktail
EDITH WILSON - Virginia Gentleman-brand bourbon on the rocks
JULIA TYLER - Champagne punch
DOLLEY MADISON - whiskey punch
JULIA GRANT - Roman Punch
ABIGAIL ADAMS - Rum Cider Toddy
FLORENCE HARDING - Scotch-and-soda
IDA MCKINLEY - wine

Florence Harding served as bartender to her husband and his friends when they came to play poker in the White House—during Prohibition.

GLENDON HARTLEY
BARTENDER, CAVA MEZZE AND OCOPA RESTAURANT

TIP: "The best advice I can give visitors of the District is "trust the natives." D.C. has a unique drinking culture because most of its inhabitants are transplants from other areas of the country and the world. The best thing about drinking alcohol in D.C. is that it has more relaxed liquor laws than many states, so we can serve virtually any type of alcohol from almost anywhere on the planet. Because of this fact we have one of the most unique cocktail scenes in the United States."

WEST VIRGINIA

Montani Semper Liberi
(Mountaineers Are Always Free)

Leave no doubt, mountaineers are more than the denizens of wild, wonderful West Virginia. Mountaineers are the football team for the #1 party school in the country, West Virginia University! It goes without saying that they may have earned that reputation due to tailgating and the fallout that follows: binge drinking. But in a counterintuitive effort to curb student intoxication during football season, WVU administrators decided to start serving beer at the games (a rarity in college football)—and to lock the doors, prohibiting re-entry. For all practical purposes, the tailgate ends when the game begins, and any further drinking is done at the discretion of licensed servers. After the first year of implementation, arrests were down 35%, and WVU cleared a cool half million in revenue.

Performed at every single WVU home game since 1972, John Denver's song "Country Roads" serves as an anthem for both the university and the state. The song was played at the funeral of longtime senator and teetotaler Robert Byrd. Mountain State Brewing produces an amber ale called Almost Heaven, highlighting the lyrics of the song. Curiously, "Country Roads" is played countless times at Oktoberfest in Munich, and it's always sung in English.

Oktoberfest is a fitting home for the tune. Because when it comes to the Mountaineers, well, they drink beer. West Virginia consumes the least amount of both wine and spirits per capita in the nation, with each person shooting back less than a gallon of spirits per year. When the state got out of the liquor business in 1990, they began auctioning off permits to sell liquor (which are re-auctioned every ten years). The result is that the places where liquor is sold are scattershot throughout the state. One outlet of a particular convenience store or drug store may have a permit, while other outlets of the same store may not, so ask around.

Country music star Brad Paisley spent his youth and formative years in the Mountain State, so he should know a thing or two about time well wasted. Order another round to help your dancing, and sing along to his hit song "Alcohol" while you enjoy the best times you'll never remember as you approach the state's quite late last call of 3:00 a.m.

In an effort to raise a troubled economy and tap into agritourism dollars, West Virginia recently legalized mini-distilleries. Mini-distilleries are licensed by the state and must produce 25% of the ingredients on the property and also not purchase more than 25% of the ingredients from out of state.

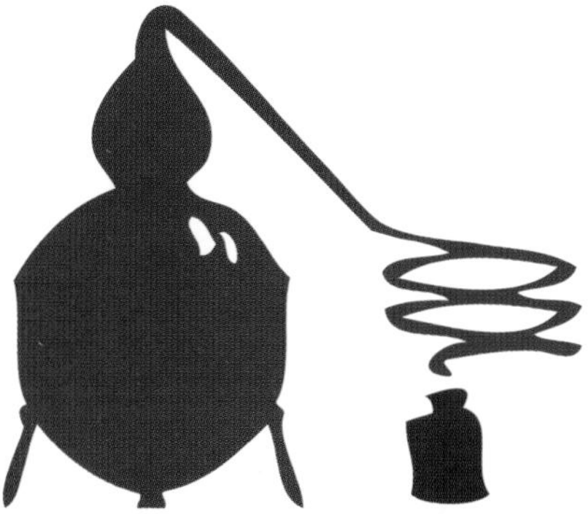

The History Channel quickly capitalized on this and created a show called **HATFIELDS AND MCCOYS: WHITE LIGHTNING**, in which descendants of these two rival families must work together to create "moonshine." The distillery featured in the show is in the tiny town of Gilbert, located in Mingo County, home to the long-standing feud.

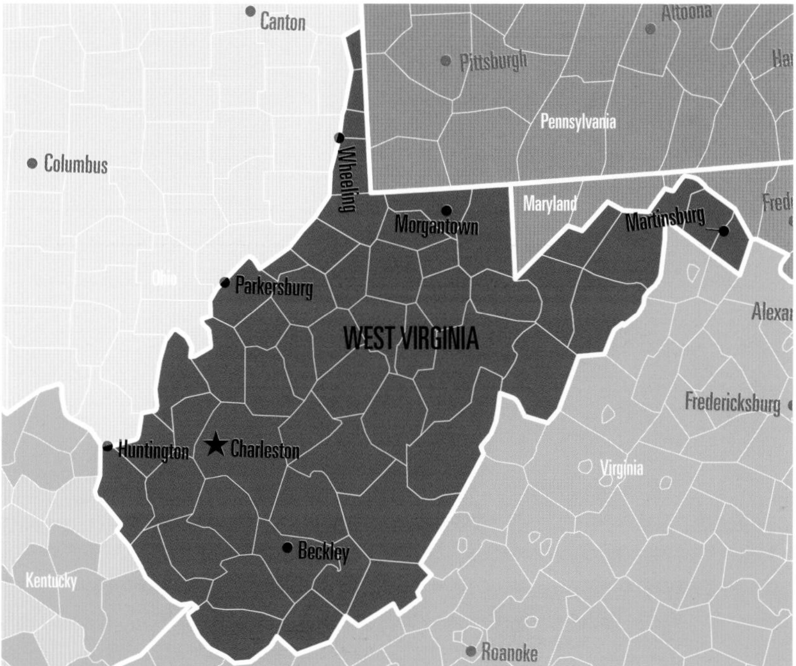

WEST VIRGINIA

WHAT'LL IT BE?

West Virginia is a control state for all beverages over 14% ABV, so package liquor and fortified wines are only available at some licensed grocery stores, convenience stores, and pharmacies. Because liquor licenses are limited, not all chain stores will sell alcohol in every location. Although these stores cannot sell alcohol on Sundays and on Christmas, their sale hours are otherwise generous and they can operate from 8:00 a.m. to midnight Monday through Saturday. West Virginia considers beer under 12% to be "nonintoxicating" and is available with wine under 14% throughout the state. Hours for package sales of nonintoxicating beer and wine are between 7:00 a.m. and 2:00 a.m. Monday through Saturday, and between 1:00 p.m. and 2:00 a.m. on Sunday. On-premise hours for bars and restaurants are the same as for beer and wine package purchases.

West Virginia allows for local jurisdictions to limit the sale of alcohol. Currently no counties prohibit the sale of alcohol, although some limit the number of liquor licenses or place restrictions on licensees.

QUICK REFERENCE

WHAT YOU CAN DO

- Purchase package liquor at a liquor store between 8:00 a.m. and midnight Monday through Saturday.
- Purchase package wine and beer at a licensed grocery store, convenience store, or pharmacy between 7:00 a.m. and 2:00 a.m. Monday through Saturday, and between 1:00 p.m. and 2:00 a.m. on Sunday.
- Order a drink at a bar or restaurant between 7:00 a.m. and 2:00 a.m. (3:00 a.m. if it has a club license) Monday through Saturday, and between 1:00 p.m. and 2:00 a.m. on Sunday.
- Enjoy happy hour specials.
- Fill a growler at a brewery, brewpub, or licensed retailer.
- Smoke in bars and restaurants, depending on local ordinances.

WHAT YOU CAN'T DO

- Purchase more than 10 gallons of liquor at a time.
- Purchase package liquor on Christmas.
- Purchase package liquor on Sunday.
- Order a drink between 2:00 a.m. and 7:00 a.m. (or between 3:00 a.m. and 7:00 a.m. at an establishment with a club license) Monday through Saturdays or between 2:00 a.m. and 1:00 p.m. on Sunday.
- Purchase package wine or beer between 2:00 a.m. and 7:00 a.m. Monday through Saturday, or between 2:00 a.m. and 1:00 p.m. on Sunday.

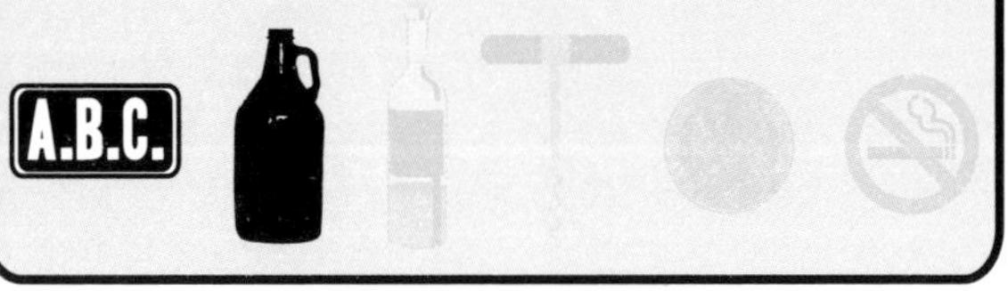

Source: West Virginia Alcohol Beverage Control Administration

White Sulphur Springs, home to the Greenbrier Resort, was a summer destination for much of the Southern gentry in the early 19th century. Reports of Greenbrier guests drinking the classic Southern cocktail, the Mint Julep, begin to appear as early as 1816. The resort is also home to **THE BUNKER**, a declassified Cold War-era fallout shelter designed to hold the entire US Congress. It's now open to the public and is available for meetings and events. The Greenbrier staff can provide a James Bond theme (presumably martinis, shaken not stirred), and a *M*A*S*H* theme (presumably not homemade gin from Hawkeye's still).

LONG DRY SPELL BEGINS IN THE MOUNTAIN STATE

PROHIBITION began in West Virginia in 1914, four years before the passage of the Eighteenth Amendment. Enforcement was lax, however, and bootlegging from surrounding wet states flourished, especially in mining camps of immigrants who were unable to vote against Prohibition in the first place. Most miners, largely of Italian and Slavic descent, saw alcohol as a small consolation for the poor working man and an essential element of their Old World culture.

BRIAN HUTCHISON
BARTENDER AT BRIDGE ROAD BISTRO IN WEST VIRGINIA

TIP: "Our blue laws say that bars with a "club license" can make last call at 3:00 a.m. on the weekends and need to have everyone out of the bar at 3:30 a.m.. If you are traveling through, you should be sure and visit the local establishments as opposed to the chains. We have a lot of great locally-owned restaurants and bars and welcome visitors from out of town."

VIRGINIA

Old Dominion

From the massive alcoholic appetites of the founding fathers to the wet and wild coeds of Virginia Beach, Virginia surely is for lovers. . . of liquor.

Virginia was home to the first permanent English settlement in the country, Jamestown. By 1790, the per capita consumption for colonists over the age of fifteen was thirty-four gallons of beer and cider, five gallons of distilled spirits, and one gallon of wine. Fittingly, the first alcohol law in the country, a law against public drunkenness, was enacted in 1619 in Jamestown. Some 400 years later, the city of Fairfax continues the crackdown on being drunk in public (or DIP as the law is known); the police there have been reported to enter bars and administer breathalyzer tests to ordinary patrons.

Virginia is the birthplace of the father of our country, George Washington. I cannot tell a lie, Washington sloshed his way into his first elected office by wetting the whistles of voters. He distributed nearly 150 gallons of hooch to polling places on Election Day. After he became General Washington, the American taxpayers would be the one paying the tab. Washington eschewed a salary, instead asking that Congress simply cover his expenses. In the span of just seven months, over $6,000 worth of alcohol swilled past Washington's wooden choppers. As president, Washington sought out the same sort of compensation. But Congress declined, saving money by paying him a $25,000 salary instead.

After office, Washington built a distillery at Mt. Vernon. Within a couple of years, and close to the time of his death, he was one of the largest distillers in the country, producing about 11,000 gallons of mostly rye whiskey. A functioning reproduction of the distillery is open from April to October to visitors near Mt. Vernon, with George Washington's Rye Whiskey (using his same recipe) periodically available in the gift shop. This is currently the only place in the country where one can view the complete distillation process (from grain crop to finished bottle).

Those first Jamestown settlers hit land at Cape Henry, in the northern part of Virginia Beach. The city is now the most populous in the state, and is also one of the most popular tourist attractions. Spring breakers, you'll be pleased to know that in Virginia you are considered twenty-one on the day before your birthday. Look for beer and wine in supermarkets and convenience stores. Liquor in the state is controlled by the ABC (Alcoholic Beverage Control) and is sold at state-run ABC stores. The top-selling ABC store is on Hilltop in Virginia Beach. Virginia Beach also has the third and fourth top-selling locations, maybe in part because of their restaurant sales. A staggering half a million Orange Crush cocktails from Waterman's Surfside Grille are drunk annually, and no drinking tour of Virginia Beach would be complete without one. More than 10,000 people attend Crush Fest, the annual féte dedicated to the refreshing cocktail. Good thing bartenders can squeeze out the citrus cooler in five seconds flat!

GEORGE WASHINGTON sloshed his way into his first elected office by wetting the whistles of voters. He distributed nearly 150 gallons of hooch to polling places on Election Day.

BAND MEMBERS may not drink at a mixed -beverage establishment until after they're finished performing or during their dinner break. Musicians can drink while they perform at places with a beer and wine license.

Half a million **ORANGE CRUSH** cocktails from Waterman's Surfside Grille are drunk annually.

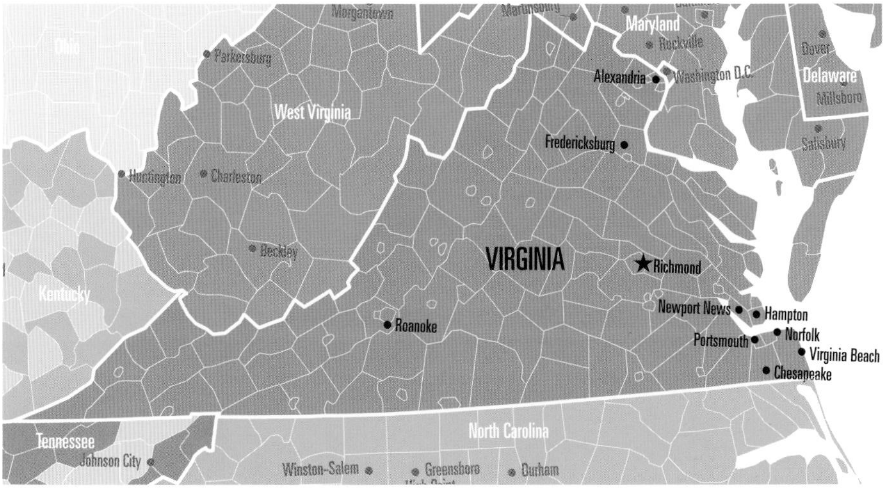

VIRGINIA

WHAT'LL IT BE?

Although Virginia is a control state for liquor, it has some of the most straightforward alcohol laws in the South. Package liquor is only available from state-run ABC liquor stores between 10:00 a.m. and 9:00 p.m. Monday through Saturday, and between 1:00 p.m. and 6:00 p.m. on Sundays. Beer and wine are available from a wide variety of retailers, including grocery stores, convenience stores, and pharmacies, from 6:00 a.m. until midnight seven days a week. Bars and restaurants can serve alcohol from 6:00 a.m. until 2:00 a.m. every day of the year.

Virginia does allow for local options, and ten counties have chosen not to allow on-premise liquor sales. Beer and wine are still available by the drink, as are package beer, wine, and liquor at licensed retailers. These counties are all in the southwestern part of the state.

QUICK REFERENCE

WHAT YOU CAN DO

- Purchase package liquor from ABC stores every day of the year. Hours are from 10:00 a.m. to 9:00 p.m. Monday through Saturday and from 1:00 p.m. to 6:00 p.m. on Sunday.
- Order a drink at a bar or restaurant between 6:00 a.m. and 2:00 a.m. seven days a week.
- Purchase package beer and wine at a grocery store, convenience store, or pharmacy, between 6:00 a.m. and midnight seven days a week.
- Bring your own bottle of wine to a restaurant.
- Take an unfinished bottle of wine from dinner home.
- Enjoy happy hour specials.
- Fill a growler at a brewery, brewpub, or other beer retailer.
- Smoke on a restaurant's outdoor patio.

WHAT YOU CAN'T DO

- Smoke in an enclosed restaurant or bar.
- Order a drink between 2:00 a.m. and 6:00 a.m.
- Purchase package beer and wine between midnight and 6:00 a.m.
- Purchase package liquor between 9:00 p.m. and 10:00 a.m. Monday through Saturday, and before 1:00 p.m. or after 6:00 p.m. on Sunday.

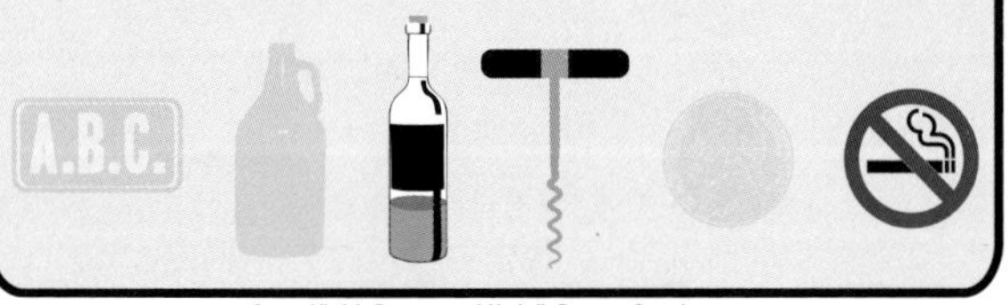

Source: Virginia Department of Alcoholic Beverage Control

Until recently, bars could only advertise **HAPPY HOUR** specials inside the building or on a small sign (17" x 22") attached to the outside of the business. Bar owners began to run afoul of the law when they would post happy hour specials on Facebook or Twitter because it was considered advertising. Recent legislation has eased those restrictions.

SANGRIA was illegal in Virginia until 2008 due to a Prohibition-era law that forbid the mixing of wine or beer with other spirits. The amended law only applies specifically to Sangria though, so don't expect to find a Kir, a Kir Royale, or any of the beer cocktails mixologists are creating elsewhere. Ironically, all manner of beer and booze mixtures (with colorful names like Whistle Belly, Bellowstop, Bogus, and Flip) were part of daily life in Colonial Williamsburg and elsewhere in the colonies.

JOHN BARLEYCORN was alcohol personified. His origin stems from an ancient British folk song and his name is a combination of the two main ingredients in making beer and spirits. When Prohibition began, an evangelical preacher named Billy Sunday presided over a "funeral" for John Barleycorn in Norfolk that attracted 15,000 supporters. Newspaper reports described twenty pallbearers carrying a twenty-foot coffin led by the devil himself in a crimson suit. Sunday's vitriolic eulogy signaled victory for the thousands of Virginians in attendance and concluded with these words: "Farewell, you good-for-nothing, God-forsaken, iniquitous, bleary-eyed, bloated-faced, old imp of perdition."

ASHLEY VINCI
BARTENDER, BILLY'S RESTAURANT IN ROANOKE

TIP: "One requirement to hold a liquor license in Virginia is to maintain a certain percentage of food sales. This means there is no such thing as a typical 'bar' in the state. All bars are restaurants, but not all restaurants have bars. Also, if you want to have a casual drink, go early. If you are looking for more of a social bar scene, you might want to wait until later at night."

NORTH CAROLINA

Esse Quam Videri
(To Be Rather Than to Seem)

After the Revolutionary War, North Carolina set out to establish a new state capital. State senator Joel Lane had a parcel of land in Raleigh he was eager to sell, so he invited the search committee to visit. After their tour of the plantation, he took them to a tavern for a little Southern hospitality. Reportedly, they enjoyed a potent local bourbon tipple called Cherry Bounce throughout the evening. Legend has it that the committee didn't realize until the fog in their heads had cleared the next morning that they had agreed to buy the land. Raleigh became the state capital in 1792. A drink called the Cherry Bounce is still on the menu at an old Raleigh haunt, The Deep South Bar. Folks say it tastes like a spiked version of Cheerwine, a local soda.

Two legendary drinkers were residents, albeit temporary, of North Carolina: the wrestler Andre the Giant, and the writer F. Scott Fitzgerald. When The Giant retired from wrestling he settled on his ranch in Ellerbe. He weighed in at more than 500 pounds and had a drinking appetite the size of his famous physique: he once pile-drived down 119 beers in a single sitting. In a 1981 edition of *Sports Illustrated*, Terry Todd reported his daily consumption at a case of beer, a couple bottles of wine, multiple shots, and a half dozen mixed drinks. Fitzgerald chose the small town of Hendersonville to work on his novel *The Great Gatsby*, saying, "I didn't know anybody there and wouldn't be bothered." He was the chronicler of the Lost Generation who led a glittering life built on a Martini firmament and famously noted: "First you take a drink, then the drink takes a drink, then the drink takes you." North Carolina would not take Mr. Fitzgerald (he absconded back to Hollywood), but it would take the life of his sparkling wife, Zelda. Left behind in a mental institution in Asheville, she would perish in a fire there at the age of forty-seven.

Asheville, known as Beer City USA, has the most breweries per capita of any other city in the country, with one brewery for every 8,000 people. Big beer behemoths (and the second and third largest craft breweries in the country) Sierra Nevada and New Belgium have outposts here as well. Several seasonal festivals round out the beer drinking experience, from Winter Warmers in January, a Firkin fest in the spring, and June's Asheville Beer Week, which culminates in the Asheville Beer City Festival. An entire planet's worth of beer descends upon Durham in October and Raleigh in April for the World Beer Festivals, held annually for nearly twenty years.

In the 1930s, all efforts to repeal Prohibition in North Carolina failed, leaving that task to less temperate states. When the twenty-first Amendment was ratified in 1933, North Carolina formed the ABC store system to control the sale of alcohol. That very same year, musician and activist Nina Simone was born into a poor Methodist family in Tryon. Simone crooned out soulful renditions of "Feeling Good" and "Sinnerman" with a voice seasoned by cigarettes and alcohol. In what could be used as a protest song against the state's liquor system, she also covered Bessie Smith's "Gin House Blues" with its battle cry "I'll fight the army and navy / Somebody gives me my gin!"

Nothing could be finer than buying beer in North Carolina at a drive-through. The Outer Banks is home to **BREW THRU**, a small chain of drive-through beer stores. Offering everything from bottles to kegs and micros to macros, you simply pull your vehicle into their cooler-lined loading zone, tell them what you want, and pop the trunk. They do all the work.

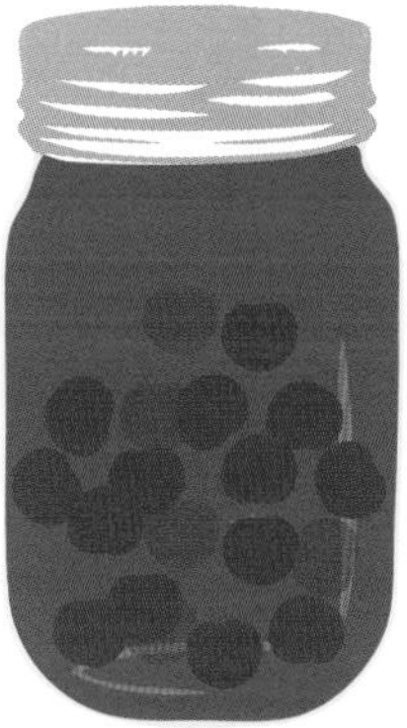

The legendary **CHERRY BOUNCE** cocktail

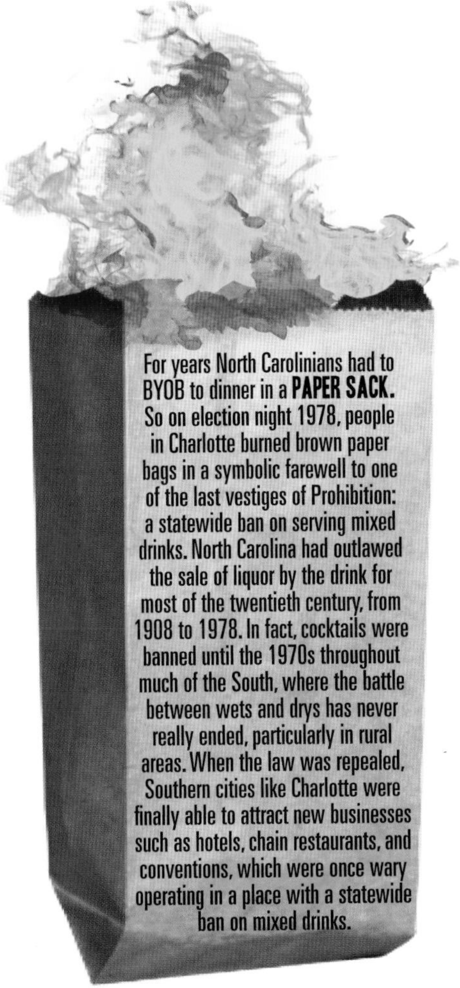

For years North Carolinians had to BYOB to dinner in a **PAPER SACK.** So on election night 1978, people in Charlotte burned brown paper bags in a symbolic farewell to one of the last vestiges of Prohibition: a statewide ban on serving mixed drinks. North Carolina had outlawed the sale of liquor by the drink for most of the twentieth century, from 1908 to 1978. In fact, cocktails were banned until the 1970s throughout much of the South, where the battle between wets and drys has never really ended, particularly in rural areas. When the law was repealed, Southern cities like Charlotte were finally able to attract new businesses such as hotels, chain restaurants, and conventions, which were once wary operating in a place with a statewide ban on mixed drinks.

NORTH CAROLINA

WHAT'LL IT BE?

North Carolina's alcohol laws are complicated because they are primarily controlled at the county and town level, but there are some general rules that apply statewide. North Carolina is also a control state for liquor and fortified wine, which are only sold for off-premise consumption at state-run ABC stores. State law requires these stores to close by 9:00 p.m. Monday through Saturday and remain closed on Sunday. They also do not sell beer or wine. Beer and wine are sold in grocery stores, convenience stores, and pharmacies between 7:00 a.m. and 2:00 a.m. Monday through Saturday, and between noon and 2:00 a.m. on Sundays. Bars can keep the same hours. On- and off-premise sale hours are consistent statewide, and there are no days in which beer and wine are not sold. Liquor sales by the drink can be restricted by county and town laws.

North Carolina is a local option state. The sale of alcohol is determined at both the county and town level by local elections. Alcohol sales are broken down into five categories: malt beverage, unfortified wine, fortified wine, ABC stores, and mixed beverages. Counties then vote to determine which of these they will allow. Towns can vote to allow alcohol sales that a county prohibits, but towns cannot vote to be more restrictive than the county—if a county allows a particular type of sale, so must the town.

QUICK REFERENCE

WHAT YOU CAN DO

- Buy beer and wine every day of the year between 7:00 a.m. and 2:00 a.m. Monday through Saturday, and between noon and 2:00 a.m. on Sunday.
- Buy package beer and wine in grocery stores and convenience stores.
- Buy package liquor and wine at state-run ABC stores before 9:00 p.m. Monday through Saturday.
- Order a drink in bars and restaurants between 7:00 a.m. and 2:00 a.m. Monday through Saturday, and between noon and 2:00 a.m. on Sundays.
- Take an unfinished bottle of wine from dinner home.
- In counties that prohibit the sale of mixed alcoholic beverages, restaurants can apply for a "brown-bagging" permit, which allows patrons to bring their own.
- Fill a growler at a brewery, brewpub, or grocery store.

WHAT YOU CAN'T DO

- Buy package liquor after 9:00 p.m. Monday through Saturday or anytime on Sunday.
- Purchase package beer and wine after 2:00 a.m. seven days a week.
- Order a drink in a bar after 2:00 a.m.
- Smoke in bars and restaurants.

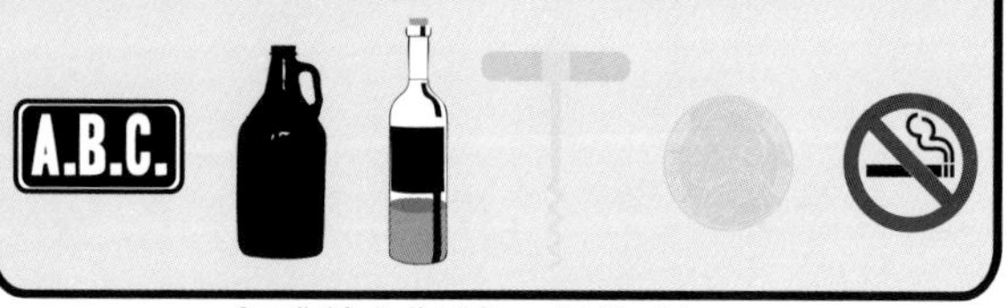

Source: North Carolina Alcoholic Beverage Control Commission

ASHEVILLE BEER WEEK™

Asheville's designation as **BEER CITY USA** is largely due to the efforts of Highland Brewing's Oscar Wong, a man often regarded as the "godfather" of craft brewing in western North Carolina. He founded his brewery in 1994, paving the way for many other Asheville craft brewers. More recently, western breweries, such as Colorado's New Belgium and California's Sierra Nevada, have been setting up brewing facilities in the area.

Carbonated beverages are called **"SOFT DRINKS"** to distinguish them from the harder stuff. However, when the beverages were transitioning from the soda fountain to the bottle, the trend was to name them after types of alcohol. This practice gave us products that are still around today, like ginger ale, root and birch beer, and North Carolina regional fave Cheerwine, who has been making their cherry-red soda since 1917.

When **SIR WALTER RALEIGH'S** explorers related their impressions of the area around Roanoke Island in 1584. They said the land was "so full of grapes as the very beating and surge of the sea overflowed them." Future settlers became among the nation's first vintners. Many used cuttings from the Mother Vine, a 400-year-old scuppernong vine that is believed to be the oldest vine in the nation.

JASPER ADAMS
BARTENDER AT THE IMPERIAL LIFE IN ASHEVILLE

TIP: "We have an awesome community of bartenders who source quality ingredients and work together to acquire unique spirits. We work together to explore contemporary techniques like hand-cut ice, percolation, and barrel-aged cocktails, for example. The control state limits our access to spirits, so we are a group of bartenders that spend extra time and energy to procure spirits that we share between our bars to make sure we all serve a great product."

SOUTH CAROLINA

Dum Spiro Spero
(While I Breathe, I Hope)

For thirty-three years, and up until 2006, the only liquor allowed to be poured in South Carolina bars and restaurants came from mini-bottles—the kind that you would find in a hotel minibar or an airplane. They were both instituted and recalled in the name of temperance. The new free-pour system seems to have had no effect on sales or drunk-driving fatalities (they are among the highest in the nation). A drink is a drink is a drink.

Loosening liquor legislation in South Carolina has led to the opening of more and more distilleries. The myriad of wonderful products that they produce are notable: Dark Corner Distillery's Moonshine, Six & Twenty Whiskey, and Firefly's Sea Island Rum and original Sweet Tea Vodka are but a few. Firefly uses tea leaves from America's only tea garden, the Charleston Tea Plantation. The Plantation's American Classic Tea is the official tea of the White House, as well as the official Hospitality Beverage of South Carolina.

Though not borne of the South (its dubious origin was probably a Caribbean island), Planter's Punch was certainly popularized here. Staking a claim in its provenance was the antebellum Planter's Hotel in Charleston. The old Planter's Hotel is now a theater, but a potent Planter's is served at Charleston's Peninsula Grill (housed in the similarly named Planters Inn). As with many punches of the day, Planter's Punch was concocted to cover up the taste of bad rum. A little rhyme was popularized to remember the recipe: "One of sour, two of sweet, three of strong, and four of weak" (that is, one part lemon juice, two parts sugar, three parts rum, and four parts water). There are dozens of variations of Planter's Punch, including one that uses sweet tea, but all of them use at least one type of rum.

It was a bad marriage and a nagging wife that made Major Stede Bonnet turn from a career as a prosperous Barbados planter to a life of rum piracy on the high seas. Aboard his sloop *Revenge*, he made his way up and down the Eastern Seaboard robbing trade ships, often burning the ships and their crew. (Dead men tell no tales.) Stede was known as the Gentleman Pirate, not just for his former life as an aristocratic plantation owner, but for the way he treated his crew. However, in 1718 he would meet his maker in Charleston, at the end of a rope. His pirate career lasted for just over a year.

Visitors to historic Charleston can see the site of the Gentleman Pirate's hanging, along with many other notable places, including the oldest building in the city, called the Tavern. It dates from 1686 and is reportedly the oldest continually-operating liquor store in the country. Shop for your grog after 9:00 a.m. and before 7:00 p.m., and not on Sunday. Time flies when you're having rum.

FYI

For the industrious: South Carolina grapes that are grown, harvested, processed, fermented, bottled, and sold at the vineyard are granted an exception to the Sunday wine ban.

For many years, the Palmetto State didn't allow liquor by the drink. The local workaround was to simply allow people to bring their own bottle to the bar and charge them for mixers and ice. People became concerned with over-imbibing and drinking and driving, so in 1973 a law was passed that stopped BYO and made the 1.5 ounce **MINI-BOTTLE** the standard pour in the state. When the liquor industry switched to the metric system in the '80s, the mini-bottle became a 1.7-ounce pour. In 2004, again in response to overindulgence and safety, the minis were scrapped and South Carolina bartenders had to learn the art of the free-pour.

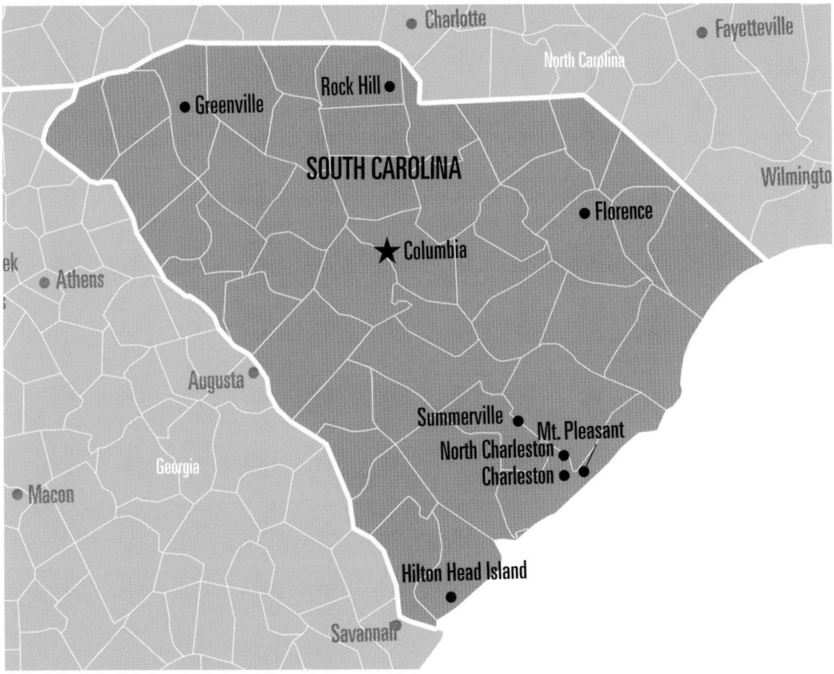

SOUTH CAROLINA

WHAT'LL IT BE?

Alcohol is more readily available in South Carolina than in much of the South. The state allows beer and wine to be sold twenty-four hours a day Monday through Saturday from grocery stores, convenience stores, and pharmacies. Off-premise beer and wine sales are prohibited between midnight on Saturday and "sunrise" Monday statewide, but some municipalities allow a Seven Day Permit, which can allow the sale of beer and wine 24/7. Liquor is only sold at liquor stores, which can also sell beer and wine, unlike in neighboring North Carolina. Liquor stores can operate between 9:00 a.m. and 7:00 p.m. Monday through Saturday, but are closed on Sundays. Bars and restaurants can serve from 10:00 a.m. to 2:00 a.m. most days of the week. Sundays require a special permit to serve liquor by the drink. Without one, liquor sales end at midnight on Saturday and don't resume until 10:00 a.m. on Monday.

South Carolina law allows for cities and counties to restrict the hours of sale of alcohol with local referendums, although they cannot prohibit alcohol completely.

QUICK REFERENCE

WHAT YOU CAN DO

- Buy package beer and wine anytime from sunrise Monday through midnight Saturday (essentially twenty-four hours a day) and on Sunday with a Seven Day Permit, if local laws allow.
- Buy package liquor between 9:00 a.m. and 7:00 p.m. Monday through Saturday.
- Order beer and wine in bars and restaurants between 10:00 a.m. and 2:00 a.m. Monday through Saturday, and until midnight on Sunday.
- Bring your own bottle of wine to a restaurant.
- Take an unfinished bottle of wine from dinner home.
- Fill a growler at a brewery, brewpub, or grocery store.
- Smoke in bars and restaurants. However, nine of the ten largest cities in South Carolina have passed local ordinances banning smoking in the workplace.

WHAT YOU CAN'T DO

- Buy package beer and wine between midnight on Saturday and sunrise on Monday, unless Sunday sales are approved by local voters.
- Order beer and wine after 2:00 a.m. and before 10:00 a.m. Monday through Saturday, or after midnight on Sunday.
- Buy package liquor on Sundays or between 7:00 p.m. and 9:00 a.m. Monday through Saturday.
- Order liquor by the drink on Sundays, subject to local option and permits.

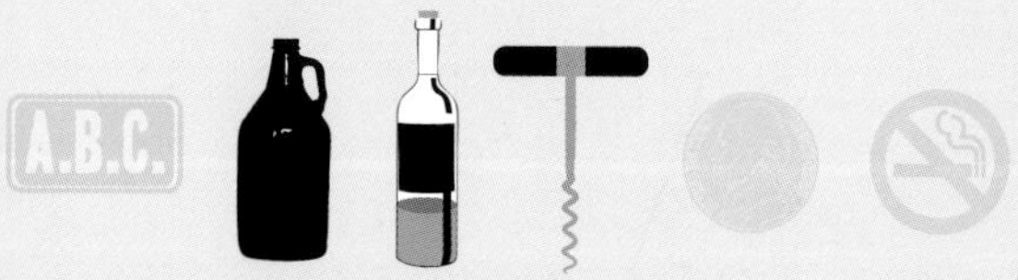

Source: South Carolina Department of Revenue

South Carolina allows retail beer and wine sales on **SUNDAYS** in counties and cities where voters have approved it. Currently, eight counties do: Richland, Lexington, Georgetown, Charleston, Beaufort, Horry, York, and Newberry. Cities where voters have approved this option include Columbia, Spartanburg, Greenville, Aiken, Rock Hill, Summerville, Santee, Daniel Island, and Tega Cay.

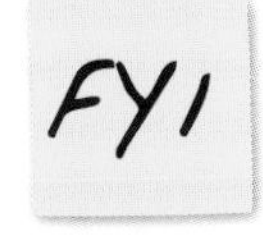

No drunken bungee jumping.
No tattoos for the drunk.
No body piercings for the drunk.

The Dispensary System was South Carolina's experiment in monopolizing liquor sales from 1893 to 1907, requiring all liquor sold within its borders to be bottled and sold through state-run facilities. It was the first and last of its kind. The dispensaries sold liquor, but not by the drink, not to be consumed on the premises, and not after dark. A *New York Times* article from 1895 described the dispensaries as "not convenient for revelry, or even for conviviality." To fill the revelry gap came **"BLIND TIGERS."** Functioning as an earlier version of the speakeasy, one legend claims the name comes from the practice of charging patrons to see a non-existent creature and providing complimentary cocktails once inside. When the customers left they often stumbled home "blind."

JEREMIAH SCHENZEL
BARTENDER AT THE COCKTAIL CLUB IN CHARLESTON

TIP: "Charleston is the food and drink capital of the south, but only recently has had the privilege of buying full liquor bottles. Up to a few years ago a bar could only carry mini bottles, so it became common practice to split shots. Most places still offer this unique ability. So if you want to sample a lot of drinks or liquors, ask a bartender for a split shot and let the good times roll."

GEORGIA

Wisdom, Justice, Moderation

Georgia is home to the Peaches, the Braves, and one president, Jimmy Carter. Though the president famously legalized homebrewing during his administration, Carter himself not only abstained, but kept a dry White House (excepting for wine at state dinners). His mother, "Miz Lillian" Carter, seemed more the kin of beer-binging brother Billy when she remarked, "I'm a Christian, but that doesn't mean I'm a long-faced square. I like a little bourbon."

It's also home to historic Savannah, The Hostess City, a city so beautiful that they surrendered rather than let Sherman set it ablaze. It's also one of the great cities in America where you can drink in public on city streets! While drinking in Savannah's historic district is legal, public drunkenness is not. So exercise moderation and respect the wondrous gift that is outdoor drinking by being polite.

Technically, drinking in public is not illegal in the state, but most counties have opted out of that regulation. The state's 159 counties each have their own liquor and beer laws, with a few counties choosing to remain dry. There are some statewide laws to keep in mind: alcohol may not be purchased anywhere before 12:30 p.m. on Sunday, and anything with an ABV of 21% or higher is considered liquor. Both possession and transportation of personal amounts of alcohol are legal throughout the state.

One of America's favorite sports, NASCAR (The National Association of Stock Car Auto Racing), has deep roots in Georgia. It was named by Atlanta mechanic Louis Jerome "Red" Vogt. NASCAR was created out of the spirit of competition that arose between "trippers" (drivers who transported moonshine from the stills to the sellers). After Prohibition, the state still had numerous dry counties. And even though liquor was legal in some counties, there was still no real outlet or distribution system. In the end, the bottom line was money. Moonshiners originally evaded the law, but after Prohibition, they were evading the tax man. Many of the trippers who drove in those first NASCAR races were moonlighting, so to speak. Their main source of income was still running moonshine at night.

"Awesome" Bill from Dawsonville was one of the legendary NASCAR-racing trippers, and Dawsonville, Georgia, is still the moonshine capitol of the world. Capitalizing off that history, the Dawsonville Moonshine Distillery recently started a legal distillery right inside city hall! To learn more about moonshining, trippers, and NASCAR, visit Dawsonville's Thunder Road Museum, or take in the Georgia Moonshine Festival there at the end of October. Many legal "moonshine" brands are sold in stores, including Shine On Georgia Moon Corn Whiskey. Be wary of sipping it straight, though. Aged less than thirty days, it once came with the slogan/warning: "First ya swaller, then ya holler!"

Georgians began making **MOONSHINE** in the late 18th Century after Scots-Irish immigrants introduced distilling to the mountain region of Northern Georgia. When Georgians returned to the Union after the Civil War, they found themselves subject to a new federal liquor tax. It was not illegal to produce moonshine in the nineteenth century, but it was illegal to not pay tax on it. So from the end of the Civil War to around the turn of the century, Georgian moonshiners and federal revenuers engaged in a heated battle. The increased violence between moonshiners and revenuers and the rise of the temperance movement shifted public opinion away from the moonshiners.

BILLY BEER was introduced by Billy Carter the same year that brother Jimmy took office. An urban legend persists that Billy Beer cans are valuable. They aren't.

GEORGIA

WHAT'LL IT BE?

Like neighboring Florida, most alcohol regulation is left up to local option in Georgia, particularly regarding the sale of alcohol over 21% ABV. Package liquor is only available from liquor stores, but beer and wine are widely available from licensed retailers, which can include grocery stores, convenience stores, pharmacies, and gas stations. Sundays are the only statewide no-sale days for package liquor, but localities can choose to allow Sunday sales between 12:30 p.m. and 11:30 p.m. The hours for all other alcohol sales for both on- and off-premise consumption, if not set by local ordinance, are 6:00 a.m. to midnight, seven days a week.

Georgia does allow for local option. Counties can restrict the sale of both package and by-the-drink alcohol. They can also set hours of sale, which can be more or less restrictive than state law. Municipalities can choose to ban the sale of alcohol on Christmas and Election Day. Most counties do not limit the sale of liquor, but eleven counties do. These county ordinances do not affect beer and wine, which are widely available throughout the state.

QUICK REFERENCE

WHAT YOU CAN DO

- Purchase package beer and wine at grocery stores, convenience stores, and pharmacies between 6:00 a.m. and midnight seven days a week.
- Purchase package liquor between 6:00 a.m. and midnight Monday through Saturday, and between 12:30 p.m. and 11:30 p.m. on Sunday, if allowed by local ordinance.
- Order a drink at a bar or restaurant between 6:00 a.m. and midnight seven days a week.
- Bring your own bottle of wine to a restaurant that has a wine license.
- Take an unfinished bottle of wine from dinner home.
- Enjoy happy hour specials.
- Fill a growler at a brewery or grocery store, depending on local ordinances.
- Smoke in bars and restaurants, depending on local ordinances.

WHAT YOU CAN'T DO

- Fill a growler at a brewpub.
- Purchase alcohol between midnight and 6:00 a.m. Monday through Saturday.
- Purchase package liquor between midnight and 6:00 a.m. Monday through Saturday, and before 12:30 p.m. or after 11:30 p.m. on Sunday.

A.B.C.

Source: Georgia Department of Revenue, Alcohol and Tobacco Division

THE WILLIAM BARKER WHISKEY BONDING BARN in Molena, Georgia, is on the National Register of Historic Places. A bonding barn was a sort of federal warehouse that allowed distillers to age their whiskey in barrels and delay paying federal excise tax until it was bottled. The Bottled-in-Bond Act of 1897 was one of the first federal laws to set standards for spirits production. Bonded bourbon is to be the product of one distiller, at one distillery, in one season; it needs to be aged for a minimum of four years; and it needs to be bottled at 100 proof. There were five distilleries in Pike County around the turn of the century that likely bonded their product in Molena.

FROM THE *NEW YORK TIMES*, NOVEMBER 17, 1915:

"The Georgia Legislature met in special session on Nov. 3 for the purpose of making the prohibition laws rum-tight. A fervid Dry in that body proposed to make 'the smell of liquor illegal in Georgia.' This counsel of perfection seems not to have been followed."

One of the most popular bootlegging films of all time, **SMOKEY AND THE BANDIT**, involved getting a truckload of Coors beer from Texas to Georgia at a time when Coors beer wasn't available east of the Mississippi. For many years Coors held a certain mystique in American culture because it was only available in the western half of the country. So, despite leading Sheriff Buford T. Justice from the dry community of Texarkana in an epic car chase across the driest of the dry states in America, the plot actually hinged on the fact that Coors simply wasn't distributed in Georgia yet. By the time Smokey and the Bandit Part 3 was released in 1983, Coors was available nationwide and the Bandit's payload was a large stuffed fish.

CHARLES FREELAND
BARTENDER AT THE PAINTED PIN IN ATLANTA

TIP: "Georgia liquor laws vary widely by county and municipality, which can make getting a drink difficult on Sundays in some places, and many places don't allow happy hour specials. Atlanta's cocktail scene is strong and growing, so always ask for a drink list. It's your best clue to the quality of drinks you can expect. If you see classics on the list, they probably know how to make good drinks."

FLORIDA

The Sunshine State

From the white sugar beaches and twenty-four-hour liquor stores of Miami to the bountiful bar scene and lax enforcement of open containers in Key West, travelers who find their way to Florida are in for a good time. Legend has it that Florida was discovered in 1513 when Ponce de Leon, thirsty for treasure and a restorative drink from the Fountain of Youth, dropped anchor at St. Augustine. The town has been continuously populated ever since. St. Augustine is also home to the Taberna del Gado, which has been serving sailors and landlubbers alike for more than 275 years.

¡Bienvenido a Miami! More than 30% of Miamians identify as Cuban, and the island is just 333 miles away. You'll be entertained and eating well if you wander down Calle Ocho, the busy backbone of Miami's Little Havana neighborhood, but what should you be drinking? How about a Mojito, the native drink of Cuba? The name "Mojito" might come from the African mojo, meaning "to place a little spell," or possibly from the Spanish, meaning "little wet one." The drink is similar to a Brazilian Caipirinha and the South's Mint Julep, all of which beat the heat in warmer climes. For a Mojito, muddle mint, sugar, and lime, add rum, and top with club soda.

Ernest Hemingway was said to have loved the Mojito when he lived in Havana and Key West—but was there any drink that Papa didn't love? His good friend and sailing partner "Habana" Joe Russell was a rum runner who also operated a bar in Key West. Hemingway suggested that Russell name the place after their shared love for the Havana dive bar Sloppy Joe's. The Key West Sloppy Joe's still stands on Duval Street, and even holds an annual Hemingway look-alike contest. Just two blocks away from Sloppy Joe's, Key West's first legitimate distillery, Chef Distilled, opened recently—and naturally named its inaugural liquor Key West First Legal Rum.

The notorious rum runner and bootlegger William (Bill) McCoy got his start in Florida. A teetotaler himself, McCoy specialized in procuring genuine Scotch and Canadian whiskies during a time when the household hooch was bathtub gin. The urban legend goes that he was so great at getting the good stuff that people called his booze "The Real McCoy." Curiously, the most likely origin of the phrase traces back to a brand of Scottish whisky whose slogan was "A drappie o' the real McKay" and has been cited in print long before Prohibition and Bill McCoy's rum running exploits.

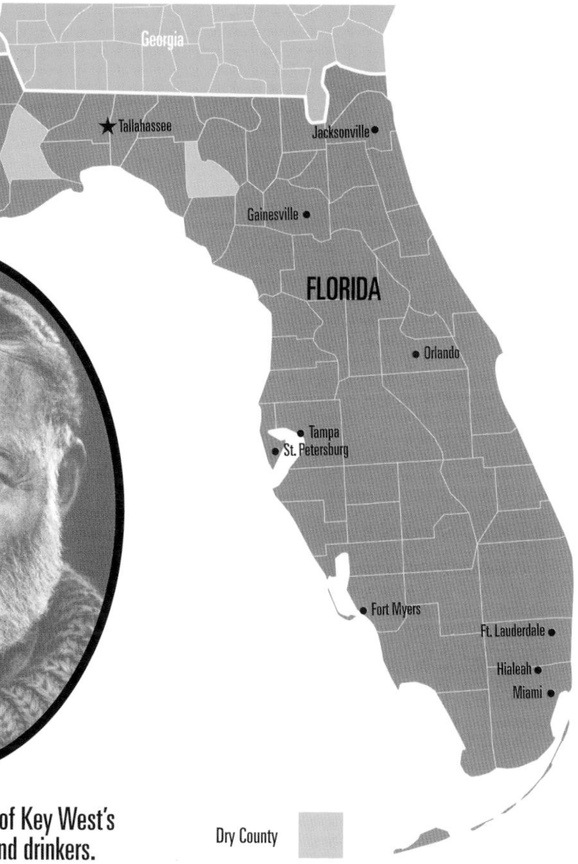

ERNEST HEMINGWAY, one of Key West's most famous inhabitants-and drinkers.

"SPANISH MARIE" WAITE, one of the most notorious rum runners in Florida, got her start by taking over her husband's business after his death in 1926. Operating out of Havana, Spanish Marie ran the Florida coast between Palm Beach and Key West. She was one of the only female rum runners in a game dominated by men and was known for her beauty, business sense, and ruthlessness. Her boats were fast, her men were armed, and her profits were huge, until she was caught one night in Miami in 1928. She was released on a $500 bond after begging the authorities to let her leave to see her children. But she didn't report to court the next day and was never seen or heard from again.

FLORIDA

WHAT'LL IT BE?

Florida's liquor laws are straightforward, with most of the details left up to local ordinances. Package beer and wine are available at grocery stores, convenience stores, and pharmacies, while package liquor is only available from liquor stores. Alcohol is widely available for on-premise consumption in bars and restaurants. If not otherwise specified by the municipality, sale hours for both on- and off-premise purchases are 7:00 a.m. to midnight, every day of the year.

Florida does allow for a local option. Municipalities and counties may set hours for alcohol sales, which can be either more restrictive or more lenient than state law. Florida takes this to both extremes. In Miami, for example, grocery stores can sell beer and wine twenty-four hours a day, as long as they are still selling groceries. Bars and restaurants can serve until 3:00 a.m. if they have a standard license, and until 5:00 a.m. if they are classified as a nightclub or "supper club." There are also three dry counties in the northwestern corner of the state. All alcohol sales for both on- and off-premise consumption are prohibited in Lafayette, Liberty, and Washington counties.

QUICK REFERENCE

WHAT YOU CAN DO

- Purchase package spirits at a liquor store from 7:00 a.m. to midnight seven days a week, depending on local ordinance.
- Purchase package beer and wine at a grocery store, convenience store, pharmacy, or gas station between 7:00 a.m. and midnight seven days a week, depending on local ordinance.
- Order a drink at a bar or restaurant between 7:00 a.m. and midnight seven days a week, depending on local ordinance.
- Bring your own bottle of wine to a restaurant that has a wine license.
- Take an unfinished bottle of wine from dinner home.
- Enjoy happy hour specials.
- Fill a growler under 32 ounces or over 128 ounces at a brewery or retailer.
- Smoke in a stand-alone bar.

WHAT YOU CAN'T DO

- Take a glass container on the beach.
- Fill a growler at a brewpub.
- Fill a standard 64-ounce growler.
- Drink from an open container in Key West, despite street vendors, walk-up windows, bars offering to-go cups, and hordes of people (and police) who ignore the law. Technically, it's illegal.
- Smoke in enclosed restaurants. Florida has a smoking ban for enclosed work spaces, which includes restaurants but excludes stand-alone bars.
- Purchase package beer, wine, or liquor between midnight and 7:00 a.m.

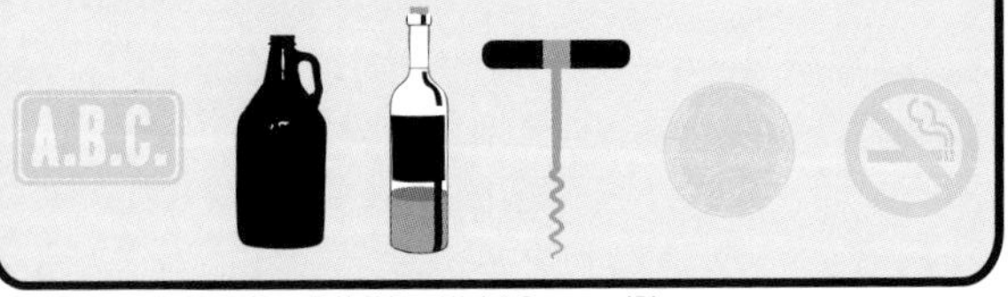

Source: Florida Division of Alcoholic Beverages and Tobacco

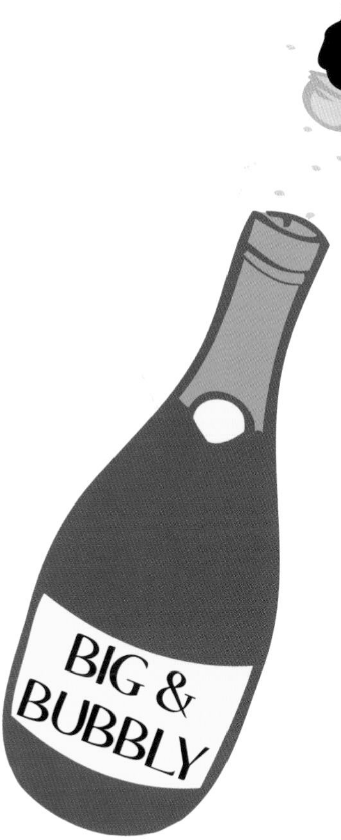

A magnum of **CHAMPAGNE** is the equivalent of two bottles of bubbly. However, the traditional, larger bottles of Champagne, which have impressive names such as Methuselahs, Salmanazars, Balthazars, and Nebuchadnezzars—the largest of which can contain the equivalent of twenty bottles—are illegal in Florida.

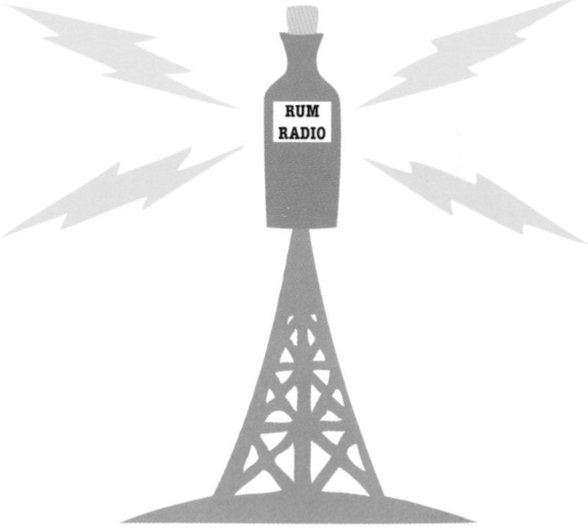

During Prohibition, smugglers relied on **RADIO** to coordinate the transfer of their freight to faster ship-to-shore boats in international water off the coast of Florida. Since the Coast Guard was able to monitor these transmissions, the rum runners developed sophisticated codes to evade capture. The radio operations of the rum runners were comparable in size, technical skill, and organization to those that would be used by enemy agents in World War II. In fact, the skills the Coast Guard developed intercepting transmissions and decrypting codes during Prohibition were of immense value in the coming years when America faced a menace much greater than rum.

FYI

Florida vendors are required to stop selling alcohol in the event of a riot or mob.

PHILIP KHANDEHRISH
MIXOLOGIST AT THE SETAI IN MIAMI BEACH

TIP: "Miami's cocktail scene has come a long way in a short time. Five years ago the best you could get was a vodka and Redbull, but now we have many bars that serve a great Manhattan, Sazerac, and other classic cocktails. Plus, with access to amazing produce from farms in Homestead, we can create an array of tropical drinks. So, please feel free to order more than a Mojito."

ALABAMA

Audemus Jura Nostra Defendere
(We Dare Defend Our Rights)

Welcome to the Heart of Dixie, where the tea is sweet and humidity, religion, and football rule the day. Twenty-six of the state's counties—almost 40%—are dry. But with 2011's Brewery Modernization Act, the recent legalization of home brewing, and local liquor laws falling like faded camellia petals, thirsts are sure to be slaked in sweet home Alabama.

Before the legislation, breweries could only sell their beer at their own pubs and were limited to brewing beer under 6%. Now that breweries are able to distribute, you'll find a much wider selection of local beer at your corner watering hole. Before legislation, eighty of the country's top 100 best-rated beers could not be sold in the state. Now that the alcohol content limit has been raised to 13.9%, you can have that pint of Pliny! And there's more to come: the volume of beer brewed in Alabama has doubled in the years following the legislation, and growth is expected to continue. In response to the state's beer boom, Auburn University now offers a brewing science graduate certificate.

Each fall, a half million acres of Alabama farmland appear to be dusted in snow. It's cotton picking time, and with it comes the Iron Bowl. Perhaps no more contentious rivalry is known than the 120-year battle between the University of Alabama Crimson Tide (ROLL TIDE!) and the Auburn University Tigers (WAR EAGLE!). Though the stadiums (which alternate hosting) seat only around 90–100,000, hundreds of thousands begin rallying the night before the game. Want to tailgate more than one day a year? Head on over to the Talladega Superspeedway in Lincoln, where days before the race even begins, tens of thousands of NASCAR fans start tailgating, camping out in RVs in the parking lots ringing the arena. It's the longest, fastest, and most dangerous track on the NASCAR circuit. Shake 'n bake! Beer, wine, or liquor may be brought into the race, but check their website for ever-changing cooler limitations.

Coolers and alcohol are not allowed at the annual Helen Keller Festival held in her hometown of Tuscumbia. Keller, a socialist, suffragist, and pacifist (among many other things), is pictured on the state quarter, along with her name written in braille. She left Alabama to study, eventually traveling the world, giving lectures, and writing. Living life to the fullest, she regularly enjoyed a preprandial nip of Scotch whisky. No word on whether she took it neat or with a little W-A-T-E-R.

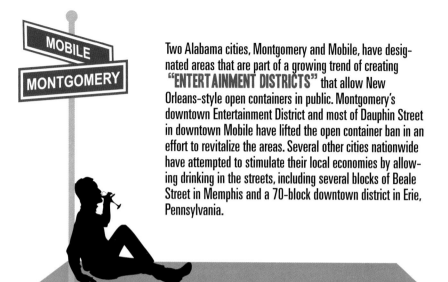

Two Alabama cities, Montgomery and Mobile, have designated areas that are part of a growing trend of creating **"ENTERTAINMENT DISTRICTS"** that allow New Orleans-style open containers in public. Montgomery's downtown Entertainment District and most of Dauphin Street in downtown Mobile have lifted the open container ban in an effort to revitalize the areas. Several other cities nationwide have attempted to stimulate their local economies by allowing drinking in the streets, including several blocks of Beale Street in Memphis and a 70-block downtown district in Erie, Pennsylvania.

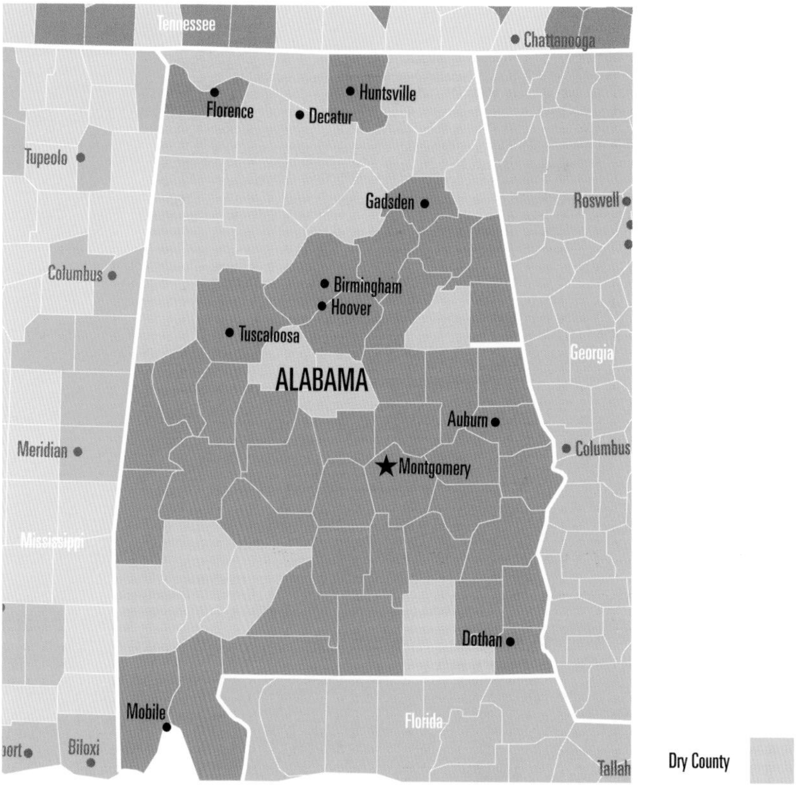

ALABAMA

WHAT'LL IT BE?

Like other states in the South, Alabama leaves much of the regulation of alcohol up to the counties and local governments. Package liquor is available through state-run ABC liquor stores Monday through Saturday. Beer and wine are available at grocery stores, convenience stores, and pharmacies Monday through Saturday with varied hours, and after noon on Sundays. Bars and restaurants can serve liquor, wine, and bottled or canned beer, but draft beer is only available if the county or municipality allows it. The state does not set sale hours for alcohol, leaving them to be determined by individual communities.

Twenty-five of Alabama's sixty-seven counties are dry, prohibiting the sale of alcohol for both on- and off-premise consumption. Most of these counties are in the northern part of the state, but some of the southern counties are dry as well. Although the sale of alcohol is prohibited in these counties, possession and consumption are not. Moreover, private clubs are allowed to sell alcohol even in dry cities. All dry counties have at least one wet city, and alcohol is available in all of the larger cities. Draft beer and Sunday sales are both subject to local option.

QUICK REFERENCE

WHAT YOU CAN DO

- Purchase package liquor at an ABC liquor store Monday through Saturday. Hours vary.
- Purchase package beer and wine from a grocery store, convenience store, or pharmacy seven days a week. Hours vary.
- Order a drink at a bar or restaurant Monday through Saturday (hours vary), and from noon to midnight on Sunday.
- Bring your own bottle of wine to a restaurant that has a wine license.
- Take an unfinished bottle of wine from dinner home.
- Enjoy happy hour specials.
- Fill a growler at a grocery store.

WHAT YOU CAN'T DO

- Order a draft beer at a bar or restaurant, depending on local ordinances.
- Fill a growler at a brewery or brewpub.
- Order a drink at a bar or restaurant on Sunday before noon, depending on local ordinances.
- Purchase package liquor on Sunday statewide.
- Purchase package beer and wine on Sunday, depending on local ordinances.

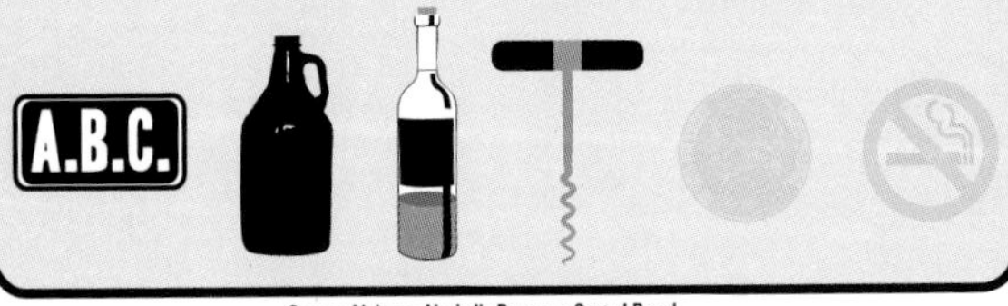

Source: Alabama Alcoholic Beverage Control Board

The **ALABAMA ALCOHOLIC BEVERAGE CONTROL** has made some interesting decisions regarding imagery and language on labels. They banned the California wine Cycles Gladiator because it depicted a nude nymph flying alongside a bicycle. The vintner, whose label riffed on a famous piece of French advertising from 1895, quickly began marketing his product as "Banned in Bama" and "Taste What They Can't Have in Alabama." The Alabama ABC also banned the sale of Michigan-based Dirty Bastard beer because of profanity on the label. Curiously, Fat Bastard wine and Raging Bitch beer are available in the state.

Before the **BREWERY MODERNIZATION ACT** in 2011, breweries could only sell their beer at their own pubs and were limited to brewing beer under 6%. Now that breweries are able to distribute, you'll find a much wider selection of local beer at your corner watering hole.

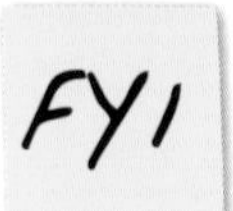

Drunk pedestrians are not allowed on highways.

Alabama has an official state spirit: **CONECUH RIDGE ALABAMA FINE WHISKEY**. The 2004 House Joint Resolution designated Clyde May's family recipe for "special Christmas whiskey" with the honor because "the bourbon, Conecuh Ridge, is produced using pure Alabama water and embodies family pride, independence, entrepreneurial drive, innovation and respect for the tradition and craftsmanship which is evident in this family tradition." Ironically, what Clyde didn't have respect for was the law. He made his name and reputation as a moonshiner and a bootlegger and once served time in a federal penitentiary.

FEIZAL VALLI
BARTENDER AT THE COLLINS BAR IN BIRMINGHAM

TIP: "At 2:00 every Saturday you are encouraged to leave almost every bar since our liquor laws still expect you to be at church the next morning. But Birmingham has historically been full of contradictions. So, if you forsake The Lord and want to keep sinning your choices are these: the biker bar under the bridge behind the Projects, the gay bar in the low-slung bunker, or the dimly lit, under-policed frat bar"

MISSISSIPPI

Virtute et Armis
(By Valor and Arms)

From the blues of Biloxi to the crossroads in Clarksdale, Mississippi is a state rich in history and in struggle. It has one of the poorest and most rural populations in the nation, with about half of its population living in small towns and the countryside. It was the last state to repeal Prohibition, and is slowly modernizing in terms of liquor law.

Nearly half of the counties in the state are dry, prohibiting the production, advertising, sale, distribution, or transportation of alcohol in varying degrees. That's right, it is even illegal to bring alcohol through a dry county. Surprisingly, state law is quite lax on open containers, allowing even the driver of a vehicle to drink, provided they stay under the legal limit. Another oddity: people between the ages of eighteen and twenty may enter a bar and drink (beer only) with their parents. Mississippi is also the only state in the country where underage military personnel are allowed to drink beer (provided it's also legal for them to do so on their base).

Mississippi beer drinkers recently celebrated two victories: homebrewing is now legal in the state, and the ABV limits of beer (that can be produced, distributed, and sold) have been raised to 10%, allowing for much more creativity in craft beer brewing. The ABV law was championed by a grassroots organization called Raise Your Pints, self-described as "just wanting to make Mississippi a better place." The state now has a handful of breweries and a brew festival called the Tops of Hops. Held annually in Biloxi, the festival is now able to pour some of the best beers in the country for Mississippians thirsty for more than Miller. Offering 120 different beers, the Keg & Barrel in Hattiesburg was recently named one of the top 100 beer bars in America by DRAFT Magazine. Expect to see craft beer growing and becoming even better as these laws gain traction.

You can't purchase cold beer in Oxford, and the entire town is dry on Sundays (excepting home game days at perennial party school University of Mississippi). Ole Miss alum and Nobel Prize winner William Faulkner said, "Civilization begins with distillation." His home, Rowan Oak, is located near campus, and his final resting place is also nearby. Tradition dictates that one enjoy a slug of whiskey with the author at his gravesite, leaving the rest of the bottle on the headstone. A fitting tribute since Faulkner also famously said, "A man shouldn't fool with booze until he's 50; then he's a damn fool if he doesn't."

Sharing a bottle at the gravesite of famous Mississippi author, **WILLIAM FAULKNER.** His gravesite is located not far from the campus of the University of Mississippi.

Raise your pints at the Mississippi **TOP OF THE HOPS** Festival.

FYI

Since 1966, ABC agents in Mississippi have destroyed approximately 3,000 illegal whiskey stills, averaging about 64 stills per year—more than one a week.

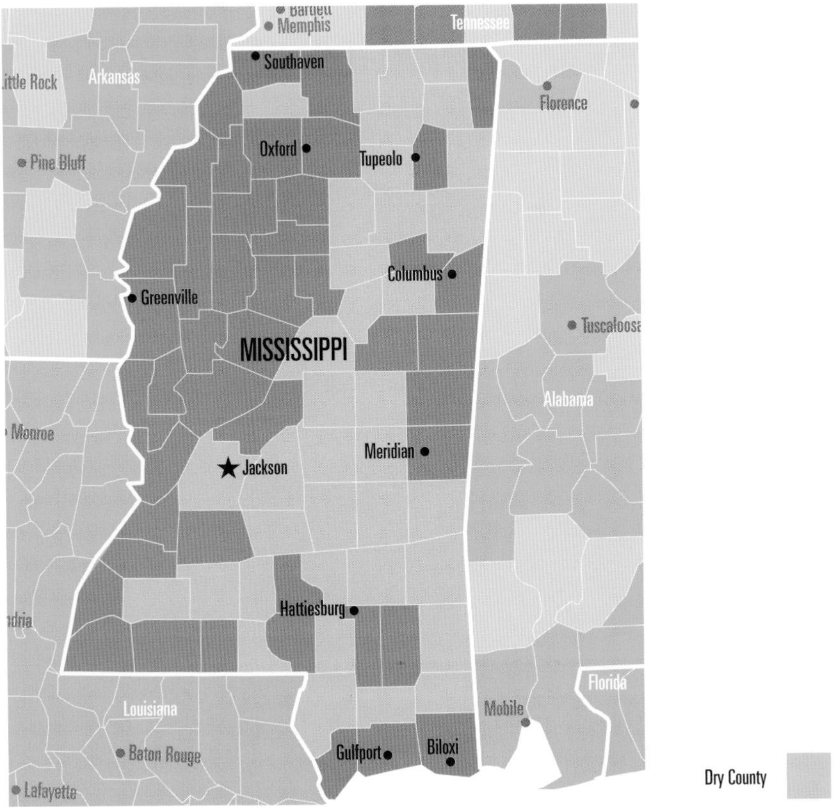

MISSISSIPPI

WHAT'LL IT BE?

Mississippi controls the sale of liquor and wine. They can only be purchased at ABC package stores, which do not sell beer. ABC stores are open from 10:00 a.m. to 10:00 p.m. Monday through Saturday and are closed on Sundays and Christmas. The state also restricts liquor by the drink on Sundays, so mixed beverages are not available in bars or restaurants without a special permit. Beer is sold at grocery stores, convenience stores, and pharmacies seven days a week, although hours are limited in places that do allow sales. Bars can serve beer and wine from 7:00 a.m. to midnight seven days a week and mixed drinks until midnight on Saturday in the absence of a special permit.

Mississippi requires a local option to allow the sale of alcohol. Local jurisdictions can choose to allow the sale of both beer and liquor. Currently, thirty-four of eighty-two counties prohibit the sale of liquor. Thirty-six counties also prohibit beer. Municipalities can be either more or less restrictive than county law, and it is possible to find a wet town in a dry county and a dry town in a wet county. The major cities, including Jackson and Biloxi, are wet.

QUICK REFERENCE

WHAT YOU CAN DO

- Buy package beer and wine at grocery stores, convenience stores, and pharmacies seven days a week, hours subject to local option.
- Buy package liquor from an ABC package store between 10:00 a.m. and 10:00 p.m. Monday through Saturday.
- Order beer and wine in bars and restaurants between 7:00 a.m. and midnight seven days a week. Some cities extend these hours by local ordinance.
- Order liquor in bars and restaurants between 10:00 a.m. and midnight Monday through Saturday. Some cities extend these hours by local ordinance.
- Fill a growler at a brewpub or grocery store.
- Smoke in bars and restaurants.

WHAT YOU CAN'T DO

- Buy liquor on Sunday or Christmas.
- Fill a growler at a brewery.
- Order alcohol in a bar after midnight, depending on local ordinances.
- Smoke in bars and restaurants in Jackson, Mississippi's largest city.

Source: Mississippi Alcoholic Beverage Control

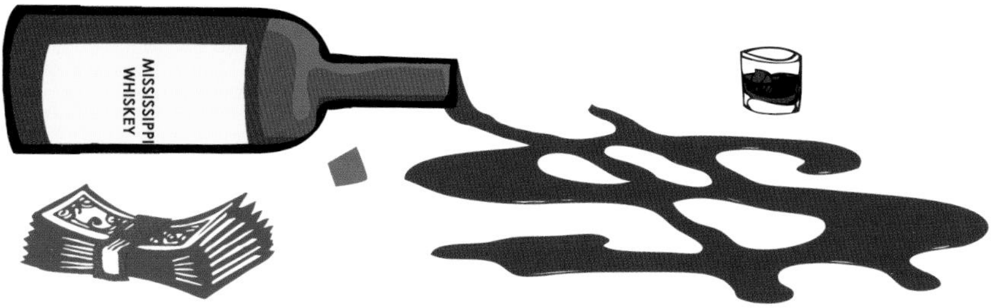

Mississippi's statewide prohibition didn't end until 1966, when a bill was passed allowing counties and municipalities to decide by local option. Prior to that, the old saying was "the drys have their law, the wets have their whiskey, and the state gets its taxes." Yes, Mississippi had a **"BLACK MARKET TAX"** on illegal liquor. Additionally, the state tax collector was allowed to keep 10% of what he was able to add to the state's coffers from the black market tax, which reportedly made the job the second-most lucrative public office in the nation—second only to President Eisenhower.

"If when you say whiskey you mean the devil's brew, the poison scourge, the bloody monster, that defiles innocence, dethrones reason, destroys the home, creates misery and poverty, yea, literally takes the bread from the mouths of little children . . . then certainly I am against it.

But, if when you say whiskey you mean the oil of conversation, the philosophic wine, the ale that is consumed when good fellows get together, that puts a song in their hearts and laughter on their lips, and the warm glow of contentment in their eyes . . . then certainly I am for it.

This is my stand. I will not retreat from it. I will not compromise."

State Representative Noah S. "Soggy" Sweat, in a 1952 speech when the state was still hotly divided between wets and drys.

For decades, a section of Rankin County known as the **"GOLD COAST"** was famous for its blues clubs and infamous for its bootlegging operations. The bootleggers came first and were openly doing business in the area by the 1930s. The clubs and juke joints followed. By the 1940s, some were hosting national acts and were staying open twenty-four hours a day, seven days a week. The party stopped abruptly in 1966 when Mississippi ended statewide prohibition. Rankin County voted to become dry and the conditions that allowed the bootleggers and club owners to thrive on the Gold Coast were gone.

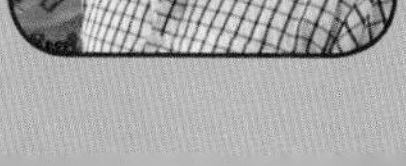

CHRIS ROBERTSON
BARTENDER AT BRAVO ITALIAN RESTAURANT IN JACKSON

TIP: "Mississippi keeps you on your toes. Drinking culture and fines vary by county and most of the time that changes by simply crossing a bridge. Remember to stock your bar on Saturday, because there will be none to be bought on Sunday. When going to brunch on Sunday, remember to go after noon because you can't drink till the preacher drinks in this town."

LOUISIANA

Union, Justice, Confidence

Louisiana was named by French colonists for King Louis XIV. The French also named New Orleans after old Orleans and its streets after French royal houses, with Bourbon Street named for Louis XIV's own family. According to bourbon historian Michael Veach, Bourbon Street in New Orleans, not Bourbon County in Kentucky, is most likely the origin of the name of bourbon whiskey. Two Frenchmen in Kentucky realized they could sell more whiskey in New Orleans if they floated it down the river in charred barrels so that it would taste more like cognac. The barrels were a hit, and soon people were asking for the whiskey that they served on Bourbon Street.

Morning, noon, night—anytime's a good time to drink in New Orleans. Bars in New Orleans are open 24/7, and the joke goes that NOLA bars only close at midnight on Ash Wednesday in deference (and to clean up). Such a drinking city is the Big Easy that it even has an official cocktail, the Sazerac. Look for the Sazerac Seal of Approval in bars that local cocktailians have determined mix the deceptively complex drink correctly—or just head to the Sazerac Bar in the Roosevelt Hotel. There's much mystery surrounding its true origin, but leading legend is that of local druggist Antoine Amedie Peychaud, who began making one of history's first cocktails with his bitters in the early 1830s. The Sazerac Coffee House, the bar where the cocktail flourished, acquired Peychaud's Bitters and other spirits and became the Sazerac Company. In 1992, Sazerac, whose headquarters are still in Metairie, purchased a run-down Kentucky whiskey distillery and renamed it Buffalo Trace. The company now produces several other high-end whiskeys: Blanton's, W.L. Weller, and Pappy Van Winkle. The bourbon barrels have floated back upstream!

Peychaud's Bitters are part of many of the drinks that found their origins in the Big Easy, like the Vieux Carre ("old square," or French Quarter), a New Orleanian take on the Manhattan. The revolving Carousel Bar in the opulent and historical Hotel Monteleone is the place to order one. Pat O'Brien's is a former speakeasy and the birthplace of the Hurricane, a fruit juice concoction originally devised to cover up the taste of cheap rum. Ninety-five percent of first time visitors to the city stop here! Whatever you do find to drink, you may tote it around with you; open containers ("go cups") are legal here, with the caveat that they must be plastic.

On Bourbon Street, you'll find walk-up windows serving "daiquiris," many made from grain alcohol and high fructose corn syrup. These candy-colored adult slushies are also available all over the state at drive-through daiquiri stands, which take advantage of a legal loophole (which is actually the hole—it must be sealed, straw on the side, to comply as a "closed container").

Two physicians from Thibodaux partnered up to turn the region's top crops into just what the doctor ordered: hooch! The Donner-Peltier distillery produces vodka made from Louisiana-grown rice, and from sugarcane (a crop transplanted here by the French) they produce rum. The French Cajun legend of the Rougarou (a werewolf that haunts the swamps) is the source of the distillery's 13 Pennies Rum. The Rougarou can't count beyond twelve, so thirteen pennies laid on a doorstep would keep the beast away from one's door.

A recent study by Harvard and the University of British Columbia found that five of the top ten happiest places in America are in Louisiana. When Louisianians get together, be it at a wedding, wake, parade, or festival, they are eating (and yes, drinking) with other people, people of all ages. There's a long tradition of good food, music, and drinking in the state. Life is a celebration here, and everyone is invited. Laissez les bon temps rouler!

Back-bar staple **TABASCO** hot sauce has been made on Avery Island for almost 150 years. The privately owned McIlhenny's Company is a fourth-generation family-run business and is estimated to own a quarter of the hot sauce market. Its peppers are fermented for over three years in old white-oak bourbon barrels from Kentucky. Bartenders have been experimenting with the ingredient since its invention as a way to provide heat and depth to their cocktails.

One of history's first cocktails was made with **PEYCHAUDS BITTERS** back in the 1830s.

The Southern Food and Beverage Museum in New Orleans is home to both the Museum of the American Cocktail and La Galerie d'Absinthe.

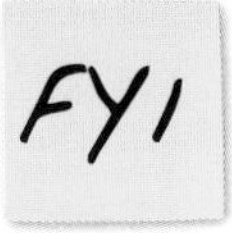

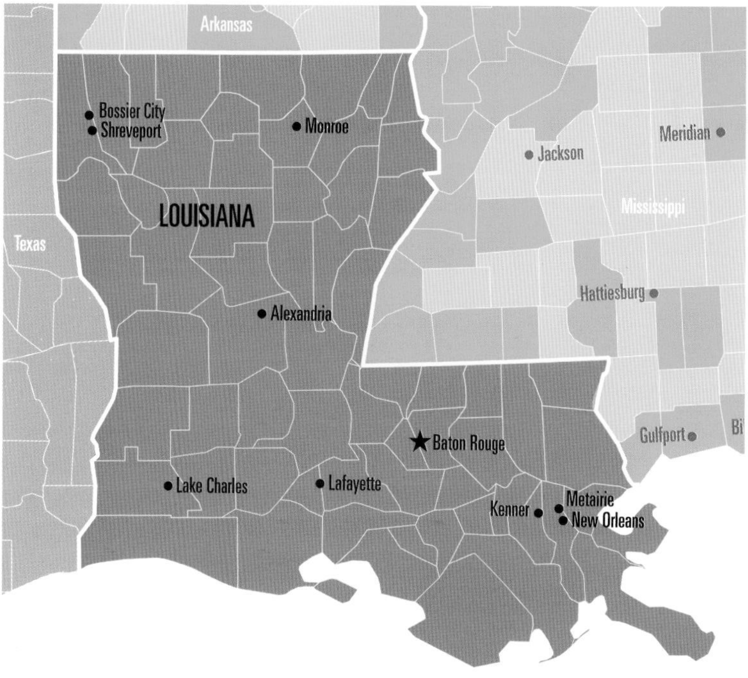

LOUISIANA

WHAT'LL IT BE?

Compared to other states in the South, the alcohol laws in Louisiana are more relaxed. Like the other southern states, though, Louisiana leaves most of the details of alcohol sales to the counties and municipalities. Package beer, wine, and liquor are widely available in grocery stores, convenience stores, and pharmacies at hours set by the municipalities. There are different levels of on-premise licenses, including wine-only, beer-only, beer and wine, and all-inclusive (beer, wine, and liquor). Beverages are available at bars and restaurants according to their license type and the hours set by the municipality. There are no statewide no-sale days.

Louisiana does allow for local option. Counties can ban liquor by the drink, set hours for package alcohol sales, or restrict Sunday sales. New Orleans, for example, allows package and on-premise sales twenty-four hours a day, every day of the year, while Baton Rouge only allows Sunday alcohol sales to start at 10:00 a.m.

QUICK REFERENCE

WHAT YOU CAN DO

- Purchase package beer, wine, and liquor at a licensed retailer, including grocery stores, convenience stores, and pharmacies, during hours set by the municipality.
- Order a drink at a bar or restaurant during the hours set by the municipality.
- Take an unfinished bottle of wine from dinner home.
- Enjoy happy hour and drink specials before 10:00 p.m.
- Fill a growler at a brewery, brewpub, or grocery store.
- Smoke on outdoor patios or in bars.
- Bring your own beverage to a restaurant, subject to local ordinances.
- Get a frozen daiquiri from a drive-through stand.

WHAT YOU CAN'T DO

- Smoke in enclosed restaurants.
- Purchase alcohol on Sunday where prohibited.

A.B.C.

Source: Louisiana Office of Alcohol and Tobacco Control

It's not surprising that New Orleans, the city that champions the "go cup," is home to frozen drink pouch pioneer Cordina. Similar to a child's juice pouch but frozen and with booze, the **MAR-GO-RITA** and the **DAIQ-GO-RI** have given beach bums a new and easy way to enjoy a frozen drink in the sand. Cordina's innovation and contribution to American culture was even recognized by the White House as part of their "Champions of Change" program in 2011, which selected founder Craig Cordes as part of its series on young entrepreneurs.

In Louisiana, donut shops hold the distinction of being the only type of restaurant unable to obtain an alcohol permit.

SUGARCANE was introduced to Louisiana by Jesuit missionaries in 1751. Soon after, large quantities of sugarcane were being used to make "tafia," a low-grade rum. In 1764, the governor stated that the "immoderate use of tafia has stupefied the entire population." In addition to being a popular drink, tafia was also used for trade. Many ordinances were passed attempting to regulate the exchange of tafia.

In Cajun French, a buveur is a drinker and a **BUVEUR DE LAIT** (literally "milk drinker") is a teetotaler, or one who does not drink alcohol.

ABIGAIL GULLO
BARTENDER AT SOBOU IN NEW ORLEANS

TIP: "I find the go-cup policy quite civilized. No need to slam down that drink in a hurry to move onto the next bar, a practice that will make you far more drunk far too fast. No, leisurely sip that delicious cocktail and have it cool your hand as you stroll to your next destination. Pure class and elegance...especially if it is a good cocktail, of which there are many here in New Orleans!"

ARKANSAS

Regnat Populus
(Let the People Rule)

More than half of Arkansas' counties are dry, making it one of the driest states in the country—finding the Arkan-sauce can be a challenging endeavor for a newcomer. Dotting dry counties are private clubs: restaurants that have petitioned the state for liquor permits, and which require a nominal membership fee in order to drink. Retail alcohol outlets ring dry counties like luxurious liquor bracelets, though the drive to them can be arduous. Just to make things more disjointed, towns in wet counties may elect to go dry; however, towns in dry counties may not elect to go wet.

As much as a dry county's population would like to become wet, doing so in Arkansas is a Herculean undertaking. A 1993 law stipulates that signatures from 38% of a county's population must be submitted just to put the initiative on the ballot. Before Benton County recently voted to go wet, 127 private club permits existed. Those restaurant owners couldn't purchase alcohol in a dry county with no liquor stores, nor could they have alcohol delivered. Moreover, when they purchased beer, wine, and liquor from an adjacent wet county they were forced to pay retail for it. Walmart is headquartered in Bentonville in Benton County, and the campaign to go wet was supported in large part by heirs to the Sam Walton fortune. Unfortunately, the Bentonville Walmart store was not at press time granted a retail liquor license, since the state limits them to one per company.

Bentonville not-withstanding, Walmart, in addition to being the world's largest private employer, also sells more beer than any other retailer in America. And the top-selling beer in America is Budweiser. Budweiser beer is one of the most consistent-tasting beers brewed. Some might find it surprising that Budweiser's grain bill is made up of 30% rice. With Arkansas producing nearly twice as much rice as any other state in the country, it's no surprise that Anheuser-Busch has a massive milling plant in Jonesboro. In Lavacca, look for the giant Budweiser can painted on a grain silo, an homage to the artist's favorite beverage.

There's a long list of boozy, bluesy Arkansas musicians that could provide a soundtrack for crying in your beer. West Memphis, just over the bridge and across the state line from the more famous music city, is the home of legendary radio station KWEM. Sonny Boy Williamson's radio show on the station featured such burgeoning blues legends as BB King, Ike Turner, and Howlin' Wolf, who for a time even shared the same roof as Sonny Boy (he was his brother-in-law). Elvis Presley's first appearance was on KWEM, and so was that of Kingsland native Johnny Cash, who actually had to pay to play. Many years and beers later, the Man in Black would give us perhaps the best hangover song ever written, "Sunday Morning Coming Down".

Look for the giant Budweiser can painted on a grain silo in Lavaca, Arkansas.

ELVIS had his first appearance on radio at KWEM in West Memphis, Arkansas.

Combative sports elimination contestants must have a breathalyzer test before the bout to ensure their blood alcohol content is 0.2% or less.

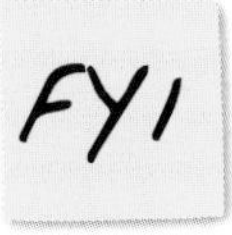

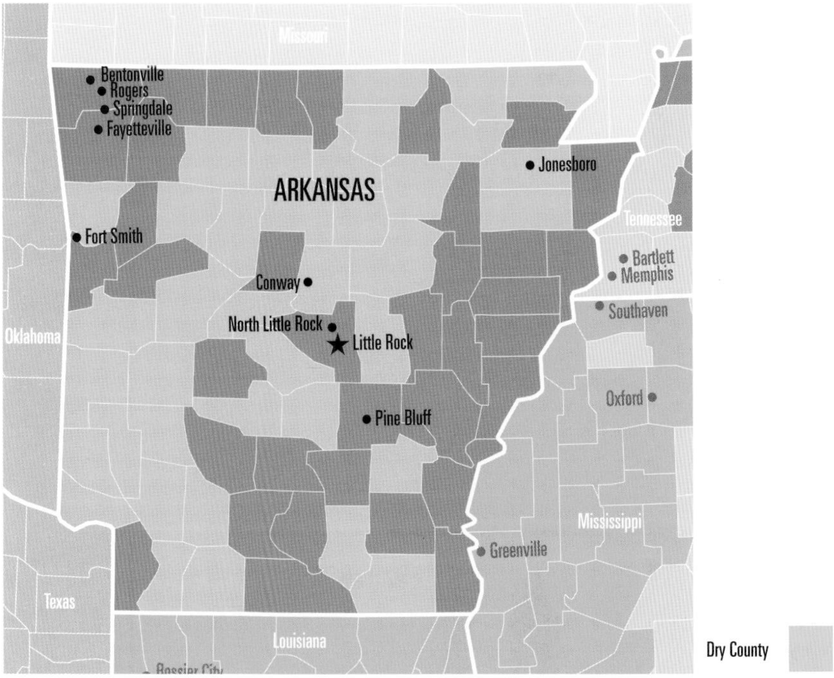

ARKANSAS

WHAT'LL IT BE?

About half of Arkansas is completely dry and the sale of alcohol is prohibited. Where alcohol sales are allowed, package beer, wine, and liquor are available from licensed stores, which can include grocery stores, convenience stores, and pharmacies. Sale hours are between the hours of 7:00 a.m. and 2:00 a.m. Monday through Friday, and between 7:00 a.m. and midnight on Saturday. Most towns do not allow Sunday package sales, although private clubs are permitted to sell package alcohol on Sundays. Beer, wine, and liquor are available from bars and restaurants between 7:00 a.m. and 1:00 a.m. seven days a week, and nightclubs can stay open until 2:00 a.m. or 5:00 a.m., depending on their license. State law bans both package and on-premise alcohol sales on Christmas.

Arkansas does allow for local option. Localities primarily restrict the sale of different types of alcohol and, to a lesser degree, set hours for alcohol sales. Of the state's seventy-five counties, thirty-seven are completely dry and do not allow alcohol sales of any kind. Municipalities can be more restrictive than counties, and there are dry towns within wet counties. Of the wet counties, only eleven are completely wet; the remaining twenty-nine all have dry towns.

QUICK REFERENCE

WHAT YOU CAN DO

- Where cities or counties allow, purchase package beer, wine, and spirits between 7:00 a.m. and 2:00 a.m. Monday through Friday, and between 7:00 a.m. and midnight on Saturday.
- Where cities or counties allow, order a drink at a restaurant or bar from 7:00 a.m. to 1:00 a.m. seven days a week.
- Order a drink at a club until 2:00 a.m. or 5:00 a.m., depending on the type of club.
- Bring your own bottle of wine to a restaurant.
- Take an unfinished bottle of wine from dinner home.
- Enjoy happy hour specials.
- Fill a growler at a brewery or brewpub.

WHAT YOU CAN'T DO

- Purchase alcohol on Christmas.
- Purchase package alcohol on Sundays in most places.
- Purchase package alcohol between 2:00 a.m. and 7:00 a.m.
- Order a drink at a bar or restaurant between 1:00 a.m. and 7:00 a.m. seven days a week.

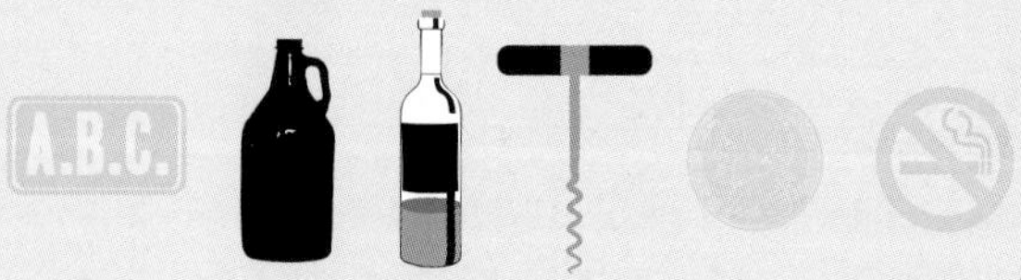

Source: Arkansas Alcoholic Beverage Control Division

The annual **WIEDERKEHR WEINFEST** celebrates the Swiss-German heritage of those who settled in the region in the 1880s. When the festival began in 1963, there was a law that prohibited advertising alcohol in dry counties. To circumvent this law, the winery owners used Schweizerdeutsch (Swiss-German) spellings on the billboards. The law no longer exists, but the founders kept the traditional spellings of Weinfest and Weinkellar as a tribute to their heritage

Hot Springs was a frequent vacation getaway for **AL CAPONE** during Prohibition. Attracted to its healing waters, gambling, high-class nightlife, and the robust moonshining culture of the Ozarks, Capone kept a room at the Arlington Hotel. It's believed that Capone hid Arkansas moonshine in water bottles and kegs and used trucks and railcars labeled Mountain Valley Water to distribute his product nationwide. Hot Springs-based **MOUNTAIN VALLEY SPRING WATER** (which claims no ownership of these stories) was an upscale brand of spring water in the early twentieth century and the first bottled water to be available coast-to-coast.

Prior to 2010, there were no distilleries in Arkansas. Then came Little Rock's **ROCK TOWN DISTILLERY**, the first in the state since prohibition. There are now a handful of craft distillers in the state and more are springing up each year.

ANDY CRITTENDEN
BAR MANAGER AT THE WINE CELLAR IN FAYETTEVILLE

TIP: "Arkansas is a strange land to navigate if you're a professional barfly. We have tons of dry counties where booze is hard to find. There is also an alarming number of 18+ bars, which kind of sucks. If you're ever in NW Arkansas, go check out Dickson St. in Fayetteville, but don't forget about Block St. at the top of the hill."

TENNESSEE

America at Its Best!

The drinking laws in Tennessee are so convoluted, you would think that all those local legislators had been drinking when they wrote them. More than thirty of the state's ninety counties are dry, and have been so for more than 100 years (predating Prohibition). That being said, if you'd like a stiff drink in a dry county in Tennessee, the best advice is to just keep driving. If it isn't wet where you're at, it will be somewhere up the road. It is not illegal to possess, transport, and consume alcohol in Tennessee, and you won't be arrested for bootlegging if you have to pack in your six-pack. The laws only regulate how and where you buy alcohol. Keep in mind that what dry counties lose in tax revenue, they make up for in tickets. Dry counties tend to have higher DUI arrests than wet counties.

Tennessee-crafted beer options abound. Boscos in Memphis makes a rare, unique steinbier named Famous Flaming Stone. It's made by lowering hot (700-degree) stones into the kettle during the boil, caramelizing the sugars and creating rich flavor. Nashville's Yazoo Brewing is the state's first brewery to acquire a distillery license, a requirement if you want to brew anything higher than 8%. Their first high-gravity concoction, a beer named Sue, clocks in at 9% and is a medal-winning best seller.

Whether your travel plans have you walking in Memphis or going to Graceland, it's a great idea to add a distillery tour to your itinerary. The Jack Daniel's Distillery is the oldest registered distillery in the country. You'll pass by the wood-burning shacks where they make their own charcoal, and the iron-free spring whose waters help make Jack the top-selling whiskey in the country. Standing guard over the spring is a bronze likeness of the distillery's diminutive founder, anatomically correct down to the ankles. The only difference is that the sculpture wears a size nine shoe; when it sported the original's size fours, the statue toppled over. The commemorative bottle you can buy in the gift shop is the only liquor that's sold in dry Lynchburg.

More than twenty distilleries now operate in the state, several of them producing moonshine. But the first to do so legally was the Ole Smokey distillery. Visit them (in their namesake holler) in Gatlinburg, with live music all day and night, comfy rocking chairs, and all the moonshine you need to keep you a-pickin' and a-grinnin'. When Tennessean Davy Crockett set out to marry his beloved Polly, he observed the frontier tradition of sending a group of friends with an empty jug to the home of his intended wife. The patriarch of the family returned the jug filled with liquor, approving the union. Now that's Southern hospitality. Pass the jar and 'shine on!

MOUNTAIN DEW was invented in Knoxville and is named after a slang term for moonshine. Originally concocted as a mixer for liquor, its label at one time featured jug-toting Willy the Hillbilly shooting at a man emerging from an outhouse. It was even marketed as "zero proof hillbilly moonshine." Pepsi acquired the brand in 1964, and in 1973 they dropped the hillbilly and moonshine themes in order to appeal to younger markets. Mountain Dew is currently the fifth bestselling soda in America.

BOSCOS FAMOUS FLAMING STONE BEER is made by lowering hot rocks into the kettle during the boil.

JACK DANIELS himself (in bronze form), standing guard over the oldest registered distillery in the country.

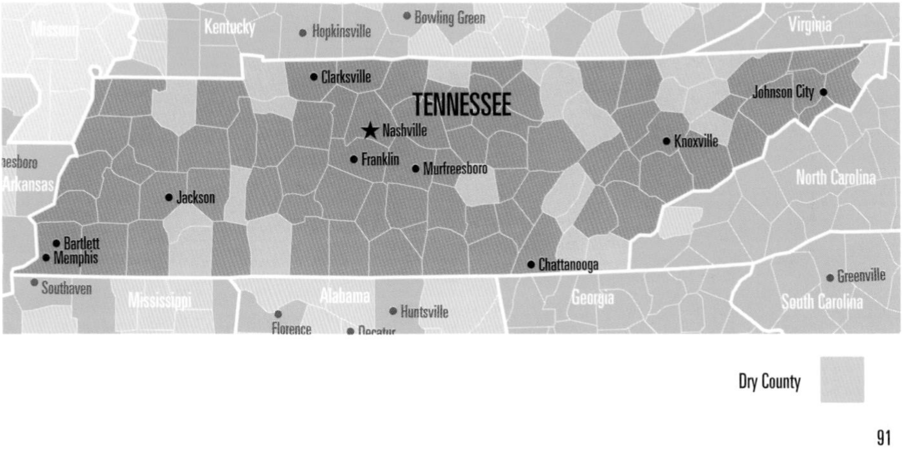

TENNESSEE

WHAT'LL IT BE?

In Tennessee, beer under 5% ABW (6.4% ABV) is available at grocery stores, convenience stores, and pharmacies between 6:00 a.m. and midnight Monday through Saturday, and after 10:00 a.m. on Sunday. Bars can also sell beer for off-premise consumption. Package liquor, wine, and beer over 5% ABW are available only at liquor stores, which only operate from 8:00 a.m. to 11:00 p.m. Monday through Saturday. On-premise sales are more permissive. Bars and restaurants can serve alcohol between 8:00 a.m. and 3:00 a.m. Monday through Saturday, and between 10:00 a.m. and 3:00 a.m. on Sundays, depending on the local options. Alcohol is available on all holidays.

Tennessee is dry by default and counties must choose whether or not to permit the sale of alcohol. Beer sales under 5% ABW are regulated by the counties, while spirits wine and strong beer are governed by state law. Of Tennessee's ninety-five counties, twenty-six are completely dry. A further sixty counties limit the sale of alcohol in some way, either by restricting package sales, "liquor by the drink," or both. Nine counties are completely wet and have no restrictions on the sale of alcohol. All major cities are wet.

QUICK REFERENCE

WHAT YOU CAN DO

- Order a drink at a bar between 8:00 a.m. and 3:00 a.m. Monday through Saturday, and 10:00 a.m. and 3:00 a.m. on Sunday. If the local government has opted out of the extended hours, Sunday alcohol service begins at noon.
- Purchase beer under 5% ABW at a grocery store, convenience store, or pharmacy between 6:00 a.m. and midnight Monday through Saturday, and after 10:00 a.m. on Sunday.
- Purchase package liquor, wine, and beer over 5% ABW at a liquor store between 8:00 a.m. and 11:00 p.m. Monday through Saturday.
- Bring your own bottle of wine to a restaurant.
- Take an unfinished bottle of wine from dinner home.
- Enjoy happy hour specials.
- Fill a growler at a brewery, brewpub, or grocery store.
- Smoke on an open-air patio or in a bar not attached to a restaurant, hotel, or bowling alley.

WHAT YOU CAN'T DO

- Purchase package liquor, wine, and beer over 5% ABW on Sunday.
- Smoke in an enclosed restaurant or a bar that allows minors to enter, such as those attached to a restaurant, hotel, or bowling alley.
- Order a drink at a bar between 3:00 a.m. and 8:00 a.m. Monday through Saturday, or between 3:00 a.m. and 10:00 a.m. on Sunday.
- Purchase beer, wine, or liquor between 11:00 p.m. and 8:00 a.m.

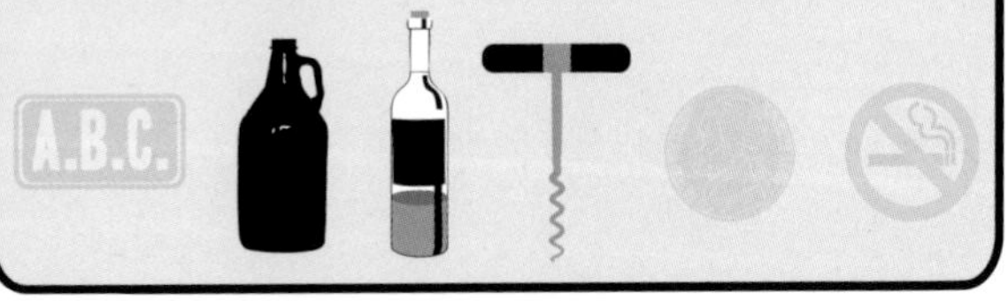

Source: Tennessee Alcoholic Beverage Commission

Johnson City was known as "Little Chicago" in the 1920s because of its speakeasies, bootleggers, and vice. It's also notable for the number of reported cases of JAKE LEG, a type of paralysis that came from drinking improperly distilled or contaminated liquor that plagued America during Prohibition. "Jake" was a medicinal alcoholic extract of Jamaican ginger root, legal under the Volstead Act because it technically wasn't beverage alcohol. A small bottle, however, contained about the equivalent of about four shots of Scotch. Jake was a go-to source of alcohol for the poor and others without access to bootlegged liquor throughout Prohibition, although it did come with a price.

Tippling License

Tennessee was one of the first states to issue what we would today call an on-premise liquor license. TIPPLING HOUSES (an antiquated term for saloons) were issued Tippling Licenses and authorized to sell "spirituous liquors." An 1837 report to the General Assembly stated "the law was complied with; enabling all who chose, to indulge occasionally in a social glass. This then appeared commensurate with the wants of the people. Scarcely an instance of complaint was heard, that the rights and privileges of any citizen were curtailed, or his liberties infringed upon."

FYI

In 2014, Tennessee raised the alcohol limit for beers sold in grocery and convenience stores. Previously capped at 5% ABW (6.25% ABV), the new limit allows for beers with an ABW of 8% (10% ABV). But don't get too excited; the new law is not slated to take effect for a few years.

MATT TOCCO
BEVERAGE DIRECTOR AT PINEWOOD SOCIAL IN NASHVILLE

TIP: "Though Tennessee has some stringent liquor laws, our bars stay open until 3 a.m. every night. So while you can't go to the liquor store on a Sunday, you can stay up plenty late enough Saturday night."

KENTUCKY

United We Stand, Divided We Fall

By act of Congress, bourbon whiskey is an official spirit of the United States. The familiar names of the founding fathers of bourbon line liquor store shelves, but who did what and when is largely a mystery. Initially, un-aged Kentucky whiskey was shipped by river to New Orleans. By the end of the journey, the white dog whiskey would take on a caramel red color from the inside of the charred barrels in which they made the trip. By the early 1800s, this aging became an integral part of the process, and Kentucky whiskey became something like contemporary bourbon.

Tasting bourbon should be a top entry on your Kentucky bucket list. Keep an open mouth when smelling the spirit, and don't forget the Kentucky chew ("chew" the whiskey, moving it around to all parts of your mouth). There's no better place to taste bourbon than Bardstown, host of the annual Kentucky Bourbon Festival and the location of several distilleries. Within driving distance is Heaven Hill's Bourbon Heritage Center, Jim Beam's American Stillhouse (which opened right after Prohibition ended), Wild Turkey, and Four Roses. Also nearby is Maker's Mark, the country's oldest working distillery on its original site, and a national historic landmark. In nearby Versailles is Labrot & Graham's Woodford Reserve, the official bourbon of the Kentucky Derby.

For a place producing so many excellent American whiskies, there is a lot of local legislation to deal with. A sizeable portion of the state is dry or moist, and it's illegal to buy, sell, or even give away alcohol in a dry county. The irony of a considerably dry state with more than two dozen bourbon distilleries drawing half a million visitors annually is enough to drive a person to drink! But don't worry about driving through a dry county with distilled souvenirs, though, as that's one thing that's legal statewide. Buy your beer on someday other than Sunday and before midnight the rest of the week.

The greatest two minutes in sports, the Kentucky Derby, takes place in May in Louisville. The big-hatted and the bowtied stand cheek-to-jowl in the stands and in the 80,000-person party on the huge grassy meadow known as the infield. Before you go lifting too many of those silver julep cups, secure a safe ride home, since it is illegal in the state of Kentucky to operate a horse while intoxicated.

To make the perfect Mint Julep, as legendary Louisville newspaper editor Marse Henry Watterson instructs, "pluck the mint gently from its bed, just as the dew of the evening is about to form upon it. Select the choicer springs only, but do not rinse them. Prepare the simple syrup and measure out a half tumbler of whiskey. Pour the whiskey into a well-frosted silver cup, throw the other ingredients away and drink the whiskey."

No whiskey produced in the state can use the word **"KENTUCKY"** on the label unless it has been aged in oak barrels for at least one year, with the exception of listing the name and address of the distiller as required by federal law.

Have a frosty **MINT JULEP** in a tin cup at the 80,000-person party known as the Kentucky Derby.

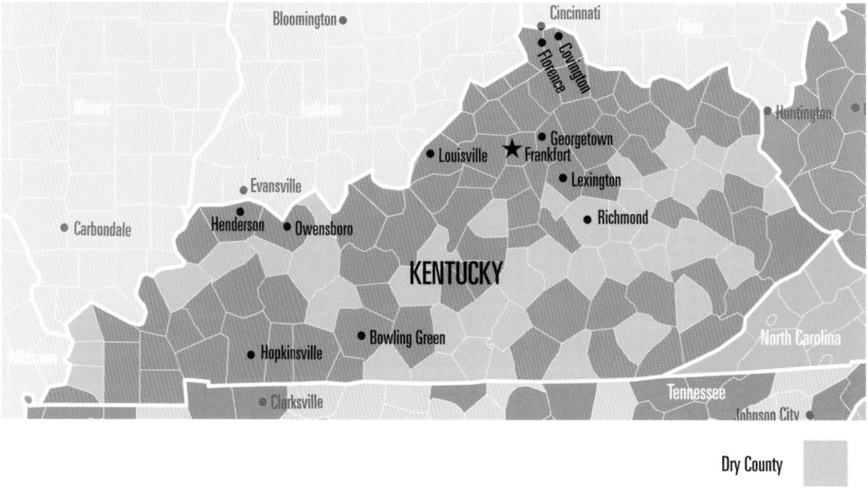

KENTUCKY

WHAT'LL IT BE?

Kentucky's alcohol laws are confusing, but if the county or town is wet, beer and weak cider (under 7% ABV) can be found in grocery stores and package spirits and wine in liquor stores. Unless there is a local ordinance to the contrary (which there usually is), state law allows sales for both on- and off-premise consumption from 6:00 a.m. to 2:00 a.m. Monday through Saturday, and from 1:00 p.m. to 2:00 a.m. on Sundays.

In Kentucky, counties can vote to become dry, prohibiting both on- and off-premise sales. A county can also have "limited" sales, where alcohol by the drink is only allowed in restaurants with at least fifty seats and with 70% of their income from food sales. Of Kentucky's one hundred and twenty counties, thirty-four are completely dry, mostly in the southeastern part of the state; there are fifty more counties that are moist or limited. City ordinances, however, can trump state and county laws, so it's possible to find a dry town in a wet county (or a wet town in a dry county). The larger cities, including Louisville and Lexington, are all wet.

QUICK REFERENCE

WHAT YOU CAN DO

- Purchase package beer and weak cider from grocery stores, convenience stores, and pharmacies.
- Purchase package liquor and wine from liquor stores.
- Transport liquor through dry counties.
- Take an unfinished bottle of wine from dinner home.
- Drink in a bar in Louisville until 4:00 a.m.
- Enjoy happy hour specials.
- Fill a growler at a brewery, brewpub, or grocery store.
- Be drunk in public. Public intoxication laws exclude alcohol.

WHAT YOU CAN'T DO

- Sell, purchase, barter, or even give away alcohol in a dry county.

**** Local options make it difficult to generalize about what is prohibited state-wide.

Source: Kentucky Department of Alcoholic Beverage Control

SOUTH

Kentucky no longer has a state-wide ban on alcohol sales on **ELECTION DAY.** In 2014 the state eased restrictions, leaving the question of Election Day sales to be decided at the local level. The law was a relic from a time when saloons were sometimes used as polling stations and ballots could be bought with booze. South Carolina was the only other state with a similar state-wide ban, but it was lifted in 2014 as well. State law also prohibits Election Day sales in Massachusetts and Alaska, but communities typically pass a local option making them exempt.

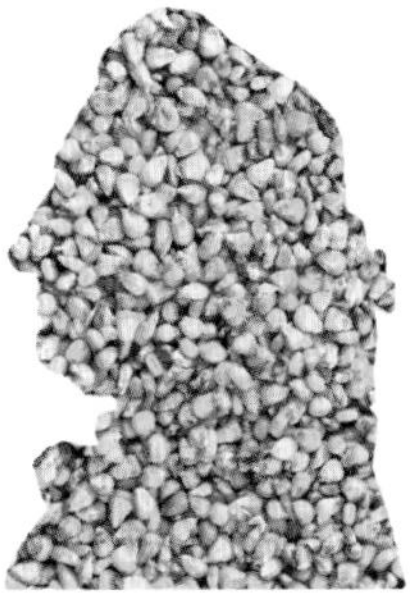

Because bourbon is at least 51% corn, a traditional Kentucky folk term for being drunk is to be **"FULL OF CORN."** Supreme Court Chief Justice John Marshall had this in mind when he wrote the following lines in 1825:

IN THE BLUE GRASS REGION
A PARADOX WAS BORN:
THE CORN WAS FULL OF KERNELS
AND THE COLONELS FULL OF CORN.

The Filson Historical Society in Louisville offers a **BOURBON ACADEMY** taught by Filson Bourbon Historian Michael Veach. These one-day, brand-neutral classes provide a review of the Society's archives, special collections, and tastings. The classes are open to bourbon enthusiasts, historians, and industry professionals who want to learn more about one of Kentucky's most famous products.

JACQUELYN ZYKAN
DOC CROW'S SOUTHERN SMOKEHOUSE & RAW BAR

TIP: "When drinking whiskey, remember this: if the proof of the whiskey is higher than your weight, avoid shooting it straight. Also, we know you're from out of town if you order a Mint Julep. Try to drink like a local instead and order an Old Forester Bourbon. If you think you've had one too many bourbons, know that according to Kentucky law you are considered sober until you cannot hold on to the ground."

OHIO

With God, All Things Are Possible

Novelist Louis Bromfield observed that his home state of Ohio is the "farthest West of the East and the farthest North of the South." As their slogan says, Ohio is the heart of it all, and that's not just because of its shape. It's Middle America, at its finest and not so finest. It's the birthplace of aviation, and it's also where Paul Newman was allegedly expelled from college for rolling a keg down a hill (and into the president's car). Hey! Ho! Way to go Ohio.

Ohio is not just home to the Rock and Roll Hall of Fame, it's also the where "Rock and Roll" (the term, that is) originated. Cleveland DJ Alan Freed came up with the phrase, and, true to art, met his end thanks to a rock and roll lifestyle. He died of kidney failure at the age of forty-three, just twenty days after entering the hospital with cirrhosis. He was inducted into the Hall of Fame posthumously in 1986.

The state is known as the "Mother of all Presidents," since seven were born within her borders: one of the two Harrisons, Harding, Hayes, Grant, Garfield, McKinley, and last but certainly not least, America's largest president, William Howard Taft. Two of those presidents died of natural causes while in office and two were assassinated, but the one with the greatest appetite, Taft, lived to see the end of his term. Taft was a man of many indulgences. The man who famously got himself stuck in his bathtub elicited the outrage of several clergymen when he asked for a Bronx cocktail at breakfast. For the record, the Bronx cocktail of Taft's time was just a gin Martini with a shot of OJ thrown in to assuage guilt.

The Bronx cocktail played a significant role in the life of another famous Ohioan. It was the very first of entirely too many drinks that Akron resident Bill Wilson consumed. That name might go unrecognized to all but the friends of Bill W., the Alcoholics Anonymous founder. Not a quitter? Clevelander Drew Carey has some advice for the troubled that are not on the twelve-step path: "There's a support group for that. It's called EVERYBODY, and they meet at the bar." The annals of great fake beer names must list Buzz Beer, the coffee/beer combo from *The Drew Carey Show*, whose motto was simply "stay up and get drunk all over again."

The beverage best consumed in a breakfast Bloody or on a plane (or in a breakfast Bloody on a plane) also happens to be the state beverage of Ohio: tomato juice. Pour it into beer and you're ordering a Red Eye. If you're aiming to drink before dawn, keep in mind that Buckeye state bars may begin serving at 5:30 a.m. Too many Bloody Marys at breakfast? Heed the counsel of famous addled Ohioan Dean Martin: "If you're drunk don't drive, don't even putt." Born in Steubenville in 1917, Dino drove liquor across state lines during Prohibition before breaking into show business under the name of Dino Martini. In the '60s and '70s he hosted television shows where he entertained America with his persona of an alcoholic lush, an act that was more schtick than truth.

Because alcohol that is 21% ABV or less can be sold without a full liquor license, there are "DILUTED SPIRITS" available alongside beer and wine in grocery stores, pharmacies, and convenience stores. These products are cut with water by their manufacturer to 21% (about 40 proof) and are marked "diluted" on the label.

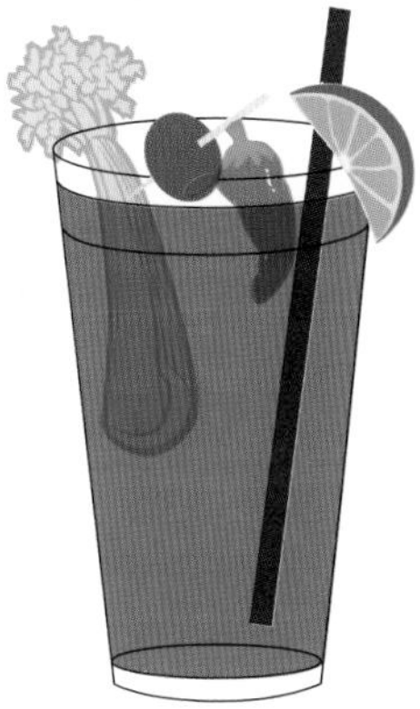

You can't make a Bloody Mary without **TOMATO JUICE**, Ohio's state beverage.

WHAT'LL IT BE?

Ohio is a control state. The sale of liquor and fortified wine over 21% ABV is closely regulated and the sale of beer over 12% ABV is prohibited. Spirits over 21% are only available at a limited number of private businesses with a full liquor license that serve as agents of the state. While many state liquor agencies are stand-alone liquor and beverage stores, some grocery stores and markets can also have a full liquor license. Ohio does allow businesses without a full liquor license to sell alcohol at or under 21%, so package beer, wine, and "diluted spirits" are widely available from a variety of businesses, including grocery stores, convenience stores, and pharmacies. On-premise consumption is allowed between 5:30 a.m. and 2:30 a.m. seven days a week, every day of the year.

Ohio allows for a local option, which results in a few dry spots around the state. However, the number of places that completely prohibit the sale of alcohol are relatively few and dwindling with time. The greatest impact local options have on consumers is the start time of Sunday liquor sales. Although state law allows an 11:00 a.m. start to Sunday liquor sales, some towns start later.

QUICK REFERENCE

WHAT YOU CAN DO

- Buy beer, wine, and liquor every day of the year.
- Buy package beer, wine, and "diluted spirits" in licensed grocery stores, convenience stores, and pharmacies between 5:30 a.m. and 1:00 a.m. Monday through Saturday.
- Buy undiluted liquor greater than 21% ABV in liquor stores Monday through Saturday between 5:30 a.m. and 1:00 a.m. and after 11:00 a.m. on Sunday (depending on local option).
- Order a drink in a bar between 5:30 a.m. and 2:30 a.m. seven days a week.
- Take an unfinished bottle of wine from dinner home.
- Fill a growler at a brewery, brewpub, or grocery store.

WHAT YOU CAN'T DO

- Smoke in bars and restaurants.
- Play organized drinking games in a bar or win alcohol as a prize in a contest.
- Buy cider higher than 6% ABV.
- Buy alcohol for off-premise consumption between the hours of 1:00 a.m. and 5:30 a.m.
- Buy liquor over 21% in most grocery stores, convenience stores, or pharmacies.
- Bring your own bottle of wine to a restaurant.
- Bring a loaded firearm into a business that serves alcohol.

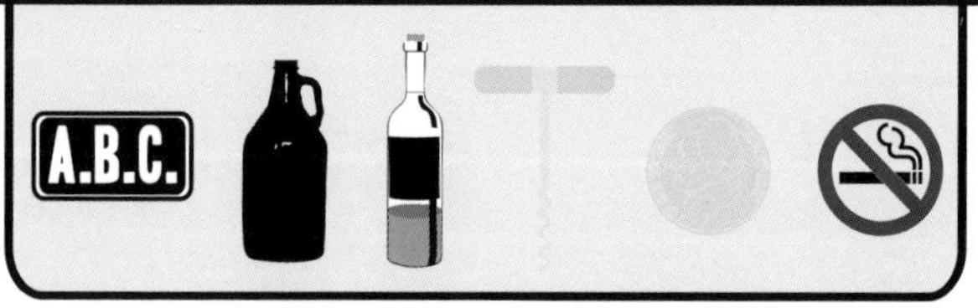

Source: Ohio Department of Commerce, Division of Liquor Control

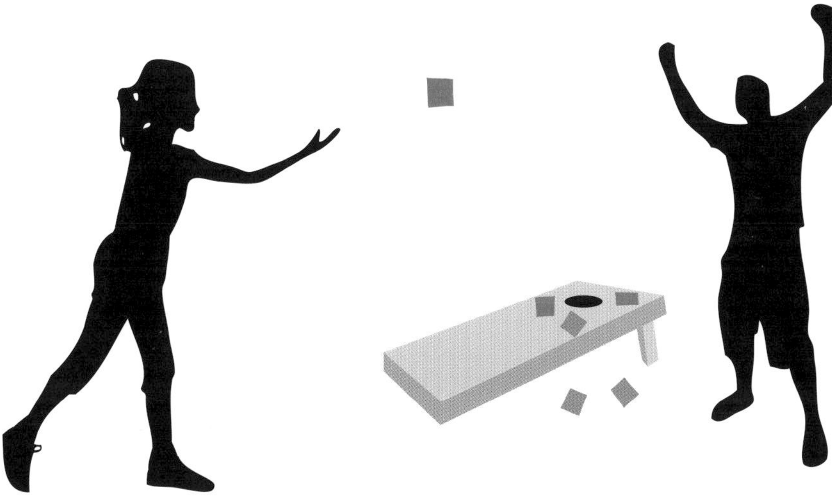

Nobody knows the exact origins of **CORNHOLE,** a game played by tossing bags of corn through a hole, but it has taken bars by storm lately. Although the game's past is open to speculation, what isn't open to dispute is that people from Cincinnati love them some Cornhole and that the city (and particularly the west side) has had a large influence on the game's recent surge in popularity.

Prior to the Civil War, Ohio was considered America's most important wine producing state. In the areas around the Ohio River where the south-facing slopes gently rolled down to the banks of America's first highway, settlers in the 1830s aspired to rival the great wine-producing regions of Europe. They even christened themselves with the ambitious title: **"THE RHINELAND OF AMERICA."**

CRIS DELAVI
BARTENDER AT M RESTAURANT IN COLUMBUS

TIP: "Ohio is one of a handful of control states in the U.S., which means our spirit options are limited because of laws dating back to Prohibition. Rather than hindering us, it has allowed the bartenders in our state to be even more creative and inspired. Columbus has a fantastic cocktail scene with nationally recognized bars and bartenders."

INDIANA

The Crossroads of America

Songwriter Cole Porter, born in Peru, Indiana, wrote many a ditty about drinking, including "Say it With Gin," "Absinthe Drip," and "Make it Another Old Fashioned, Please." But he could have been referencing the positively Prohibitionistic liquor laws of his home state when he sarcastically toasted the author of the Eighteenth Amendment in his 1929 musical comedy, *Fifty Million Frenchmen:* "Here's a long life to Volstead! And I hope he dies of thirst!"

Indiana is one of twelve states that still operate under that classic Blue Law, the off-premise Sunday liquor sales ban. It is the only state, however, that bans the retail sale of everything alcoholic—absolutely no beer, wine, or liquor will be sold over the counter in the Hoosier State on Sundays. Plan ahead or head to the pub!

Even during the rest of the week, satisfying the craving for a cold one in the comfort of one's home can be challenging in Indiana. The state also has a unique, peculiar, and frustrating rule related to temperature. Though beer and wine are available at gas stations, and beer and wine plus liquor are for sale in grocery stores, they all must be sold at room temperature. You cannot buy chilled alcohol of any kind anywhere other than at a liquor store. And those liquor stores may not sell cold mixers, cold soft drinks, or even milk.

Over 300,000 people attend the Indy 500, the largest sporting event in the country, held every Memorial Day Sunday. The Indianapolis Motor Speedway itself is huge, a 2.5-mile-long track, allowing for a gigantic party on the infield. Inside turn three, you'll find the notorious Snake Pit, a blowout of a bash which allows BYOB, so shop ahead of time and make sure there's no glass in your cooler. Chill down that case quickly with equal parts water and ice and a healthy pour of salt. Stir for two to five minutes, and then gentlemen, start your engines!

Frequently voted one of the best breweries in the world is Munster's own Three Floyds Brewing, which is astounding considering their beer isn't even distributed outside of the Midwest. One day a year, known as Dark Lord Day, thousands of people from across the country descend on the brewery to purchase their extremely limited Russian Imperial stout known as the Dark Lord. What ostensibly began as an early queuing to buy the rare beer has grown into an all-day exotic bottle share and beer fest, complete with a roster of metal bands. Tickets sell out in minutes.

Famous tippling Hoosiers include Michael Jackson (not the Beer Hunter, he of the Jesus Juice) and Dr. Rolla N. Harger, inventor of the Drunkometer (the first alcohol-measuring breath sobriety test). Fun fact: after Harger invented the Drunkometer in 1936, he went on to sponsor both state and national drunk driving regulations.

Kilgore Trout once wrote a short story which was a dialogue between two pieces of yeast. They were discussing the possible purposes of life as they ate sugar and suffocated in their own excrement. Because of their limited intelligence, they never came close to guessing that they were making champagne.

-INDIANA NATIVE KURT VONNEGUT, *BREAKFAST OF CHAMPIONS*

INDIANA

WHAT'LL IT BE?

Alcohol is available in Indiana for on-premise purchase between 7:00 a.m. and 3:00 a.m. seven days a week, every day of the year except Christmas. Off-premise purchases are more limited. There are no package sales on Sundays, except from wineries and breweries. Room-temperature package alcohol is available Monday through Saturday between 7:00 a.m. and 3:00 a.m. from grocery stores, convenience stores, and pharmacies. Cold beer and other chilled alcoholic beverages are only available for package purchase at liquor stores.

Indiana does not allow for a local option. Laws relating to alcohol are consistent statewide.

QUICK REFERENCE

WHAT YOU CAN DO

- Purchase package beer, wine, and liquor from liquor stores, grocery stores, and pharmacies between 7:00 a.m. and 3:00 a.m. Monday through Saturday.
- Order a drink at a bar or restaurant between 7:00 a.m. and 3:00 a.m. seven days a week.
- Purchase package beer and wine from a brewery or winery between 7:00 a.m. and 3:00 a.m. seven days a week.
- Bring your own homemade wine to consume at a restaurant without a wine license.
- Fill a growler at a brewery, brewpub, or grocery store.
- Smoke in a bar or on a restaurant patio.
- Take an unfinished bottle of wine from dinner home.

WHAT YOU CAN'T DO

- Purchase package beer, wine, and spirits on Sunday, except at breweries or wineries.
- Smoke in an enclosed restaurant.
- Bring your own commercially-produced alcoholic beverages to a restaurant.
- Purchase alcohol on Christmas.
- Order a drink between 3:00 a.m. and 7:00 a.m.
- Purchase cold beer at a grocery store, convenience store, or pharmacy.
- Purchase package alcohol between 3:00 a.m. and 7:00 a.m.

Source: Indiana Alcohol and Tobacco Commission

HEOROT PUB AND DRAUGHT HOUSE in Muncie takes its name from the Anglo-Saxon mead hall that was thrashed nightly by Grendel in the epic poem *Beowulf*. They do indeed serve mead, but it's the well-curated list of 450 types of craft beer from around the world that regularly puts Heorot on the list of the best beer bars in America.

Indianapolis police tested the **DRUNKOMETER**, the first scientific field sobriety test on New Year's Eve, 1938. It involved blowing into a balloon filled with chemicals that would change color the more alcohol was present.

Temperate Indiana was dry even before Prohibition was the law of the land. The Hoosier state went one step further, though, with their **WRIGHT "BONE DRY" LAW** (1925), which closed the loophole in the Volstead Act for medicinal uses of alcohol. This hard-line stance was difficult to maintain, especially when it was revealed that Indiana's attorney general, governor, and even the head of the state's Anti-Saloon League had all used or provided alcohol to family members for medicinal purposes.

ERIN EDDS
FOUNDER, HOOSIER MOMMA BLOODY MARY MAKER IN INDIANAPOLIS
TIP: "If you are going to be in town for the weekend, make sure you stock up on your spirits by Saturday night because there are no Sunday retail alcohol sales allowed in the state of Indiana. The only exceptions are breweries and wineries, if they make their product on site. Or you could just go to a bar."

MICHIGAN

Si Quaeris Peninsulam Amoenam Circumspice (If You Seek a Pleasant Peninsula, Look About You)

From Mackinac to K-zoo, no matter where you travel in Michigan, you're never further than an eighty-five minute drive from a Great Lake. Michiganders are great outdoorsmen. The mitten-shaped state has more registered snowmobiles than any other, and good hunting and fishing abound. Save your beers until after operating a snowmobile, a boat, or gun, however, as there are penalties for mixing alcohol with any of the three.

One out of five Michigan jobs depends on the auto industry. The Big Three (Ford, GM, and Chrysler) all have their headquarters here. Henry Ford invented the assembly line in Detroit in 1913, and with it, the Motor City began to flourish. Ford was a staunch teetotaler who not only forbade his employees to drink, but also threatened to stop production of his vehicles if Prohibition were ever overturned: "For myself, if booze ever comes back to the United States, I am through with manufacturing.... I wouldn't be interested in putting automobiles into the hands of a generation soggy with drink."

Detroit's desire for drink was more than a match for Mr. Ford's will against it, as was evidenced by Prohibition protesters that numbered in the tens of thousands. The city's infamous Purple Gang controlled a pipeline smuggling Canadian whiskey into the country via the Detroit River. Twenty-eight miles long and at points just a mile wide, the Detroit River was part of a network of waterways in the region that collectively supplied the United States with a whopping 75% of the bootleg liquor consumed during Prohibition. Smuggling was Detroit's second-largest industry during Prohibition, only outgrossed by automobile manufacturing. Consequently, Michigan was the first state to ratify the Twenty-First Amendment.

Recent legislation has made Michigan an easier place to get beer to go. Now any licensed bar, restaurant, or even hotel may sell tapped beer in growlers to go. From one beer lover to another, you should know that Michigan boasts more than eighty craft breweries, making it one of America's top states for hosting beermakers. Kalamazoo's Bell's Brewing has been producing award-winning beer for more than twenty-five years. Five of the state's six largest craft breweries are also located in the region, making it an ideal spot for a beer-cation. It all started with Stroh's, though (originally known as Lion's Head Beer), which was sold door-to-door by apple cart. Stroh's popularized what might be the swiller's greatest comfort: the thirty-pack. There's more than just peace of mind in that extra sixer. Deposits are a dime apiece in Michigan, making all those bags of dead soldiers in the mud room a sizeable beer fund. The state's redemption rate is more than 95%; however, it estimates that it loses between 10% and 13% to bottle bootleggers trucking empties across state lines.

HENRY FORD

forbade his employees to drink and threatened to stop production if Prohibition were overturned.

LIONS HEAD BEER,

which became Stroh's, was originally sold door-to-door by apple cart.

MICHIGAN

WHAT'LL IT BE?

Michigan is a control state, but only for liquor. The state does not operate retail stores and only controls the wholesale of distilled spirits. Package beer, wine, and liquor are widely available from a variety of licensed businesses, which can include grocery stores, convenience stores, and pharmacies. Sale hours for both on- and off-premise consumption are between 7:00 a.m. and 2:00 a.m. Monday through Saturday. Hours for Sunday sales in Michigan are dependent on two permits. The first permit allows Sunday sales between noon and 2:00 a.m. Establishments can also purchase a second Sunday permit allowing sales between 7:00 a.m. and noon, if the local government allows. No alcohol sales are permitted between midnight on Christmas Eve and noon on Christmas.

Michigan does allow for a local option, although there are very few places that are dry. They primarily reduce the hours of sale on Sundays and restrict the sale of alcohol on Election Day.

QUICK REFERENCE

WHAT YOU CAN DO

- Buy package beer, wine and liquor between 7:00 a.m. and 2:00 a.m. Monday through Saturday in grocery stores, convenience stores, and pharmacies.
- Order a drink in a bar or restaurant between 7:00 a.m. and 2:00 a.m. Monday through Saturday.
- Buy alcohol for on- and off-premise consumption between 7:00 a.m. and 2:00 a.m. on Sunday, if the local government allows it and the business has both additional special permits.
- Bring your own bottle of wine to a restaurant.
- Take an unfinished bottle of wine from dinner home.
- Fill a growler at a brewery, brewpub, or grocery store.
- Get your dime back from bottle and can deposits.
- Buy alcohol from wholesale stores like Sam's Club and Costco without a membership.
- Drink in a bar until 4:00 a.m. on New Year's Eve.

WHAT YOU CAN'T DO

- Smoke in bars and restaurants, including outdoor patios.
- Drink alcohol in branded glassware.
- Dance in a bar unless they have a "dance permit."
- Be drunk on a train.
- Buy package beer, wine, or liquor between 2:00 a.m. and 7:00 a.m. Monday through Saturday or before noon on Sundays, unless the seller has a Sunday permit.
- Order a drink in bar between 2:00 a.m. and 7:00 a.m. Monday through Saturday and before noon on Sundays, unless the seller has a Sunday permit.
- Buy alcohol between midnight on Christmas Eve and noon on Christmas.

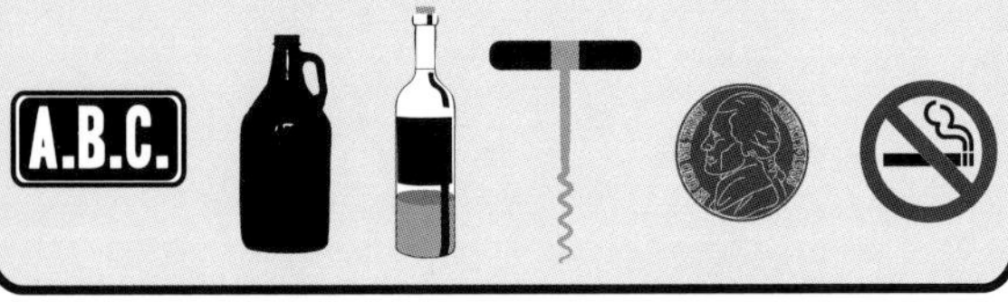

Source: Michigan Department of Licensing and Regulatory Affairs, Liquor Control Commission

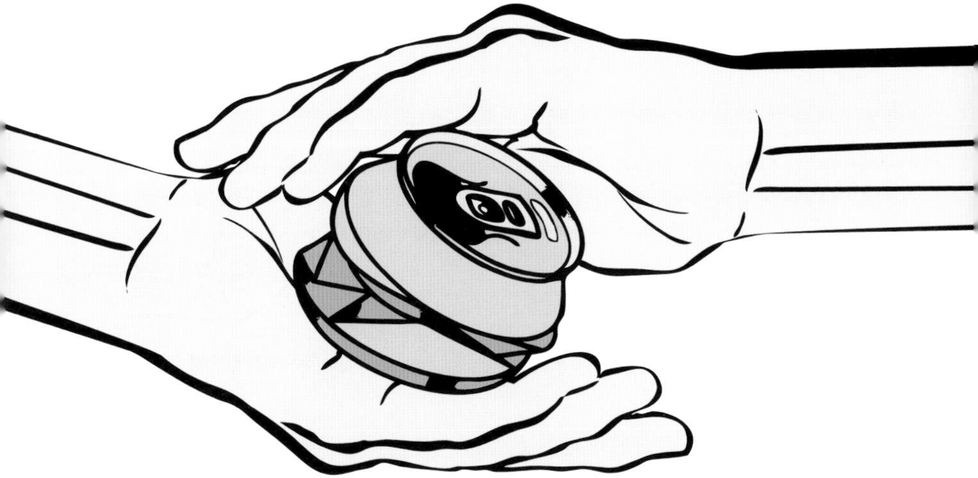

A smuggling ring involving thirteen people, millions of beverage cans, and a half million dollars in cash was taken down by Michigan authorities in **OPERATION CAN SCAM** in 2007. The scheme, which was also once the premise of a *Seinfeld* episode, involved collecting cans from nearby states and redeeming them in Michigan for their 10-cent deposit. The state loses about $13 million annually to can smugglers.

MICHIGAN

is one of only two states, the other being Kentucky, that prohibits bars from using items such as glassware, coasters, napkins, and clocks with the logos of beer, wine, or liquor on them. Wholesalers claim the ban keeps larger brands from giving away free promotional materials that smaller brands can't afford. Retailers claim they want to support local Michigan craft breweries by using promotional items—they don't just want freebies. The debate is ongoing.

FYI

In Michigan, convenience stores and other places that sell alcohol are called "party stores." As in: *"Excuse me, where's the closest party store?"*

JOSH HALLWACHS
BARTENDER AT HOLIDAY INN GRAND RAPIDS DOWNTOWN IN GRAND RAPIDS

TIP: "To all visitors coming to my state, I would stress the importance of "Craft Bars". We are not just abundant in craft beers, but all over the state you will find craft wineries, craft cidermills, and craft distilleries. The entire state is devoted to giving exceptional service, whether it's pairing drinks and food or describing the flavors of our local wines or craft beers."

WISCONSIN

Oh Wisconsin, Land of My Dreams

Hello Wisconsin, and welcome to America's beer belly! Thanks to four men with immediately recognizable surnames—Frederick Miller, Captain Frederick Pabst, Joseph Schlitz, and Valentine Blatz—Milwaukee is known as the birthplace of American beer. And by the end of the nineteenth century, Milwaukee was the top producer of beer in the world.

Right after the Great Chicago Fire of 1871, the Schlitz Brewery stepped up and donated thousands of barrels of beer to the city (which had lost many of its breweries). Its sales grew by 100%! "The Beer That Made Milwaukee Famous," one of the world's largest brewers after Prohibition, is now owned by Pabst. Pabst was using over thirty million feet of blue ribbon to decorate the necks of the bottles of their beer in the 1900s. The Pabst brand grew, acquiring more than a dozen regional breweries over the years, including Stroh's, Olympia, Rainier, Lone Star, Old Milwaukee, National Bohemian, and Old Style. Everything old is new again—PBR is the hipster drink of choice. And in Milwaukee, you can still tour the luxurious mansion that Captain Pabst built. They even hold an annual Retro Beer Night fundraiser, which showcases all the classic beers that your dad drank.

The state remains a beer powerhouse. MillerCoors is the second largest brewer in the United States. New Glarus is not just an award-winning brewery, but also the nineteenth-largest craft brewer in the country—and they don't even distribute outside of the state! One of the best beer festivals in the country is Madison's Great Taste of the Midwest. It's the second-longest-running beer festival in the nation, and has grown to the point where they now pour over 1,000 different beers.

Wisconsonites drink about 26.3 gallons of beer per person annually. And almost any club or institution can get a license to sell alcohol, so you'll find beer being sold at many events, from basketball games to curling clubs to outdoor festivals, like Milwaukee's music festival, Summerfest. Friday night fish frys are held by churches all over the state in the summer months. And many of those churches also have beer licenses, so pull over!

La Crosse was recently named the most romantic place in America by Redbox Film Rental because they rented more "romantic" movies than anywhere else. What's not to love when La Crosse is also the home to the world's largest six-pack, which holds 22,000 gallons of beer? That might just be enough to slake the town's thirst on New Year's Eve, when beer bars in Wisconsin do not close.

Lovely Wisconsin: where heads are made of cheese, hands are holding bratwurst, and bars outnumber supermarkets!

During Prohibition all of the major brewers began producing **"NEAR-BEERS,"** which were non-fermented concoctions of malt and hops. Miller made Vivo; Schlitz made Famo; Stroh made Lux-O; Anheuser-Busch made Bevo; and Pabst made Pablo (get it?). While these drinks helped keep the major breweries in business during the dry years, a common quip of the time summed up the public's reaction: "Whoever called it near beer was a poor judge of distance."

In the 1900s, Pabst used over thirty million feet of ribbon to decorate their bottles.

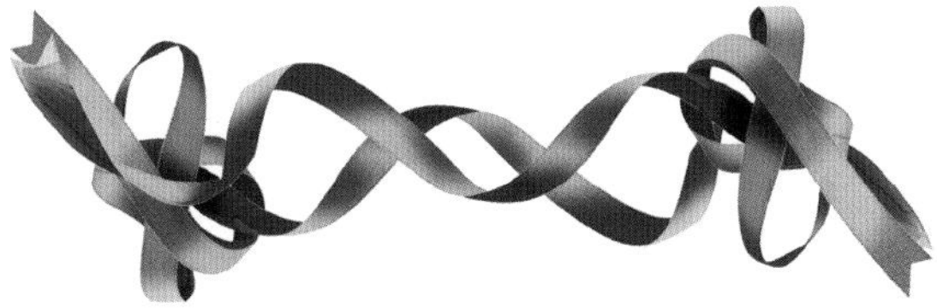

WISCONSIN

WHAT'LL IT BE?

Wisconsin's liquor laws are straightforward. Stores with a liquor license can sell beer, wine, and liquor, but some stores only have a license to sell beer. Beer, wine, and liquor are widely available from licensed retailers, which can include grocery stores, convenience stores, and pharmacies. Wine and liquor are available for purchase between 6:00 a.m. and 9:00 p.m. Beer sales are permitted until midnight. All varieties of alcohol are available in bars and restaurants between 6:00 a.m. and 2:00 a.m. seven days a week, every day of the year. Establishments may choose to stay open until 2:30 a.m. on Friday and Saturday nights.

Wisconsin does allow for a local option, and municipalities can limit the hours when alcohol is available for purchase.

QUICK REFERENCE

WHAT YOU CAN DO

- Order a drink in a bar or restaurant between 6:00 a.m. and 2:00 a.m. seven days a week, and until 2:30 a.m. on Friday and Saturday.
- Purchase package beer between 6:00 a.m. and midnight from grocery stores, convenience stores, and pharmacies.
- Purchase package wine and liquor between 6:00 a.m. and 9:00 p.m.
- Enjoy happy hour specials.
- Fill a growler at a brewery, brewpub, or licensed retail outlet such as a grocery store or liquor store.
- Take an unfinished bottle of wine from dinner home.
- Drink all night in bars on New Year's Eve.

WHAT YOU CAN'T DO

- Bring your own bottle of wine to a restaurant.
- Order a drink between 2:00 a.m. and 6:00 a.m. Monday through Friday, or between 2:30 a.m. and 6:00 a.m. on Saturday and Sunday.
- Purchase package beer between midnight and 6:00 a.m. seven days a week.
- Purchase package wine and spirits between 9:00 p.m. and 6:00 a.m. seven days a week.

Source: Wisconsin Department of Revenue

You can visit the Miller Beer Caves, a system of caverns carved into a bluff at the company's historic PLANK ROAD BREWERY. The caves were used to keep beer cold in the days before mechanical refrigeration. Blocks of ice were carved from Lake Pewaukee in the winter and brought by horse and wagon to the caves where they were covered in sawdust and hay to keep the beer chilled throughout the summer months. Miller wasn't the only brewer lagering their beer underground. Although they couldn't dig into the side of a bluff, Schlitz, Pabst, and Blatz relied on underground cellars to keep their beer cold, too.

HAPPY NEW BEER'S EVE!

The repeal of Prohibition took several acts of Congress, the first of which allowed 3.2 beer to be exempt from the Volstead Act. The night of April 6, 1933, is known as **"NEW BEER'S EVE"** because on April 7 breweries in Milwaukee and elsewhere could begin selling 3.2 beer again. Crowds estimated in excess of 50,000 people amassed at Milwaukee's breweries the night before and brought home beer by the barrelful when the breweries opened for business. The party wasn't contained to Milwaukee, though. Americans put away 1.5 million barrels of beer in the first twenty-four hours that beer was back.

BRIAN ELLISON
FOUNDER AND PRESIDENT, DEATH'S DOOR SPIRITS IN MADISON

TIP: "In Madison and Wisconsin in general, Friday nights are about fish fry and Old Fashioned cocktails. Traditional to Wisconsin is the Brandy Old Fashioned. If you don't specify your spirit, you will likely get a brandy cocktail. The next thing to decide is how you want it finished. "Sour" means topped with Squirt citrus soda; "Sweet" means topped with Sprite or 7-Up; and "Pres" is short for "Presbyterian" which means topped with club soda."

ILLINOIS

State Sovereignty, National Union

Alphonse Gabriel Capone was just twenty and already a hardened criminal when he and his gang of thugs set upon the city of Chicago. It was 1919, and the Eighteenth Amendment had just been ratified, making the manufacture, transportation, and sale of alcohol illegal. In just a few years—and through murder, brute force, bribery, and a little luck—Capone ended up as the crime capo of Chi-town. By 1925, Capone not only controlled alcohol in Chicago, his bootlegging empire extended to the entire Eastern Seaboard, with connections in Canada and the Bahamas as well. At his peak, Scarface was the most famous bootlegger alive. He was thoroughly covered in the press and was reported to have earned $60 million a year (in 1920s money) off of just the alcohol part of his crime syndicate. Public Enemy #1 was eventually captured and began serving a sentence for income tax evasion in 1932. Prohibition ended just a year later, in 1933.

Several Prohibition-era bars are still serving in the Windy City, including a favorite haunt of Scarface, the Green Mill Tavern. The uptown lounge still has a trapdoor behind the bar for both easy escapes and incoming illicit liquor. The region's unofficial spirit, Jeppson's Malört, was a fixture in Capone's time and is still served at the Green Mill as well as at hundreds of other area establishments. Jeppson's Malört, a Swedish wormwood liquor with a flavor the comedian John Hodgman described as tasting "like pencil shavings and heartbreak," is by its own admission a spirit that only one in forty-nine men will tolerate. Knock back a Malört and chase it with an Old Style pounder for a true local experience. Thankfully, a shot and a beer counts as one drink here (it is illegal in Illinois to serve more than one drink per person at a time).

For a time, liquor (whiskey in particular) was a big industry in the Prairie State. Pre-Prohibition, the city of Peoria's whopping seventy-three distilleries (which produced about 18 million gallons of liquor a year) paid more in liquor excise taxes to the government than any other city in the country, and Peoria was known as the whiskey capitol of the world. Legislation has paved the way for a new craft distilling boom in the state. There are now about twenty-five distillers operating, a number that's projected to DOUBLE. Award-winning and well-respected spirits are everywhere. Look for Few Spirits from Evanston and North Shore Distillery out of Lake Bluff.

But beer has always been an Illinois mainstay. In the 1850s, when faced with the possibility of Sunday pub closures and outrageous bar license fees, Chicagoans took to the streets in what was to become known as the Chicago Lager Beer Riots. Later that year, a statewide Prohibitionist referendum was soundly defeated. Now, more than 100 breweries operate in the state, and craft beer bars abound. Chicago is also the birthplace of the definitive barfly, George Wendt, who occupied the barstool in Cheers as Norm. "Pour you a beer, Mr. Peterson?" "All right, but stop me at one. . . make that one-thirty."

In 1855, temperance advocates interested in moral reform instituted laws in Chicago that were clearly anti-immigrant. The ensuing **CHICAGO LAGER BEER RIOTS** and their aftermath in 1856 yielded a heavy German and Irish turnout at the polls, which defeated the extremist incumbents.

AL CAPONE,
aka Scarface,
Public Enemy #1 during
the Prohibition era.

WHAT'LL IT BE?

All varieties of alcohol are readily available in Illinois every day of the year. Package beer, wine, and liquor can be purchased at grocery stores, convenience stores, pharmacies, and gas stations. Due to the low cost of retailer liquor licenses, full bars are common, so all drinks are readily available in bars and restaurants. The state does not set alcohol sale hours.

Hours for alcohol sales are set by municipalities, so expect significant variation from town to town. In Chicago, for example, on- and off-premise sales are permitted between 7:00 a.m. and 2:00 a.m. Monday through Friday night, and until 3:00 a.m. on Saturday night. A complete list of sale hours is available from the Illinois Liquor Commission's website. Municipalities also have a voice in the liquor licensing process. Some choose not to allow package sales.

QUICK REFERENCE

WHAT YOU CAN DO

- Purchase package beer, wine, and liquor at a grocery store, convenience store, or pharmacy during the hours permitted by the municipality.
- Order a drink at a bar or restaurant during the hours set by the municipality.
- Bring your own bottle of wine to a restaurant, unless it's prohibited by the municipality.
- Take an unfinished bottle of wine from dinner home.
- Fill a growler at a brewery or brewpub.

WHAT YOU CAN'T DO

- Order more than one drink at a time; however, "boilermakers" (a shot and a beer) count as one drink. Pitchers, carafes, and buckets are also exempt.
- Fill a growler at a grocery store.
- Play drinking games in a bar or win alcohol as a prize for a non-drinking game.
- Smoke in bars and restaurants. Illinois has a smoking ban for all workplaces.

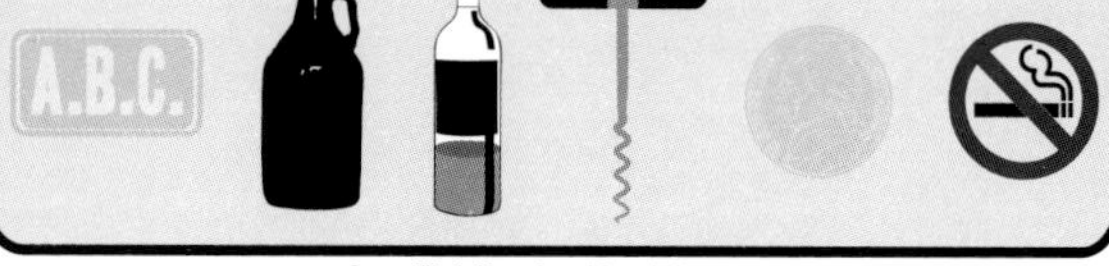

Source: Illinois Liquor Control Commission

Two beers with a long history in Chicago are **OLD STYLE** and **SCHLITZ**. Schlitz, brewed in nearby Milwaukee, reached the height of its popularity prior to Prohibition when the company built many bars that only served their product. It's said that prior to Prohibition, Schlitz owned more property in Chicago than anyone except the Catholic Church. Indeed, the Schlitz logo can still be found inlaid into the brickwork of many Chicago buildings that were bars at the time. Old Style was brewed by Wisconsin's H. Heileman Brewing Company from 1858–1996. Today both Old Style and Schlitz are brewed under contract by Pabst Brewing Company.

The Prairie State is the home of **ARCHER DANIELS MIDLAND** (ADM), the "Supermarket to the world." They could also be known as the distiller to the world because the company is one of the major producers of grain neutral spirits (GNS) for the industry. Many vodkas, gins, and whiskeys—mass-produced brands as well as boutique varieties—start as GNSs. The industry trade mag *Ethanol Producer* reported that the ADM plant in Peoria, IL, produces a high-proof grain neutral spirit that is used as a stock to make beverage alcohols like vodka. The stock is then sometimes filtered and flavored, and sometimes re-distilled. Factory-produced GNSs aren't necessarily a bad thing; indeed, they are as colorless, odorless, and tasteless as can be produced. The next time you are raising your glass of "locally-produced," "artisanal," or "craft" premium vodka, though, consider toasting Illinois' ADM as well. They may very well have brought your beverage to the table.

MIKE RYAN
BARTENDER AT SABLE KITCHEN AND BAR IN CHICAGO

TIP: "Coming to Chicago? Great! Buckle your drinking shoes since there are two licenses in the city: 2:00 a.m. and 4:00 a.m., which means you can really hit it hard. On Saturdays everyone gets an extra hour on their license, and there are also "members only" clubs, like the VFW, that allow you to purchase a one-night membership at the door—and they never close."

MISSOURI

Salus Populi Suprema Lex Esto
(Let the Welfare of the People Be the Supreme Law)

Missourians enjoy a host of imbibing liberties—and if you're just visiting the state, there's an abundance of reasons to consider a move here. Beer, wine, and liquor can be purchased at almost any retail point, including gas stations. Closing time is 3:00 a.m. in the state's larger cities (including St. Louis and Kansas City), and there are no laws against intoxication. The party is on in the Show Me State!

Alcohol isn't just easier to get in Missouri, it's cheaper, too. Missouri has some of the country's lowest excise taxes on alcohol (and cigarettes and gas, too). This price break, combined with the availability of alcohol, means that there's a lot of border crossing going on from neighboring states.

Thanks to the recipe for a lager beer from the Bohemian town of Budweis, the Anheuser-Busch brewery made St. Louis synonymous with beer in America. By the time Prohibition came around, Budweiser was distributed nationwide. Anheuser-Busch weathered the storm of Prohibition—when hundreds of other smaller breweries couldn't—by producing many non-alcohol-related products, including ice cream, soft drinks, truck bodies, and yeast. By 1938, Anheuser-Busch was back on top, hitting the two million barrels sold mark. Budweiser, the King of Beers, is the unofficial beer of the state. Budweiser and Bud Light combined are the biggest selling beers on the planet. It's no secret that the Anheuser-Busch brewery in St. Louis produces more beer than any other in the country. Visitors to Busch Stadium in St. Louis will definitely find their favorite schwag on tap, as well as an impressive selection of craft brews not produced by the beer behemoth.

Kansas City was known for flat-out ignoring Prohibition. Jazz, gambling, drinking, and prostitution flourished there under the watchful eye of the politician "Boss Tom" Pendergast. Axe-wielding temperance advocate Carrie Nation once came to the "Paris of the Plains," leaving smashed liquor bottles in her wake. She was immediately arrested, hauled into court, and fined $500 ($13,400 in 2011 dollars). The judge's harsh ruling effectively barred Nation's return. Nowadays, Kansas City is still liberal with liquor. It's home to the nine-block Power and Light District, adjacent to the Sprint Center downtown, where one may stroll with the adult beverage of their choice.

The state's reputation as a source of great drinking isn't just limited to beer, however. The American white oak used for aging Glenmorangie Scotch whisky is culled from the thinning of Mark Twain National Forest. The forest was named after the pseudonym of Hannibal native Samuel Clemens, who used his hometown as the setting for the Tom Sawyer and Huck Finn books. Twain once wisely advised, "Too much of anything is bad, but too much good whiskey is barely enough."

Missouri had a substantial wine-making industry prior to Prohibition. German immigrants established wineries such as **STONE HILL**, which by the turn of the century was the second-largest winery in America and produced over 1.25 million gallons of wine a year. During Prohibition, though, Missouri's wine industry literally died on the vines. Unlike the breweries of St. Louis, which were able to diversify and make everything from trucks to yeasts to ice cream in order to weather the dry years, the best Stone Hill could do was use their spectacular arched underground cellars (the largest series of vaulted cellars in the nation) to grow mushrooms. Today, Stone Hill Winery produces about a million gallons of wine less than they did a century ago.

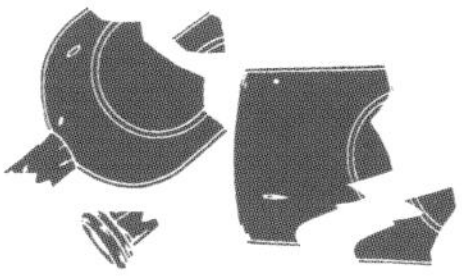

CARRIE NATION was barred from Missouri after smashing bottles over Missouri's defiance over Prohibition.

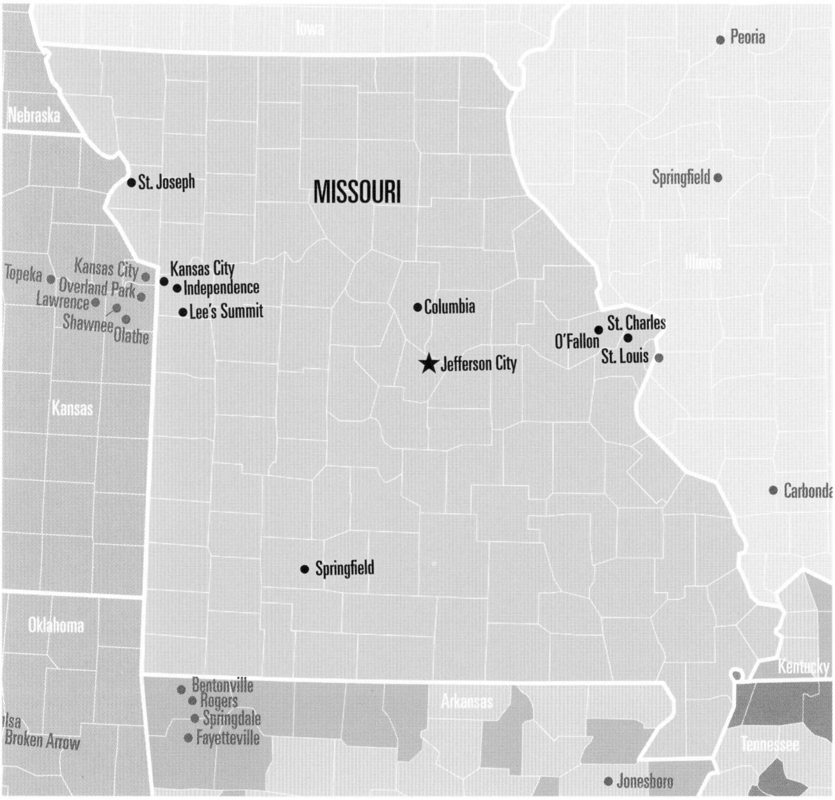

MISSOURI

WHAT'LL IT BE?

Missouri has some of the most permissive alcohol laws in the country. All forms of "intoxicating spirits" are treated equally, regardless of potency. Licenses to sell intoxicating spirits can be obtained by a variety of businesses, which makes beer, wine, and liquor widely available at grocery stores, convenience stores, and pharmacies. Purchase for on- and off-premise consumption is permitted between 6:00 a.m. and 1:30 a.m. Monday through Saturday, and between 9:00 a.m. and midnight on Sundays if the establishment has a Sunday permit. No special permit is required to sell alcohol for on-premise consumption on the following holidays, even if they fall on a Sunday: New Year's Eve, New Year's Day, St. Patrick's Day, Independence Day, and Super Bowl Sunday. No Sunday permit is needed for the Sundays prior to Memorial Day and Labor Day either.

Missouri allows for local option, and municipalities may limit the hours of sale. There are no dry or damp communities, because passing a local option prohibiting the sale of alcohol is forbidden.

QUICK REFERENCE

WHAT YOU CAN DO

- Buy beer, wine, and liquor every day of the year.
- Buy package beer, wine, and liquor at grocery stores, convenience stores, and gas stations between 6:00 a.m. and 1:30 a.m. Monday through Saturday and between 9:00 a.m. and midnight on Sunday.
- Order a drink in bars and restaurants between 6:00 a.m. and 1:30 a.m. Monday through Saturday, and between 9:00 a.m. and midnight on Sunday in places with a Sunday permit.
- Drink in the streets of Kansas City's Power and Light District.
- Use a table tap dispenser to pour your own beer, if available.
- Bring your own bottle of wine to a restaurant.
- Take an unfinished bottle of wine from dinner home.
- Fill a growler at a brewery, brewpub, or grocery store.
- Enjoy happy hour and drink specials.

WHAT YOU CAN'T DO

- Buy intoxicating spirits after 1:30 a.m. Monday through Saturday.
- Buy intoxicating spirits after midnight on Sundays.
- Pour alcohol directly into someone's mouth.
- Be charged with public intoxication. State law prohibits municipalities from punishing public drunkenness.

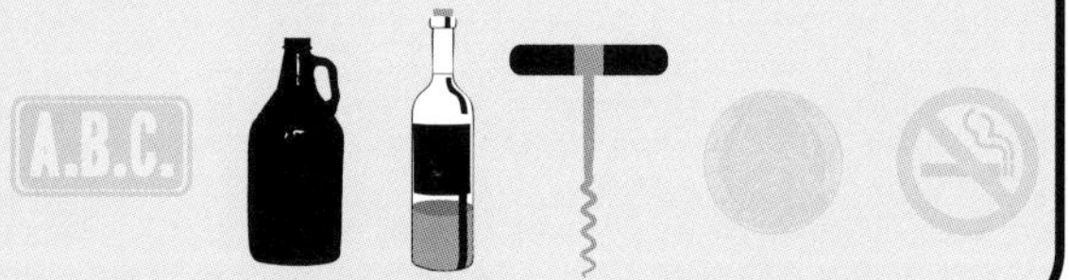

Source: Missouri Department of Public Safety, Alcohol and Tobacco Control

BUDWEISER was the first American beer to use pasteurization, and was thus one of the first that could be shipped long distances without spoiling. By the 1880s, the company was a pioneer in artificial refrigeration and introduced both refrigerated railcars and rail-side icehouses, allowing them to become America's first nationally distributed beer.

BUDWEISER CLYDESDALES

debuted on April 7, 1933, when FDR eased the ban on 3.2 beer. The six-horse team was driven down the streets of New York City in spectacular fashion to deliver a case of Budweiser to Mayor Al Smith, a longtime ally in the fight against Prohibition. The horses continued to tour New England and the Mid-Atlantic states, and they even delivered a case of beer to FDR himself at the White House.

RYAN MAYBEE
BARTENDER AT THE RIEGER HOTEL GRILL & EXCHANGE IN KANSAS CITY

TIP: "If you're visiting KC, ask the locals where to drink. Our hospitality is second to none, and we're always proud to showcase the talent in Kansas City. We're a whiskey town, so make sure you have a Pendergast and a Horsefeather using J. Rieger & Co. Kansas City Whiskey."

IOWA

Our Liberties We Prize and Our Rights We Will Maintain

From State Fair to *The Bridges of Madison County*, anyone who's been to the movies knows Iowa. It's a rolling-plained, blue-skied field of dreams. Iowa got its name from the Ayuxwa Indians who inhabited the area, whose name means "the one who puts to sleep." But leisure life in Iowa can be more than just watching the corn grow.

Just twenty miles southwest of Cedar Rapids, you'll find The Amana Colonies—seven villages of German immigrants' descendants dishing up traditional crafts, food, and drink. However, many know the colonies best from their namesake refrigerator company, which was founded in 1934. Thirty years later an epic Oktoberfest was started, which is fitting since Oktoberfests traditionally serve lager, a beer that undergoes cold fermentation. As per tradition, beer from the first barrel tapped by the Burgermeister is free until the keg runs dry. Year-round beer drinking can be had at Iowa's oldest craft brewery, Amana's own Millstream Brewery.

Commercial brewing came to Iowa about ten years after it became a territory. In Iowa City, enormous beer caverns and tunnels from some of those original breweries were recently unearthed. In the years before refrigeration, consistently cool caves were used for the cold-storage aging (or lagering) of beer. From Prohibition until 2010, the legal ABV for beer in the state was a measly, mass-market 6%. The Beer Equality Law raised the limit to 15%, which has led to much growth in the state's craft beer industry. Iowa now has dozens of craft breweries, as well as two annual state brew fests.

You'll find thirty Iowa-made microbrews on tap in the Craft Beer Tent at the iconic Iowa State Fair. Held in Des Moines in mid-August and drawing more than a million visitors, the Iowa State Fair is Americana at its finest. The fair also features a homebrew competition, a 600-pound cow made out of butter, and more than fifty food items available on a stick.

Iowans don't let their liquor laws get in the way of their leisure time. The delivery of beer, wine, and spirits is legal to homes, businesses, or even any random location, like a park. Pro tip: to quickly chill warm beer, dump the cans or bottles into a bucket and top with ice. Fill with water and add two cups of ordinary table salt. Your beer will be cold in five minutes. Simple.

There are thirty Iowa-made microbrews at the annual **IOWA STATE FAIR.**

TEMPLETON RYE, which earned the nickname of "The Good Stuff" during Prohibition, was cooked up by farmers in the tiny town of Templeton, Iowa (pop. 350). Their business was an open secret and their bootlegging operations have become legendary. The entire town was in on it, right down to the still in the basement of the Catholic Church. The brand was re-established in 2001.

IOWA

WHAT'LL IT BE?

Although Iowa is a control state, there are no state-run retail outlets. Package beer, wine, and liquor are widely available from a variety of licensed businesses, which can include grocery stores, convenience stores, pharmacies, and gas stations. Package sales are permitted between 6:00 a.m. and 2:00 a.m. Monday through Saturday, and between 8:00 a.m. and 2:00 a.m. on Sundays. On-premise sales are allowed between 6:00 a.m. and 2:00 a.m. Monday through Saturday, and between 9:00 a.m. and 2:00 a.m. on Sundays. Although alcohol sales are permitted every day of the year, Sunday sales are only allowed in establishments with a Sunday permit, so not every business sells alcohol on Sundays.

There are no dry counties or towns because state law requires counties to issue liquor licenses. Local ordinances can be more restrictive than state laws on issues like operating hours, but they cannot be more permissive. Sunday permits are issued by local licensing authorities.

QUICK REFERENCE

WHAT YOU CAN DO

- Buy beer, wine, and liquor every day of the year.
- Buy package beer, wine, and liquor in grocery stores, convenience stores, and gas stations between 6:00 a.m. and 2:00 a.m. Monday through Saturday, and between 8:00 a.m. and 2:00 a.m. on Sundays from businesses with a Sunday permit.
- Order a drink in bars and restaurants between 6:00 a.m. and 2:00 a.m. Monday through Saturday, and between 9:00 a.m. and 2:00 a.m. on Sundays from businesses with a Sunday permit.
- Bring your own bottle of wine to a restaurant.
- Take an unfinished bottle of wine from dinner home.
- Fill a growler at a brewery or brewpub.
- Enjoy happy hour and drink specials.
- Get your nickel back from bottle and can deposits.

WHAT YOU CAN'T DO

- Fill a growler at a licensed liquor retailer.
- Buy alcohol after 2:00 a.m.
- Smoke in bars and restaurants. Iowa has a statewide smoking ban.

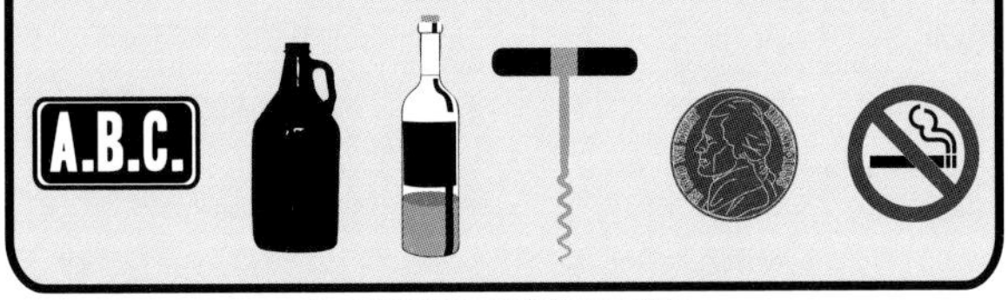

Source: State of Iowa Alcoholic Beverages Division

Iowa Prohibitionist JOHN BROWN HAMMOND drafted 95% of Iowa's laws relating to liquor and moral conduct. Hammond was a cousin of the abolitionist John Brown, who advocated violence against the sin of slavery and was hanged for his failed raid on the federal arsenal in Harper's Ferry. John Brown Hammond took a similar righteous attitude against the evils of drink. He once demolished the interior of a speakeasy in Bunker Hill, Iowa, with a chair.

The first beverage cooler was produced in Iowa's Amana Colonies in 1934. The Colonies were a utopian religious commune in the Nineteenth Century who reluctantly gave up their idealism only to double-down on commerce. AMANA REFRIGERATION soon became a leading producer of refrigerators, freezers, and air conditioners.

The temperance movement was strong in nineteenth-century Iowa. The state began passing prohibition laws as early as 1847, only a year after statehood. THE WOMEN'S CHRISTIAN TEMPERANCE UNION also had a strong presence in the state and grew to include 60,000 Iowa women among their ranks well through the 1930s.

BJORN CARLSON
BARTENDER AT MALO IN DES MOINES

TIP: "After Prohibition, any Iowa-brewed beer over 6.2% ABV was classified as liquor. This subjected it to the same regulations as whiskey and effectively halted all local production. While the national craft beer scene evolved and more high-alcohol beers were being imported from other states, our beer industry wasn't allowed to compete. Finally in 2010, Iowa allowed brewers to produce beer up to 12.5% ABV which has rapidly expanded Iowa's craft beer scene."

MINNESOTA

L'Etoile du Nord
(The Star of the North)

With one boat for every six residents, Minnesota earns its moniker of The Land of 10,000 Lakes. Minnesota issues more fishing licenses per capita than any other state in the union. And as the saying goes, friends don't let friends fish sober. It doesn't matter if you're on the lake, on the ice, or on land—drinking and fishing often go hand in hand. Open containers are allowed in boats, on the banks, and on the ice. You can even ice fish from your barstool at the Ice Hole Bar on Lida Lake in northwestern Minnesota, a temporary tavern set up literally on the lake!

Minnesota's moniker comes from the Minnesota River, which in Sioux means "water that reflects the sky." The confluence of the Minnesota and Mississippi Rivers was a stop for beaver trappers and traders in the 1800s, and was initially settled by the trapper Pierre "Pig's Eye" Parrant, nicknamed thusly for his least attractive feature: an unserviceable eyeball. Parrant became better known for his whiskey, which he distilled and served out of a ramshackle saloon in Fountain Cave, which was served by a natural spring. This area evolved into a settler's hub known simply as Pig's Eye. It was eventually renamed St. Paul after the arrival and blessing of a Catholic priest (and the ouster of poor Parrant). Pig's Eye, however, lives on thanks to the St. Paul brewery of the same name.

The Twin Cities of Minneapolis and St. Paul are the birthplace of Charles M. Schultz, F. Scott Fitzgerald, Judy Garland, and more than ten miles of elevated, climate-controlled walkways. These human-sized hamster trails are a savior in the winter months, when sub-zero temps are the norm. They connect everything from transit and parking to office buildings and malls, and, yes, even many bars! Minnesota's #1 tourist attraction is also indoors: the Mall of America. It boasts fifty restaurants, seven nightclubs, an amusement park, an aquarium, and a wedding chapel, which has married more than 5,000 couples since it opened.

If you're not afraid of a little frostbite, head outdoors for the "Coolest Celebration on Earth," St. Paul's Winter Carnival, held every January since 1886. The fest features great outdoor activities like curling, ice carving, a hockey tournament, and, of course, a 200-tap beer festival. So suit up, stay warm, and remember that Minnesota is one of the only states that doesn't consider public drunkenness a crime.

Test out your ice carving skills at the **ST. PAUL'S WINTER CARNIVAL.**

Fishing from the **ICE HOLE BAR** on Lida Lake

MINNESOTA

WHAT'LL IT BE?

Like the neighboring Great Plains states, Minnesota makes a distinction between beer under 3.2% ABW (about 4% ABV) and beverages with higher alcohol content. Liquor, wine, and beer over 3.2% are available only at licensed liquor stores, but 3.2% beer is widely available at grocery stores, convenience stores, and pharmacies. Although the state allows package sales between 8:00 a.m. and 2:00 a.m., a special permit is required to sell during the last hour. Sunday package sales of liquor, wine, and beer over 3.2% are not permitted, but low-point beer is still available. No package sales are allowed on Thanksgiving, Christmas, or after 8:00 p.m. on Christmas Eve. On-premise sales are allowed between 8:00 a.m. and 2:00 a.m. Monday through Saturday. Sunday sales for on-premise consumption are determined by local option.

Minnesota does allow for a local option. Municipalities can limit the hours when alcohol is available for purchase and choose to allow on-premise Sunday sales. Some towns may also run municipal liquor stores for package sales and decline to grant licenses to other retailers.

QUICK REFERENCE

WHAT YOU CAN DO

- Purchase package 3.2% beer in a grocery store, convenience store, or pharmacy between 8:00 a.m. 2:00 a.m. Monday through Saturday, and between 10:00 a.m. and 2:00 a.m. on Sunday where permitted.
- Purchase package liquor, wine, and beer over 3.2% from a licensed liquor store between 8:00 a.m. and 2:00 a.m. Monday through Saturday.
- Order a drink at a bar or restaurant between 8:00 a.m. and 2:00 a.m. Monday through Saturday, and on Sunday between 10:00 a.m. and 2:00 a.m. where permitted.
- Enjoy happy hour specials.
- Fill a growler at a brewery or brewpub.
- Smoke on outdoor patios.
- Be drunk in public. Drunkenness is not a crime.

WHAT YOU CAN'T DO

- Fill a growler at a grocery store or other retail outlet.
- Smoke in enclosed restaurants. Minnesota has a smoking ban for all enclosed public spaces.
- Be charged with public intoxication.
- Purchase package liquor, wine, and beer over 3.2% on Christmas, after 8:00 p.m. on Christmas Eve, or on Sunday.
- Purchase package liquor, wine, and beer over 3.2% between 2:00 a.m. and 8:00 a.m. Monday through Saturday.
- Purchase package low-point beer between 2:00 a.m. and 8:00 a.m. Monday through Saturday, or on Sundays where prohibited.
- Order a drink at a bar or restaurant between 2:00 a.m. and 8:00 a.m., or on Sunday where prohibited.

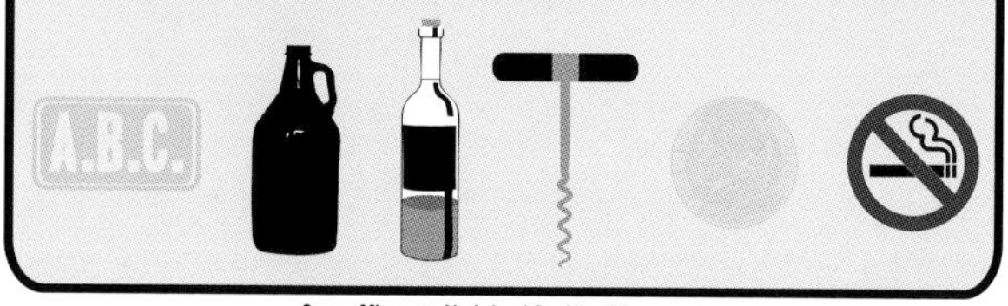

Source: Minnesota Alcohol and Gambling Enforcement

HAMM'S BREWING was founded in in 1865 in St. Paul Minnesota. It is best remembered for its cartoon bear mascot and catchy jingle celebrating its Minnesota heritage: "From the Land of Sky-Blue Waters." Hamm's is now owned by MillerCoors.

TARGET FIELD, home to the Minnesota Twins, is the first sports stadium to offer Americans self-serve beer. The stadium features machines that allow fans with ID to load up a card with beer money and then pay by the ounce at the tap. Bud and Bud Light run 38 cents an ounce while Shock Top and Goose Island 312 cost 40 cents an ounce. The self-serve taps made their debut at the 2014 All-Star Game.

"MINNESOTA 13" was a smooth, high-quality moonshine produced in huge quantities by the farmers of Stearns County during Prohibition and made with a unique strain of corn tailored for the region. The reputation of Minnesota 13 extended nationwide thanks to Al Capone's distribution networks; it was the only "branded" moonshine produced in the nation during the dry years. Historian Elaine Davis estimated that in some areas of Stearns County, 100% of the community had a hand in the bootlegging trade.

MATT LILLEGARD
BARTENDER, FIRE LAKE RESTAURANT IN MINNEAPOLIS

TIP: "If you're picking up groceries and looking for a bottle of wine, you'll search the entire store and not find anything. Don't worry though! Just purchase your groceries and enter back in through the separate liquor store entrance. Minneapolis is definitely a beer town and the neighborhoods around downtown host a wealth of microbreweries, most with tap rooms for tasting, and hopefully a food truck parked outside for some good eats."

NORTH DAKOTA

Liberty & Union Now & Forever, One & Inseparable

Often referred to as the least visited state in the union, North Dakota is probably not on your immediate list of travel plans. But if some twist of fate has you driving through this often frozen and barren landscape, then you will most certainly be in need of a drink.

North Dakota is one of the least populated states in the country, and has more bars per capita than any other (more than four times more bars per capita than the national average). And in those bars, they are drinking beer—nearly thirty gallons of beer for every adult in the state. In 2013, Fargo topped the list as the drunkest city in America, according to data compiled by the Center for Disease Control. Yah? You betcha! Look for local labels like Fargo Brewing's Woodchipper IPA and Northern Light Lager. Drinking on the cheap? Look for "Mug Night" special listings (buy the mug and get lesser-priced refills all night long). Uff-da indeed!

Teetotalers who've spent time in the state include Teddy Roosevelt, who was a rancher in the Badlands of North Dakota. He said, "I never would have been president if it had not been for my experiences in North Dakota." The Rough Rider was not a beer drinker, and in fact sued a man for calling him one. He won and was awarded 6 cents, about the price for a beer back then.

Though the "Beer Barrel Polka" was one of the most requested songs on *The Lawrence Welk Show*, the bandleader and native son was more commonly known as the King of Champagne Music. He opened his show with a theme song called "Bubbles in the Wine," and closed with a fond "Adios, Au Revoir, Auf Wiedersehen." Ah-one and ah-two (and remember, the bars close at 2:00)—good night!

Grand Forks may possibly be ground zero for the "organized trivia" played in bars every night across the country. Curt Eriksmoen debuted **"THINK AND DRINK"** at the Westward Ho Peanut Bar in 1973 and copyrighted the game the following year. Successful franchises soon spread to Bismarck and Fargo.

Experts in **NORTH DAKOTA STATE UNIVERSITY'S** barley and malt science program are working with craft brewers who want to alter their flavor profiles. North Dakota has traditionally been a major producer of American barley, and while larger breweries stick to traditional malt flavors, craft brewers are more experimental. NDSU recently set up a "heritage barley" nursery to showcase older varieties of the crop for the benefit of craft brewers.

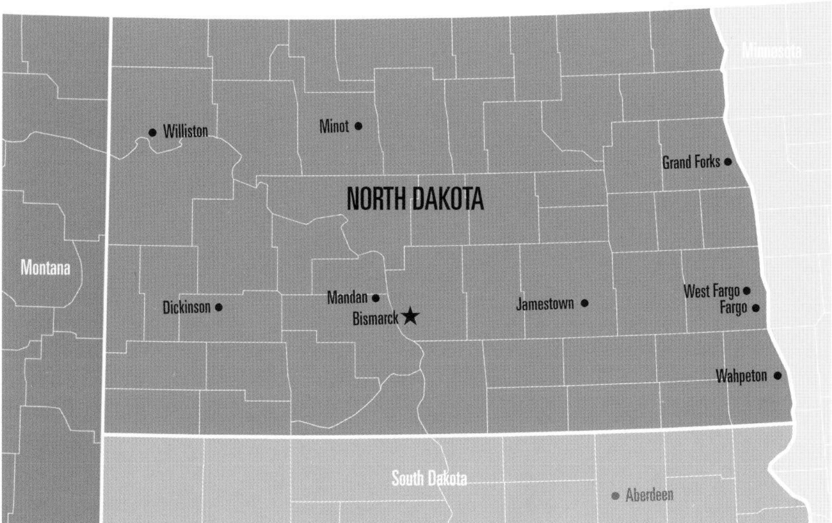

NORTH DAKOTA

WHAT'LL IT BE?

North Dakota's liquor laws are straightforward. Package alcohol is available at licensed retailers, which can include grocery stores, convenience stores, and gas stations, between 8:00 a.m. and 2:00 a.m. Monday through Saturday, and from noon until 2:00 a.m. on Sundays. There are no package sales on Thanksgiving, Christmas, or Christmas Eve after 6:00 p.m. Alcohol displays may not be immediately visible, as stores are required to have a wall separating them from the rest of the merchandise. On-premise hours and restrictions are the same as for off-premise, but drink purchases are allowed on Thanksgiving.

North Dakota does allow for local variation, primarily in regulating Sunday sales. Counties that permit Sunday alcohol sales may also choose to allow dancing at the same establishment, which requires a separate permit.

QUICK REFERENCE

WHAT YOU CAN DO

- Purchase alcohol for on- and off- premise consumption between 8:00 a.m. and 2:00 a.m. Monday through Saturday, and between noon and 2:00 a.m. on Sunday.
- Enjoy happy hour specials.
- Bring your own bottle of wine to a restaurant.
- Fill a growler at a brewery or brewpub.

WHAT YOU CAN'T DO

- Barter for beer.
- Purchase alcohol on Christmas or after 6:00 p.m. on Christmas Eve.
- Purchase package alcohol on Thanksgiving.
- Drink before 8:00 a.m. on your twenty-first birthday.
- Smoke in a bar or restaurant. There is a statewide ban on smoking in enclosed spaces, including e-cigarettes.
- Purchase alcohol for on- or off-premise consumption between 2:00 a.m. and 8:00 a.m. seven days a week, or between 8:00 a.m. and noon on Sunday.

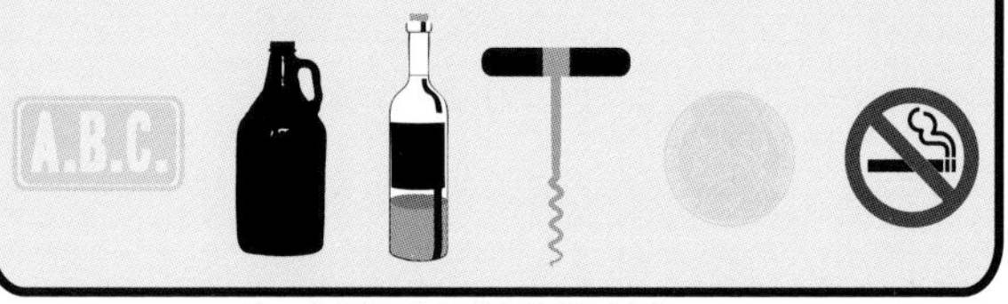

Source: North Dakota Century Code, Title 5, Alcoholic Beverages

In a hat tip to their German ancestry, a favorite song to sing at UNIVERSITY OF NORTH DAKOTA Sioux sporting events is the beer-hall polka "In Heaven There Is No Beer (That's Why We Drink It Here)."

Water freezes at 32 degrees, but lower temperatures are needed to freeze alcohol. A general rule is the higher the alcohol content, the lower the temperature required for it to freeze.

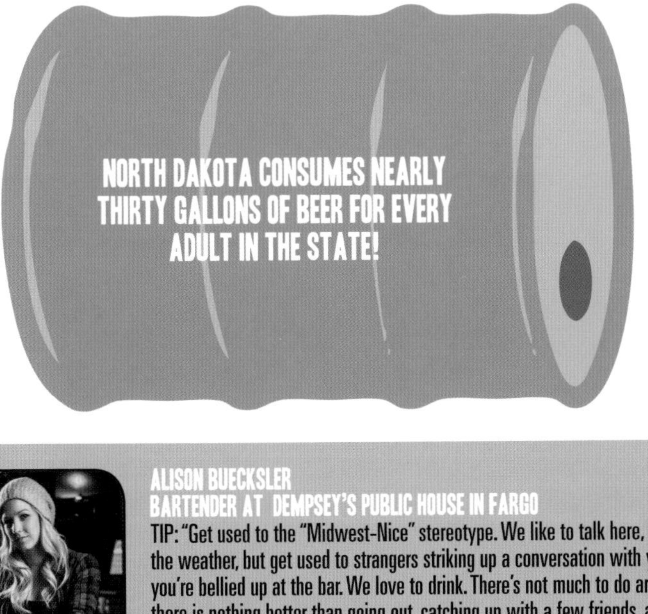

NORTH DAKOTA CONSUMES NEARLY THIRTY GALLONS OF BEER FOR EVERY ADULT IN THE STATE!

ALISON BUECKSLER
BARTENDER AT DEMPSEY'S PUBLIC HOUSE IN FARGO

TIP: "Get used to the "Midwest-Nice" stereotype. We like to talk here, mostly about the weather, but get used to strangers striking up a conversation with you when you're bellied up at the bar. We love to drink. There's not much to do around here, so there is nothing better than going out, catching up with a few friends, and kicking back a few."

SOUTH DAKOTA

Under God the People Rule

It's been called both the Sunshine State and the Blizzard State for its extreme weather, and the Artesian State for its many artesian wells. It's even been known as the Coyote State. But South Dakota's official nickname is the Mount Rushmore State, after its largest tourist attraction. While viewing those big granite noggins, ponder this: if the Mount Rushmore presidents came to life, they would be 465 feet tall, which means that if you were to pour stone-faced Washington a pint, you would have to drain 4,000 kegs.

Another stop on the tourist trail is the old gold boom town of Deadwood. The tradition of spreading sawdust on a barroom floor reportedly began in Deadwood. It was an attempt on the part of saloonkeepers to hide all of the falling gold dust, which would be swept up, sifted, and rendered at the end of the day. Deadwood is also, of course, the Wild West resting place of Calamity Jane and Wild Bill Hickok. Hickok was shot dead while playing poker, holding the "dead man's hand": black aces over eights. On the site where Hickok was shot now stands The Old Style Saloon no. 10, a self-described museum within a bar.

Indian scout, two-gunned sharp shooter, and all-around general drunk Martha Canary is better known as Calamity Jane. Throughout her life, she regaled audiences with her knife-throwing, trick-riding, and bear-taming skills. As an itinerant alcoholic constantly spoiling for a fight, however, she would lay you out as soon as look at ya and could blind a rabbit from thirty paces. Calamity would eventually meet her end in South Dakota. She died in her fifties, leaving only a stipulation in her will that she be laid to rest alongside her unrequited love, Wild Bill Hickok. You can visit their graves high above the outskirts of Deadwood in Mount Moriah Cemetery.

Say the word Sturgis to a biker and you'll be greeted as a friend. In what has been described as "Mardi Gras with chrome," the Sturgis Motorcycle Rally is the biggest in the world. What started with nine Harley Davidson riders in 1938 now draws nearly half a million bikers. Sturgis brings in all kinds of riders, from waxers and hoggers with ape hangers to weekenders sporting shiny new leathers. Rallyers don't go thirsty, what with Jack Daniels as a major sponsor, and a veritable kegger in Sturgis Memorial Park. In the end, an estimated three million gallons of beer are consumed during the festival, and liquor sales are nearly ten times the national average! Stay vertical and keep the sun on your back, your fists in the wind, and let the horizon tease you farther down a great road.

PRESIDENTIAL TRIVIA (RUSHMORE EDITION)

- After leaving office, WASHINGTON opened the largest distillery in America at his home at Mount Vernon. He was said to prefer his wife's rum punch.
- THOMAS JEFFERSON was a homebrewer, however his favorite drink was a Madeira wine.
- ABE LINCOLN owned a tavern in Illinois before he became a lawyer. However, he rarely touched the stuff.
- THEODORE ROOSEVELT was not fond of alcohol at all.

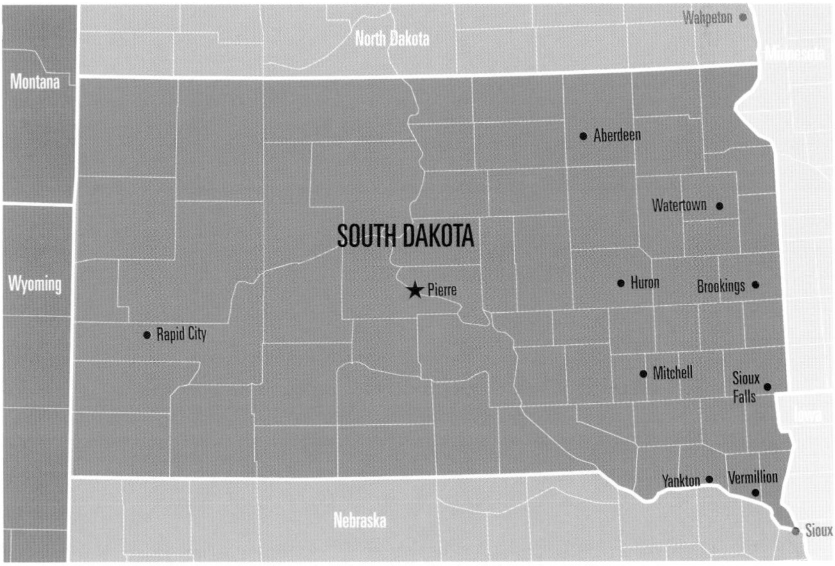

SOUTH DAKOTA

WHAT'LL IT BE?

Beer and wine are widely available for on- and off-premise consumption between 7:00 a.m. and 2:00 a.m. seven days a week. The sale of liquor is more strictly regulated, with a statewide ban on Sundays, Memorial Day, and Christmas Day. Wine and liquor are not available in convenience stores, which are only permitted to sell beer. There are no exceptions to the prohibition of on- and off-premise liquor sales on Christmas Day, though you can purchase beer and wine.

Local ordinances may be more or less restrictive with sale hours than those prescribed by the state. A city can pass a local ordinance that gives license holders an exception to the Sunday and Memorial Day liquor sales ban. A city can also determine whether it wants to prohibit the sale of wine or liquor, but not beer. It is illegal to consume or even possess alcohol on the Pine Ridge Indian Reservation in the southwest corner of the state.

QUICK REFERENCE

WHAT YOU CAN DO

- Buy package beer and wine between 7:00 a.m. and 2:00 a.m. seven days a week.
- Buy package liquor from between 7:00 a.m. and 2:00 a.m. Monday through Saturday, and on Sundays from businesses with a Sunday sales permit.
- Buy package beer in convenience stores.
- Order a beer, wine, or liquor in a bar or restaurant between 7:00 a.m. and 2:00 a.m. seven days a week. Liquor purchase is allowed on Sunday only if the establishment has a special Sunday license.
- Enjoy happy hour and drink specials.
- Bring your own bottle of wine to a restaurant.
- Take an unfinished bottle of wine from dinner home.
- Fill a growler at a brewery, brewpub, or licensed retailer.

WHAT YOU CAN'T DO

- Buy liquor anywhere on Christmas Day.
- Buy package wine or liquor in convenience stores.
- Order a drink in a bar between 2:00 a.m. and 7:00 a.m.
- Order liquor in a bar or restaurant on Sunday if the establishment does not have a Sunday license.
- Smoke in bars and restaurants.
- Possess or consume alcohol on Pine Ridge Indian Reservation.

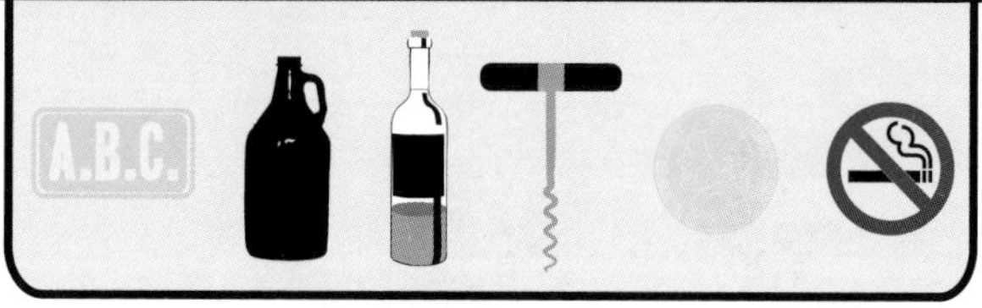

Source: South Dakota Department of Revenue

COWBOY SLANG

BEER: John Barleycorn / Purge / Hop Juice

WHISKEY: Nose Paint / Pop Skull / Prairie Dew / Rebel Soldier / Red Eye / Snake Pizen / Tarantula Juice / Tongue Oil / Tonsil Paint / Tornado Juice / Busthead / Bottled Courage / Family Disturbance / Gut Warmer / Kansas Sheep Dip

GENERAL TREAT: Buying a round of drinks

LAPPER: A hard drinker

MEALER: A partial abstainer who drinks liquor only during meals

PAINTIN' HIS NOSE: Getting drunk

PAIR OF OVERALLS: Two drinks of whiskey

RED LANE: A vulgar name for the throat, chiefly used by those drinking alcohol

RUM HOLE, RUM MILL: A small drinking establishment, saloon

SHOOT THE CROW: Obtain a drink in a saloon and leave without paying

BENZINERY: A low-grade drinking place. Cheap whiskey was sometimes called benzene

CALIBOGUS: Rum and spruce-beer

WHIP BELLY: Bad beer

Courtesy of LegendsofAmerica.com

YOU CAN HOMEBREW 200 GALLONS OF BEER OR WINE FOR PERSONAL OR FAMILY USE.

The capital of South Dakota, Pierre, rhymes with beer.

TONY DEMARO
PROPRIETOR AT MURPHY'S PUB & GRILL IN RAPID CITY

TIP: "If you're planning a road trip to South Dakota to see Mt. Rushmore, appreciate the highways. South Dakota was the last state in the union to raise its minimum drinking age to 21 in 1987, but it took losing a Supreme Court appeal and the threat of losing highway funding to do it."

NEBRASKA

Equality Before the Law

Nebraskans are happy. The state continually lands in the top ten of the country's happiest places. And what's not to be glad about when its largest city, Omaha, ranks number eight in both per capita billionaires and Fortune 500 companies? Why, the state's highway signs even call 'em as they see 'em: next exit, "The Good Life."

Five and a half percent of Nebraskans are of Czech descent, more than in any other state in the country. That Bohemian rhapsody comes together every August in the state (and national) capitol of Czech-dom, Wilber. Czech Days is a three-day celebration that swells the tiny town's population of 2,000 to tens of thousands who sing, dance, and naturally, drink. Order a kolache and a Pilsner Urquell (beer is *pivo* in Czech) and toast *Na zdraví* (to your health)! Czech people almost always consume more beer than any other country annually, around thirty-eight gallons per person. And Nebraskans come close to their Czech cousins by consuming over thirty-five gallons! If you're ordering a beer on tap in the state, just ask for a "draw." Red beer (part tomato juice, part draft beer) is popular here, too—ask for a "red draw."

If you're seeing a sea of red, that can only mean one thing: University of Nebraska Cornhusker football. Not only are the Cornhuskers a part of the Big Ten, but to Nebraska college students, big drinking is a major extracurricular activity. Nebraska ranks number two in the country in terms of binge drinkers, and on a weekly basis, thousands of students at the university hold one of the most raucous tailgates in the country. Husker power!

Drinking or being drunk is not illegal in the state. Drinking is legal in a great number of state parks, and bartenders may tip one back while behind the stick as well. Omaha-born dancer Fred Astaire admitted in his biography to once drinking on the job during the beloved Christmas film *Holiday Inn*. It was for the New Year's Eve dance scene and he took "two stiff hookers" of bourbon before the first take and another before each successive take. The seventh (and last) take is used in the film. President Gerald Ford, also of Omaha, admired the productivity of noonday nip. "The three-martini lunch is the epitome of American efficiency. Where else can you get an earful, a bellyful and a snootful at the same time?"

The company BEERS NOT BOMBS takes copper cable from decommissioned nuclear missile silos in Nebraska and South Dakota and turns them into bottle openers.

"Wherever beer is brewed, all is well-
wherever beer is drunk, life is good."
- CZECH PROVERB

Nebraska is one of the happiest (and richest) states in the country!

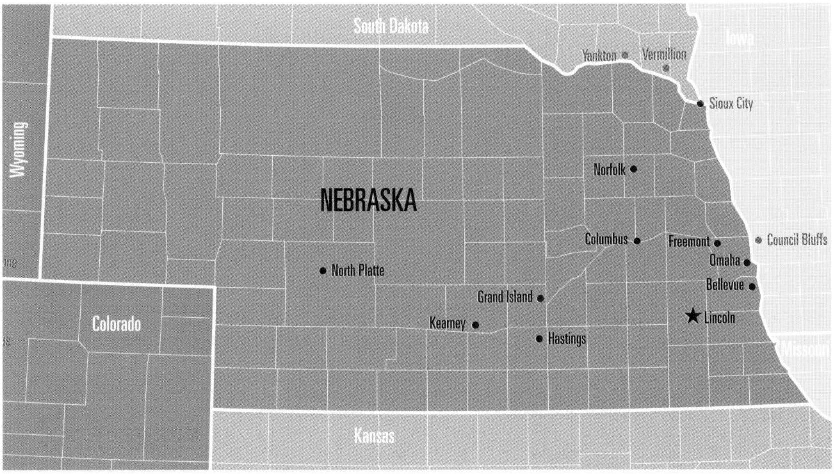

NEBRASKA

WHAT'LL IT BE?

Beer, wine, and liquor are readily available from licensed retailers in Nebraska. Package sales are allowed between 6:00 a.m. and 1:00 a.m. Monday through Saturday, with Sunday sales dependent on a local option. On-premise sales are permitted during the same hours, with the option for restaurant and bar hours to be extended to 2:00 a.m.

Nebraska does allow for local option. While municipalities cannot ban the sale of alcohol outright, they can restrict off-premise hours of sale, as well as extend on-premise hours until 2:00 a.m. There is, however, a statewide ban for on- and off-premise Sunday sales, but localities are allowed to override it. Some allow only on-premise sales, some allow only off-premise sales, and some allow both on Sundays.

QUICK REFERENCE

WHAT YOU CAN DO

- Purchase package alcohol at licensed grocery stores, convenience stores, and pharmacies between 6:00 a.m. and 1:00 a.m. Monday through Saturday, with Sunday sales dependent on local ordinances.
- Order a drink at a bar or restaurant between 6:00 a.m. and 1:00 a.m. Monday through Saturday. Sunday sales and sales until 2:00 a.m. are available where permitted by a local option.
- Enjoy some happy hour specials.
- Fill a growler at a brewery or brewpub.
- Bring your own bottle of wine to a restaurant.
- Take an unfinished bottle of wine from dinner home.

WHAT YOU CAN'T DO

- Smoke in bars and restaurants. Nebraska has a statewide smoking ban for enclosed spaces.
- Buy cider in an establishment with only a beer license. Nebraska considers cider a wine.
- Have an "upside down drink." It's illegal to pour alcohol directly into someone's mouth.
- Fill a growler at a liquor store or grocery store.
- Order a drink between 2:00 a.m. and 6:00 a.m., or on Sunday where prohibited.
- Purchase package alcohol between 1:00 a.m. and 6:00 a.m., or on Sunday where prohibited.

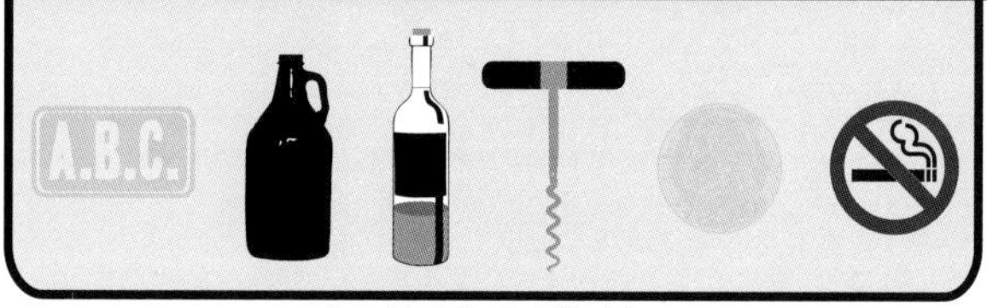

Source: Nebraska Liquor Control Commission

The tiny city of **WHITECLAY** is on the frontline of the political and economic battle over who is to blame for alcoholism. With less than a dozen residents but four package stores, Whiteclay sells between four and five million cans of beer each year, primarily to residents of the Pine Ridge Indian Reservation, where alcohol is banned, across the border in South Dakota. The conflict is ongoing and occasionally violent, with protesters setting up roadblocks for delivery trucks and Nebraska officials saying that retailers have not broken any laws, so there is nothing to be done.

When the Union Pacific Railroad began building the transcontinental railroad, frontier towns like North Platte and Fort Kearney, NE, were among the first to experience "Hell on Wheels." As the railroad progressed west, boomtowns comprised of saloons, brothels, and gambling halls sprang up to cater to the rail-workers. As the tracks moved west, so did the dens of vice, thus earning them the name **"HELL ON WHEELS."** Today, the Union Pacific Railroad has its headquarters in Omaha.

JEFF LUBY
CO-OWNER AT WILSON & WASHBURN IN OMAHA

TIP: "Omaha was built on three things: the railroad, meat packing, and vice. Unfortunately, Prohibition and The Great Depression brought a halt to our "Dirty Wicked Town". Now Nebraska is home to twelve craft breweries and dozens of wineries. The food and cocktail scene has also boomed in the last five years. So, come for the beef, stay for all the great food and drink, and live here for the award winning beer!"

Ad Astra per Aspera
(To the Stars through Difficulty)

KANSAS

From "Home on the Range,"
the state song of Kansas

Oh, give me a home where the buffalo roam
And the deer and the antelope play,
Where seldom is heard a discouraging word,
And the skies are not cloudy all day

If you find yourself in the Sunflower State, the discouraging words you're likely to hear are those that are uttered when you try to buy alcohol. Kansas was the first to enact a statewide ban on alcohol and held onto Prohibition longer than any other state in the union, from 1881–1948. It still hasn't ratified the Twenty-First Amendment. Our country's thirty-fourth president, Kansan Dwight D. Eisenhower, had an allotment of bourbon regularly delivered to his barracks when he was a general. So when it comes to drinking in Kansas, be like Ike and be prepared: "Plans are nothing; planning is everything."

Kansas sits atop what was a huge inland sea, which is why it's so flat. It averages about fifty tornadoes a year, putting it at the center of Tornado Alley (and propelling Dorothy into Oz). The state is a leader in aircraft production, and it's the birthplace of the Cessna, the Lear jet, and Amelia Earhart. Kansas is even home to one of the largest aerospace museums in the country, The Kansas Cosmosphere and Space Center in Hutchinson, second only to the National Air and Space Museum in Washington, D.C. Take flight by ordering a classic Aviation cocktail, whose color is that of the wild blue yonder!

It seems like the Wicked Witch of the West is in charge of partying here. The state has some of the strictest drinking laws in the country, making you wish you weren't in Kansas anymore. There are more than a dozen dry counties, and 3.2% beer is all that is sold in supermarkets to whet your whistle. Anything above that is sold at separate liquor stores, and those liquor stores may only sell alcohol, no mixers or snacks. By-the-drink availability varies so much by town and country that the state looks like a long patchwork quilt of yesses, nos, and maybes. So click your heels and follow the yellow brick road to one of the growing number of breweries in the state. Seek out the Free State Brewery in Lawrence, whose Ad Astra Ale reflects not just the state motto *(Ad Astra per Aspera)* but the beauty of a hard-won drink *(To the Stars Through Difficulty)*.

Kansas has a long history of embracing PROHIBITION. For example, liquor by the drink was outlawed until 1986 and, even today, of Kansas' 105 counties, 67 only allow it with the purchase of food and 13 still prohibit it altogether.

1881: Kansas becomes the first state to enact statewide prohibition.
1917: The passage of the "Bone Dry Act" makes even the possession of alcohol a crime.
1937: Kansas allows the sale of 3.2 beer, classifying it as "Cereal Malt Beverage" and exempt from liquor laws.
1948: Kansas permits the sale of liquor but only from package stores and never on Sunday. Liquor by the drink is still "forever prohibited."
1970: Kansas Attorney General Vern Miller begins enforcing Kansas liquor laws to an unprecedented degree, raiding an Amtrak train to stop illegal sales by the drink and prohibiting airlines from serving alcohol in Kansas airspace.
1986: Kansas finally allows the sale of liquor by the drink.
2005: Sunday liquor sales are allowed.
2011: Kansas lifts restrictions on tastings and allows happy hour specials.

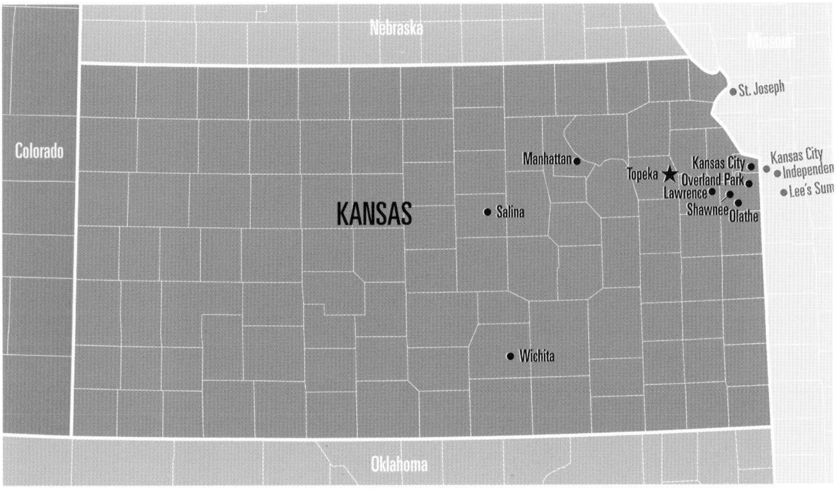

KANSAS

WHAT'LL IT BE?

Kansas liquor laws are more restrictive than those of Nebraska and the Dakotas. Beverages under 3.2% ABW (about 4% ABV) are classified as "cereal malt beverages" (CMB) and are less strictly regulated than stronger drinks. In counties that allow it, drinks are available for on-premise consumption between 9:00 a.m. and 2:00 a.m. seven days a week, every day of the year. Package liquor, wine and beer over 3.2% are available only through licensed liquor stores, which are open from 9:00 a.m. to 11:00 p.m. Monday through Saturday. If the store does not have an "extended" license, it will be closed on Sundays, Memorial Day, Labor Day, and Independence Day. All liquor stores are closed on Easter, Thanksgiving, and Christmas. Low-point beer is available from grocery stores, convenience stores, pharmacies, and gas stations between 6:00 a.m. and 1:00 a.m. Monday through Saturday, and between noon and 8:00 p.m. on Sunday (if the store has an extended license). Package CMB purchases are prohibited on Easter.

Kansas does allow for a local option, which can be either more or less restrictive than state law. Restrictions primarily apply to alcohol service in bars and restaurants. 13 counties prohibit liquor by the drink, while 63 of the 105 counties allow liquor service only if it makes up less than 30% of the establishment's business. Counties also determine whether Sunday sales are allowed.

QUICK REFERENCE

WHAT YOU CAN DO

- Purchase package liquor, wine, and beer over 3.2% from licensed liquor stores between 9:00 a.m. and 11:00 p.m. Monday through Saturday, and between noon and 8:00 p.m. on Sunday if the store has an extended license.
- Purchase low-point beer from grocery stores, convenience stores, pharmacies, and gas stations between 6:00 a.m. and 1:00 a.m. Monday through Saturday, and between noon and 8:00 p.m. on Sunday if the store has an extended license.
- Order a drink at a bar or restaurant between 9:00 a.m. and 2:00 a.m. seven days a week where permitted.
- Enjoy limited happy hour specials.
- Bring your own alcoholic beverage to consume at a restaurant.
- Take an unfinished bottle of wine from dinner home.
- Fill a growler at a brewery or brewpub.

WHAT YOU CAN'T DO

- Fill a growler at a liquor or grocery store.
- Smoke in bars and restaurants. Kansas has a statewide smoking ban for enclosed spaces.
- Purchase package CMB on Easter.
- Handle a loaded handgun while under the influence, unless you are on your own property.
- Purchase alcohol over 3.2% on Easter, Thanksgiving, and Christmas, or on Memorial Day, Labor Day, and Independence Day if the store does not have an extended license.
- Purchase package CMB between 1:00 a.m. and 6:00 a.m. Monday through Saturday, and before noon or after 8:00 p.m. on Sunday.

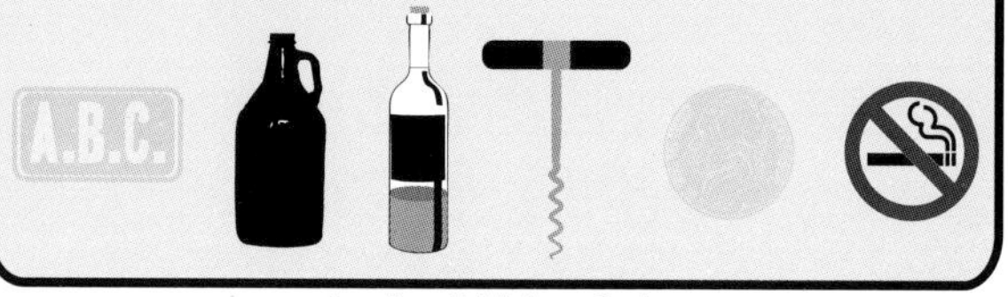

Source: Kansas Alcoholic Beverage Control

Dodge City was called the **"DEADWOOD OF KANSAS"** and had a well-earned reputation for lawlessness in the 1870s. It was both the end of a cattle drive from Texas and the end of the line for the transcontinental railroad in 1872. The Long Branch Saloon, made famous by "Miss Kitty" on the TV show *Gunsmoke*, was one of the most notorious of Dodge City's drinking establishments. Anheuser-Busch was the original beer served and it was served cold, chilled by ice from the river in the winter and on ice brought in by train from Colorado in the summer.

The sign "All nations welcome except Carrie" refers to Kansan **CARRIE NATION**, the axe-wielding teetotaler who achieved national prominence for using hatchets, rocks, and hammers to destroy saloons and the liquor inside, all in the name of temperance. She described herself as a "bulldog running along at the feet of Jesus, barking at what he doesn't like." She was arrested more than thirty times between 1900 and 1910 for leading her followers from saloon to saloon and urging them on with cries of "Smash, ladies, smash!"

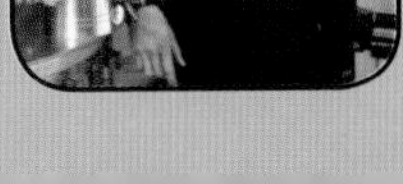

DAMIAN GARCIA
CO-FOUNDER/DIRECTOR OF SALES & MARKETING, DARK HORSE DISTILLERY IN KANSAS CITY

TIP: "When drinking spirits in Kansas, there's a lot to appreciate about what has changed in the industry. Until 2012, it was not legal to hold spirit tasting events in the state of Kansas or to offer customers samples after distillery tours. Today that is no longer the case. The state of Kansas changed its laws to allow businesses like ours the opportunity to sample spirits and provide tastings."

OKLAHOMA

Labor omnia vincit
(Labor Conquers All Things)

You want to get your drink on in Oklahoma? You better work.

Oklahoma is home to cowboys and Indians, tornadoes and trailer parks, the settling Sooners, the Trail of Tears, and the Dust Bowl. This land is also the birthplace of Woody Guthrie, Garth Brooks, and the great American trailer park poet, Toby Keith, whose red Solo cup is likely filled with low-point beer. The only alcohol available in supermarkets and convenience stores is beer with an ABW of 3.2% or less. Several states have this stipulation, and major brands like Coors and Budweiser produce special beers to meet this limit. These low-point beers are the only beverage that you can buy chilled, as well. Though 3.2 brew is the suds for sale in six states, it is by far most popular in Oklahoma, whose thirsty citizenry consumes 89% of their beer in this form and more than half of all of the low-point beer brewed in America. It's been said that getting drunk in Oklahoma is like riding a rocking horse into battle.

The long and short of it means that you just need to go out to get your drink on here—let the bartenders do all the heavy lifting for you! There's craft beer to chase your blues away. The state's first craft brewery, Huebert's, opened just in 2003, and the brewer himself had to help write the legislation to make it happen. Prior to Huebert's, Oklahoma didn't have a method of licensing microbreweries, so there were none by default. Today there are about twenty craft breweries in the state, many of which are among the more than 200 beers pouring at the annual Oklahoma Beer Festival in Oklahoma City. Tapwerks Ale House, also in OKC, has more than 200 taps as well! Or you can order up a round of shots after a day of shooting at Oklahoma City's Wilshire Gun Range, the state's first gun range with a bar! The owners say that guns are "the new golf," and like a golf course will allow members to unwind with a drink after shooting at their "guntry club." Oklahoma is also re-establishing a once thriving wine industry, which was destroyed by the one-two punch of the Dust Bowl and Prohibition. They are now producing everything from Pinot Grigio to Shiraz to Zinfandels; tasting rooms are legal (and luxurious) here. The largest is the 600-acre Woods & Waters winery in Anadarko.

The body of Geronimo, the famed Apache warrior, is buried in Oklahoma. The story goes that while being pursued in a wild chase by the American cavalry, he led them up to the top of the Medicine Bluffs and leapt, still on horseback, into the river below, shouting, you guessed it, "Geronimo!" Both Geronimo and his horse allegedly survived the leap, only to be eventually captured in 1894 and housed as a POW at Fort Sill. The once-proud warrior lived out the rest of his years there pacified by the drinks he would persuade the cavalrymen to give to him, trading in on his celebrity status by selling trinkets and posing for photos with tourists. He died in 1909 at the age of ninety, after a drunken fall from a wagon led to the contraction of a fatal case of pneumonia. The rest of the Fort Sill Apache were released four years later.

WILL ROGERS was born in 1879 on the frontier, in what would later become Oologah, OK. He once quipped that, "Prohibition was better than no alcohol at all," and predicted that Oklahoma would remain a dry state "as long as voters could stagger to the polls." He was proven wrong, but not until 1959 when Oklahoma finally repealed prohibition. Twenty-five years later, in 1985, Oklahoma finally allowed liquor by the drink, perhaps guided by Rogers' advice: "When you find yourself in a hole, stop digging."

Oklahomans are the #1 consumer of **LOW-POINT BEER** in America. 89% of suds swilled in the state are of the 3.2 variety.

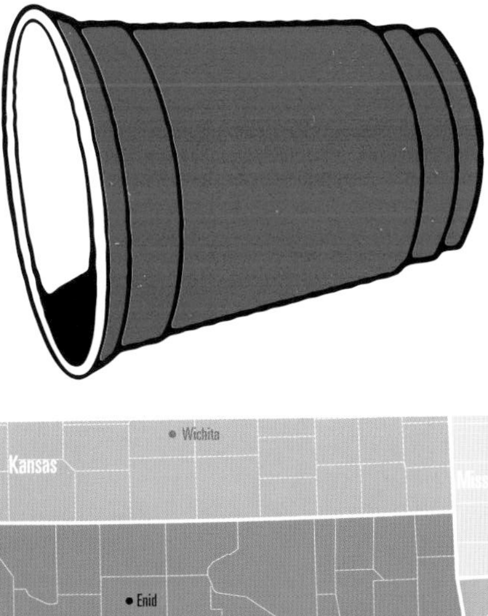

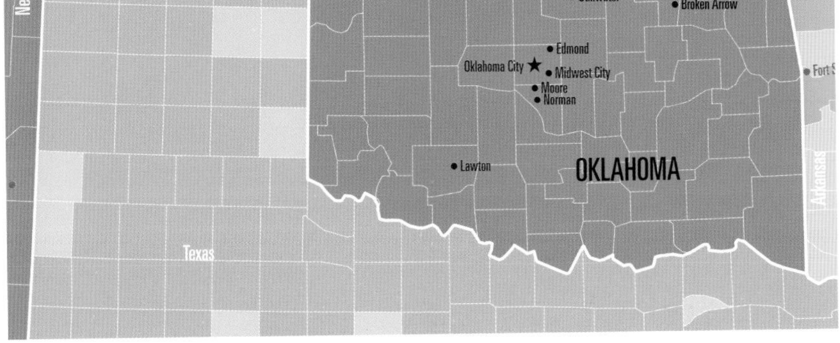

OKLAHOMA

WHAT'LL IT BE?

Like Kansas, Oklahoma's liquor laws are more stringent than those of other Great Plains states. Liquor, wine, and "strong beer" over 3.2% ABW (or about 4% ABV) are available only at room temperature through licensed liquor stores, which are open from 10:00 a.m. to 9:00 p.m. Monday through Saturday. Liquor stores are closed on Sundays, Memorial Day, Independence Day, Labor Day, Thanksgiving Day, and Christmas Day. Cold low-point beer is available from grocery stores, convenience stores, pharmacies, and gas stations from 6:00 a.m. to 2:00 a.m. seven days a week. On-premise consumption starts at 6:00 a.m. for 3.2% beer and 10:00 a.m. for stronger drinks and ends at 2:00 a.m. seven days a week

Oklahoma does allow for a local option for on-premise sales. Counties can choose to limit the hours or days alcohol is available in bars and restaurants, and twenty-nine of Oklahoma's seventy-seven counties have made such restrictions. Low-point beer is not affected by local option laws.

QUICK REFERENCE

WHAT YOU CAN DO

- Purchase room-temperature package liquor, wine, and strong beer between 10:00 a.m. and 9:00 p.m. Monday through Saturday.
- Purchase cold low-point beer for off-premise consumption from grocery stores, convenience stores, and pharmacies between 6:00 a.m. and 2:00 a.m. seven days a week.
- Order wine and spirits at a bar or restaurant between 10:00 a.m. and 2:00 a.m. seven days a week.
- Order low-point beer at a bar or restaurant between 7:00 a.m. and 2:00 a.m. seven days a week.
- Bring your own bottle of wine to consume at a restaurant.
- Smoke in "stand-alone" bars or taverns that derive more than 60% of their income from the sale of alcohol.
- Fill a growler with strong beer at a brewpub or liquor store and with 3.2% beer at a grocery store.

WHAT YOU CAN'T DO

- Have a beer at a movie theater.
- Fill a growler at a brewery.
- Smoke in a restaurant. Oklahoma has a statewide ban on smoking in enclosed spaces, with the exception of stand-alone bars.
- Order a drink at a bar between 2:00 a.m. and 10:00 a.m. seven days a week.
- Purchase alcohol for on- or off-premise consumption on Memorial Day, Independence Day, Labor Day, Thanksgiving Day, and Christmas Day.
- Purchase package alcohol over 3.2% between 9:00 p.m. and 10:00 a.m. Monday through Saturday or any time on Sunday.

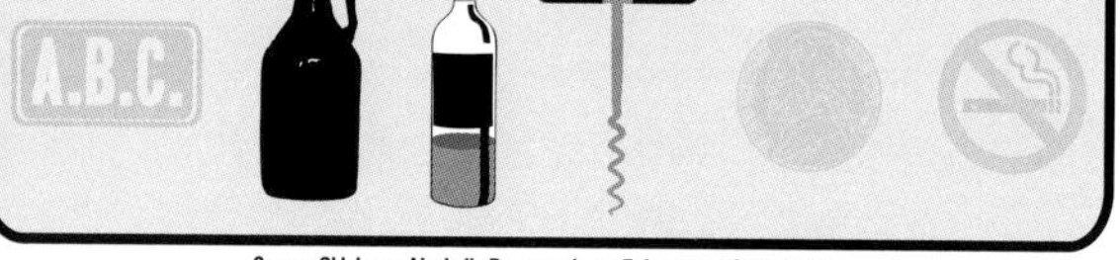

Source: Oklahoma Alcoholic Beverage Laws Enforcement Commission

Prior to 1985 and the sale of liquor by the drink, Oklahomans skirted the law by selling **"LIQUOR-BY-THE-WINK."** Private "clubs" operated where "members" kept their "own bottle" labeled with their name behind the bar. In practice, however, membership cards were handed out at the door and drinks flowed freely inside.

The number of ghost towns in Oklahoma has been estimated to be in the thousands, as communities underwent cycles of boom and bust. **"WHISKEY TOWNS"** were typical of these cycles. These towns were established with the express purpose of selling alcohol to Native Americans on neighboring reservations, where alcohol was banned by federal law. The towns flourished until Oklahoma joined the Union in 1907 as a "dry" state where liquor sales where banned just like on the reservations.

The Copper Bar sits on the fifteenth floor of **FRANK LLOYD WRIGHT'S** only realized skyscraper, the Price Tower Arts Center in Bartlesville forty-five miles north of Tulsa.

JEFFREY COLE
BARTENDER AT O BAR AT THE AMBASSADOR HOTEL IN OKLAHOMA CITY
TIP: "This is a 3.2 state, so don't plan on buying strong beer, wine, or liquor at a convenience store. There are licensed stores that legally only sell alcohol and nothing cold or "ready to drink." Also, consider the 13.5% state excise tax on alcohol when reviewing your bill at any bar or liquor store."

TEXAS

Friendship

You can all go to hell, I'm going to Texas.
Davy Crockett, died 1836, Alamo, San Antonio, TX

Everything is bigger in Texas, including the state itself—it's bigger than most countries. Here's how you can road trip your way around the Lone Star State and not look like ten miles of dirt road when all is said and done.

It's been estimated that 6% of Americans live in dry areas, and a number of those are in Texas. Most are in northern Texas, with wetter areas sinking to the bottom of the state like a soaked sponge. A drink can still be had in some restaurants in dry areas, but you might be asked to join a club to do so (often as simple as showing ID and paying a token fee). Even possession of alcohol is limited in dry counties: no more than twenty-four twelve-ounce bottles and one quart of liquor

The Margarita is America's favorite cocktail, and in 1971, Dallas restaurateur Mariano Martinez invented a fast way of making frozen ones. His Tex-Mex restaurant was having a difficult time keeping up with demand for blended margaritas, so Martinez tinkered with a soft-serve ice cream machine and the frozen margarita machine was born. Though Mariano's Hacienda still serves up deliciously limey slushies in Dallas, the original machine now sits in the Smithsonian.

You won't have a problem getting tighter than bark on a log in Houston, Texas' largest city. Here you'll find the state's oldest craft beer brewery, as well as one of the nation's preeminent cocktail bars. St. Arnold Brewing is named after one of the patron saints of brewing, and Anvil Bar & Refuge has 100 classic cocktails on its menu, calling them drinks you should "try at least once in your life. . . for better or worse."

Opened the day after Prohibition ended, San Antonio's Esquire Tavern is a Riverwalk institution which features not just classic cocktails, but also the Texas-sized, ninety-foot standing bar. Tap into a little history on the grounds of the Pearl Brewery, Texas' oldest. Ten restaurants and bars, as well as a farmer's market and a park currently reside on the twenty-two-acre site. The tallest building at Pearl, with its distinctive roofline that is visible from the highway, is the old brewhouse, now slated to become a boutique hotel. Like many other regional breweries in America, Pearl is now owned by Pabst (and brewed by Miller). Also owned by Pabst is the "National Beer of Texas," Lone Star beer.

Keeping Texas weird is the SXSW music city of Austin. Well within the Austin city limits is Tito's, a distillery producing a corn-based, pot-stilled vodka. Started in 1995 with the state's first distillery license, Tito's is one of the most respected vodkas in the world. Up the road in Waco, Balcones Texas Single Malt Whisky is a pure Texas product: the glass bottle, the water, and all of the ingredients used are produced in Texas.

America's only Texas-born president, Lyndon Baines Johnson, was a Scotch lover. When vacationing on his ranch in Stonewall, he would cool off by drinking tall Styrofoam cups of Cutty Sark and soda while driving his white Lincoln Continental around the property, a secret service vehicle trailing behind him. He signaled for a refill by extending an arm out of the Lincoln and shaking the empty cup of cubes. A member of the security detail would exit the chase car, run up to the president's, retrieve his cup, refill it, and run it back to him. Only in Texas. . .

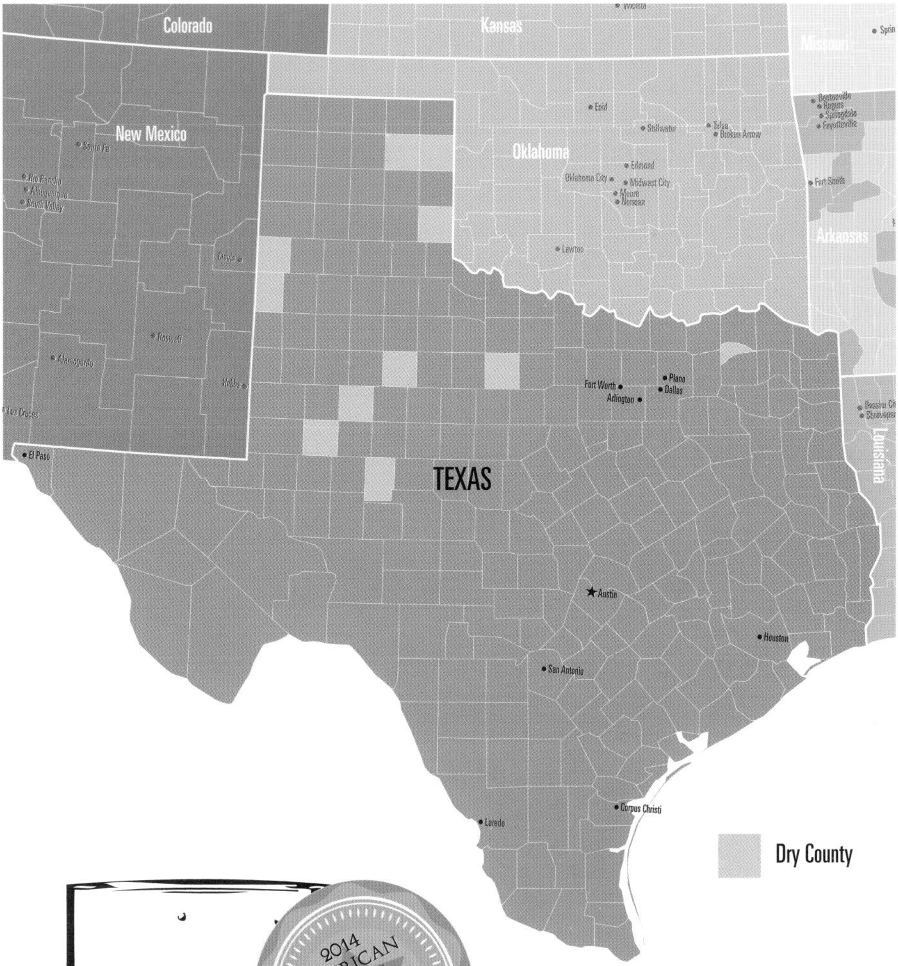

When the 2014 edition of *Jim Murray's Whisky Bible* named Garrison Brothers Cowboy Bourbon the **"AMERICAN MIRCO WHISKEY"** of the year, owner Dan Garrison announced the news on his company's website as follows: "This blog is dedicated to all of the 'professional investors' who, in the early 2000s, told me I'd never be able to make my own bourbon in Texas and should just buy it from a large producer like everyone else does. You sons-of-bitches will never know the pride I feel right now."

TEXAS

WHAT'LL IT BE?

In Texas, package liquor is only available from state-licensed liquor stores, which operate 10:00 a.m. to 9:00 p.m. Monday through Saturday. These stores are closed New Year's Day, Thanksgiving, Christmas Day, and Sundays. Beer and wine, however, are readily available at grocery stores, convenience stores, and pharmacies seven days a week during the hours listed below. Purchase times for on-premise consumption are the same as for beer and wine package purchases. Bars and restaurants are, however, able to serve alcohol until 2:00 a.m. with a "late hours permit," which is common in larger cities.

Texas does allow for local variation, and counties can choose to restrict hours or days of sale for either on- or off-premise consumption. Counties can also prohibit the sale of alcohol entirely, and eleven of the state's 254 counties are completely dry (no alcohol sales at all), while forty-nine are completely wet (no added restrictions). The remainder fall somewhere in between. Restrictions are more likely to appear in smaller communities. Large cities tend to be wet.

QUICK REFERENCE

WHAT YOU CAN DO

- Purchase package liquor at a liquor store between 10:00 a.m. and 9:00 p.m. Monday through Saturday.
- Purchase package wine or beer at a grocery store, convenience store, or pharmacy between 7:00 a.m. and midnight Monday through Friday, between 7:00 a.m. and 1:00 a.m. on Saturday, and between noon and midnight on Sunday.
- Order a drink at a bar or restaurant between 7:00 a.m. and midnight Monday through Friday, between 7:00 a.m. and 1:00 a.m. on Saturday, and between noon and midnight on Sunday.
- Order a drink until 2:00 a.m. at establishments with an extended license.
- Fill a growler with beer at a brewpub, liquor store, or grocery store.
- Bring your own bottle of wine to a restaurant.
- Smoke at a restaurant or bar, except in some larger cities.
- Enjoy happy hour specials, which must end by 11:00 p.m.

WHAT YOU CAN'T DO

- Fill a growler at a brewery.
- Smoke in a bar or restaurant in Dallas, Austin, or El Paso.
- Carry a concealed weapon in a bar with a 51% sign, where alcohol constitutes more than half of sales.
- Order a drink at a bar between midnight and 7:00 a.m. Monday through Saturday, or between 1:00 a.m. and noon on Sunday.
- Purchase beer or wine for off-premise consumption between midnight and 7:00 a.m. Monday through Saturday, or between 1:00 a.m. and noon on Sunday.
- Purchase package liquor on New Year's Day, Thanksgiving, Christmas Day, and Sundays.

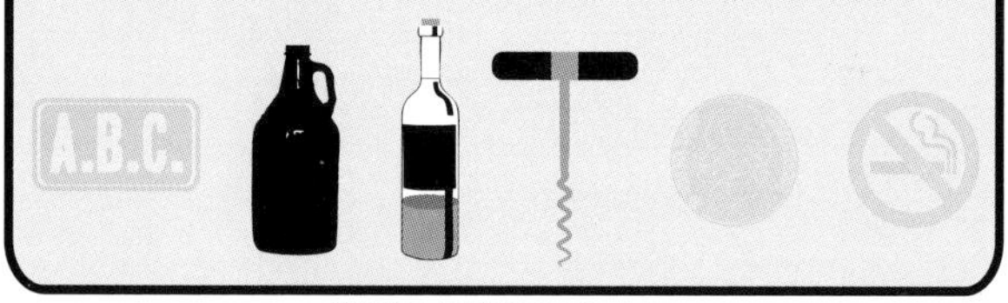

Source: Texas Alcoholic Beverage Commission

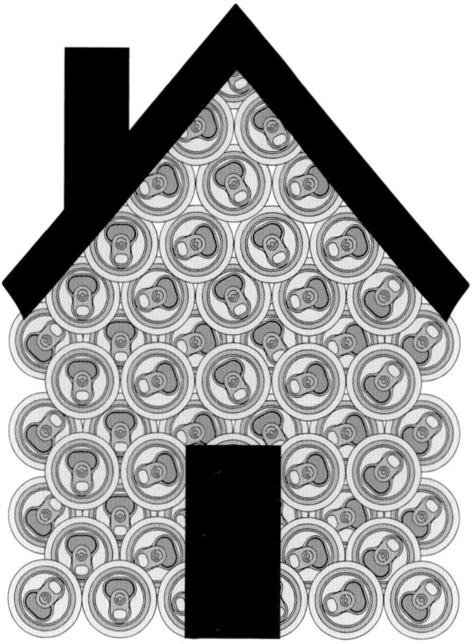

In a monument to recycling, Houston is home to the **BEER CAN HOUSE.** Former railroad worker John Milkovisch fortified his home with over 50,000 beer cans using them as aluminum siding, fencing, and general ornamentation. Drinking most of the beer himself, he always considered his hobby a pastime and not a work of art. His wife Mary said, "He didn't think anybody would ever be interested in it. He just loved drinking his beer and just loved being outside and cutting up the beer cans." The Milkovisches have both passed, but their home is still open for tours.

TEXAS BREWPUBS recently benefited from a change that allowed them to sell their beer at places other than where it was brewed. The Texas Craft Brewers Guild is predicting that this will translate into greater profits and more jobs for Texans. Texas craft beer only represents 0.7% of the beer consumed in the state, but it accounts for over half of the jobs in the sector. Experts predict that the change in this law will have a five billion dollar impact and create more than 50,000 jobs in the next five years alone.

JASON MAGEE
BARTENDER AT THE PEACHED TORTILLA IN AUSTIN

TIP: "Coming to Austin? Get the jello shots ready and the cooler packed because you'll want to spend the day floating and partying on the Guadalupe river. After that, take a downtown pedi-cab to the many local breweries, great restaurants, and hole-in-the-wall taverns filled with live music and amazing bites. Make sure your liver is prepared; Austin is, after all, the drinking capital of the world."

NEW MEXICO

Labor Omnia Vincit

(It grows as it goes)

Anyone who's driven Route 66 in the summertime knows how very hot it can get in New Mexico. By the time the glorious sun sets over the Sandias, turning the skies a namesake watermelon pink, you'll be ready for a tall, cold one. There was a time in New Mexico where you needn't even leave your car to get a case. But the state banned drive-up liquor sales in 1999. New Mexicans are careful not to drink and drive—mandatory penalties for the first offense include one year with a car breathalyzer interlock.

During the first weekend of October, you can have a part of the Whole Enchilada in Las Cruces, where the largest one of its kind is annually cooked up. "The whole enchilada" could also serve as a drinking motto for the state. Pretty much anything goes here. Liquor stores can be open as late as midnight, and bars until 2:00 a.m. The only no-nos come in the form of freebies: no all-you-can-drink nights, and no two-for-one specials.

New Mexico's liquor law extends only to state lands, however. Federal law prohibits alcohol on the rez, except by permission of the tribe. The Navajo, the largest tribe in the state, abides by the federal law and strictly prohibits any alcohol on its reservation.

New Mexico is the home state of Neil Patrick Harris, Amazoner Jeff Bezos, and the largest Balloon Fiesta in the world. In Tome, NM in 2011, nine-year-old Bobby Bradley became the youngest person to fly a hot air balloon solo. It's not known whether his father gave him the traditional celebratory champagne toast that accompanies inaugural landings, but under state law it would have been legal. So if your travels take you to Four Corners or to White Sands or to Carlsbad Caverns, here's to "soft winds and gentle landings."

In an effort to curb drunk driving among twenty-one to thirty-four-year-old Hispanic men, New Mexico engaged in a viral video marketing campaign that employed former *CHiPS* star **ERIK ESTRADA** falling out of the sky and on to the hood of a car of a young drunk driver and yelling, "What are you thinking?" Erik Estrada air fresheners were also handed out at sobriety checkpoints throughout the campaign.

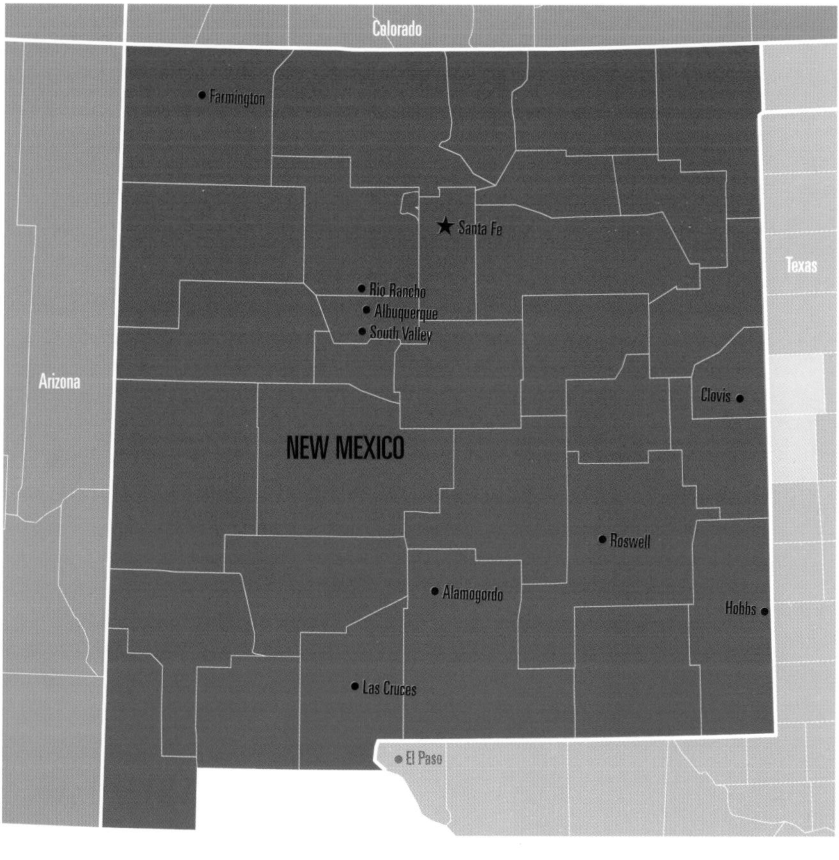

NEW MEXICO

WHAT'LL IT BE?

Package beer, wine, and liquor is available at liquor stores as well as at licensed grocery stores, convenience stores, and pharmacies between 7:00 a.m. and midnight Monday through Saturday. Full-service restaurants and bars serve beer, wine, and liquor between 7:00 a.m. and 2:00 a.m. Monday through Saturday, but some restaurants will only have beer and wine and close at 11:00 p.m. Although liquor licenses are issued based on population, sales are not limited to towns. Retailers in unincorporated areas can sell package alcohol and alcohol for on-premise consumption, but they must be at least ten miles from any other liquor license holder.

New Mexico is a local option state for Sunday sales. Counties and towns with populations greater than 5,000 can vote to allow Sunday sales of alcohol. Even if a county has voted to allow Sunday sales, towns can still vote to prohibit them. The opposite is also true: a town can vote to allow Sunday sales even if the county has voted to remain dry. A complete list of local options is available at New Mexico's Alcohol and Gaming website.

QUICK REFERENCE

WHAT YOU CAN DO

- Purchase package beer, wine, or liquor from licensed grocery stores, convenience stores, and pharmacies between 7:00 a.m. and midnight Monday through Saturday, and between noon and midnight on Sunday if a local option allows it.
- Order a drink at a restaurant that only serves beer and wine between 7:00 a.m. and 11:00 p.m. Monday through Saturday, and between noon and 11:00 p.m. on Sunday if a local option allows it.
- Order a drink at a bar or a full-service restaurant between 7:00 a.m. and 2:00 a.m. Monday through Saturday, and between noon and midnight on Sunday if a local option allows it.
- Enjoy happy hour specials.
- Fill a growler at a brewery.

WHAT YOU CAN'T DO

- Order a drink at a restaurant if the kitchen is closed.
- Bring your own bottle of wine to a restaurant.
- Purchase package beer, wine, or liquor on Sundays where not allowed by local option and on Christmas.
- Purchase package spirits on Christmas.
- Smoke in bars and restaurants
- Purchase package beer, wine, or liquor between midnight and 7:00 a.m. Monday through Saturday, or between midnight and noon on Sunday.
- Order a drink at a restaurant that only serves beer and wine between 11:00 p.m. and 7:00 a.m. Monday through Saturday, and before noon or after 11:00 pm on Sunday.
- Order a drink at bar or full-service restaurant between midnight and 7:00 a.m. on Monday, between 2:00 a.m. and 7:00 a.m. Tuesday through Saturday, or before noon or after midnight on Sunday.

Source: New Mexico Regulation and Licensing Department, Alcohol and Gaming Division

A group of Benedictine monks at the **MONASTERY OF CHRIST IN THE DESERT** outside of Santa Fe grow their own hops. In conjunction with Abbey Brewing Company, who maintains a brewery on the grounds of the monastery, they strive to create new styles of beer derived from the 1,400-year-old monastic tradition of brewing in Europe and the newer American craft beer tradition. "Our focus in all our work is to 'bring everything to perfection for the Glory of God' as the Rule of Saint Benedict instructs us." Monks' Ales are available at the monastery's tasting room and in retail locations across the state.

New Mexico has the longest history of wine production in the United States. The first wine grapes were planted by a Franciscan friar and a Capuchin monk in the **RIO GRANDE VALLEY** in 1629 to use for Communion. By 1880, the region was producing over one million gallons of wine a year. Flooding of the Rio Grande and Prohibition destroyed the industry in the twentieth century, but it is making a comeback. Currently, New Mexico's forty-two wineries produce 700,000 gallons of wine annually.

CHRIS MILLIGAN
BARTENDER AT SECRETO LOUNGE, HOTEL ST FRANCIS IN SANTA FE

TIP: "We are a high elevation state so remember that alcohol hits the body harder and faster at higher elevations. Moderation is key. Our climate is very dry too, and it is easy to dehydrate and not know it is happening, so please drink lots of water. Also, many bars in New Mexico do not accept vertical ID's, so if you have one be prepared to be turned away or bring your passport."

ARIZONA

Ditat Deus
(God Enriches)

Arizona, where summer spends the winter and hell spends summer, celebrated its 100th birthday in 2012. Sadly, for more than 100 days a year, 100 degrees is also the temperature—but as they say, it's a dry heat! Arizonans needn't even leave the cool comfort of their air-conditioned cars, because from Flagstaff to the Grand Canyon there are drive-through liquor stores in the Sunset State.

Tequila has a long history in the state, which shares a border with the Mexican state of Sonora. During Prohibition, most of the moonshine being made in Arizona (and smuggled into Arizona) was agave-based. Remember, to be called "tequila," the agave spirit must be produced in a specific geographic area of Mexico, so that Sonoran moonshine is known as bacanora, a country cousin of tequila. Bacanora only became legal in Mexico in 1992 (earning a legal Denomination of Origin in 2005). Just a few years after Prohibition ended, the Tequila Sunrise was invented in the bar of the Arizona Biltmore Hotel when a guest asked for no, not another shot of courage, but a poolside cooler. The name is derived from the way the drink looks after it has settled in the glass.

Though the Margarita wasn't invented in Arizona, many of them are served in one of the state's oldest bars, Aunt Chilada's, which predates statehood and claims to have liquor license #1. The original bar used to have a glass ceiling, upon which a scantily clad woman lolled about—the end result being that the gentlemen's heads were constantly tipped back, ready for tippling.

Legend has it that the town of Tombstone, Arizona, was founded by a prospector who was advised that the only thing he would discover was his own grave. He went on to find a silver seam and mocked the naysayers by calling it Tombstone. The silver boomtown would eventually support three newspapers, two banks, a large red-light district, and more than 100 saloons. The famous shootout at the OK Corral started with cowboy Ike Clanton drunkenly bragging in Tombstone's saloons that he'd kill an Earp. The next day, shots of whiskey would lead to shots of lead as the Earp brothers confronted Clanton and his cowboys about the town's weapon ordinance. Thirty shots were fired in thirty seconds, killing three. In 1881, twenty-four-hour saloons were legal, but carrying guns within city limits wasn't. Today it's the reverse.

Arizona has **DRIVE-THROUGH LIQUOUR STORES** throughout the entire state.

Prohibition greatly increased the amount of tourism to Mexico, with Sonora becoming a destination for Americans in search of a place to drink. America's taste for **TEQUILA** was solidified during the Prohibition years and bootlegging across the border was rampant.

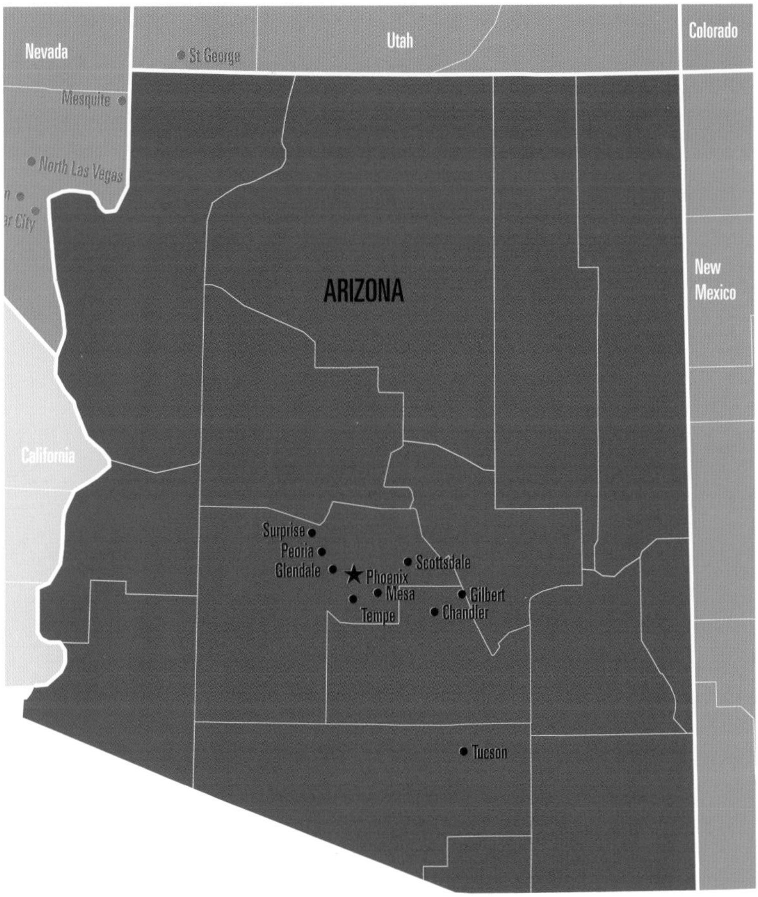

ARIZONA

WHAT'LL IT BE?

Alcohol is readily available in Arizona for both on- and off-premise consumption. Package alcohol is sold in grocery stores, convenience stores, and pharmacies, and it is also available from drive-through stores. Sales are permitted between 6:00 a.m. and 2:00 a.m. for off-premise consumption and between 6:00 a.m. and 2:30 a.m. for on-premise consumption, seven days a week.

Although there is no local option in Arizona, about 25% of Arizona's land is designated as Indian reservations, which are not bound by state law. Liquor laws there can be (and often are) more stringent. For example, the largest reservation in Arizona, the Navajo Nation, prohibits the possession and use of all alcohol, except in the casinos.

QUICK REFERENCE

WHAT YOU CAN DO

- Purchase package liquor, wine, and beer between 6:00 a.m. and 2:00 a.m. seven days a week from licensed grocery stores, convenience stores, and pharmacies.
- Purchase package alcohol from drive-through liquor stores.
- Order a drink at a bar or restaurant between 6:00 a.m. and 2:30 a.m. seven days a week.
- Bring your own bottle of wine to a restaurant that does not have a wine license.
- Fill a glass growler at a brewery, grocery store, or restaurant.

WHAT YOU CAN'T DO

- Bring a firearm into a drinking establishment that has a posted firearms ban.
- Fill a ceramic or stainless steel growler.
- Bring your own bottle of wine to a restaurant that has a wine license.
- Smoke in bars and restaurants.
- Order a drink at a bar or restaurant between 2:30 a.m. and 6:00 a.m.
- Purchase package liquor, wine, and beer between 2:00 a.m. and 6:00 a.m.
- Bring alcohol into the Navajo Nation.

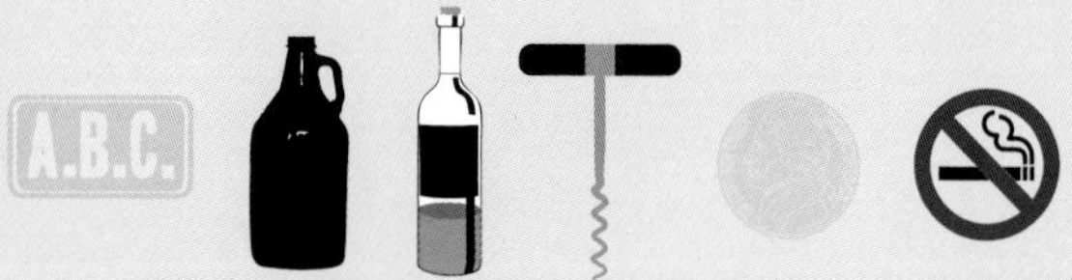

Source: Arizona Department of Liquor

There should never be a worm in your bottle of tequila. The urban legend of **"EL GUSANO"** was born in the 1940s as a marketing ploy to entice gringos with promises of being a hallucinatory aphrodisiac and it persists to this day. Some brands of mezcal, on the other hand, may contain a worm. If so, it is actually the larva of the mariposa moth, which lives in the agave plant from which Mezcal is made. As a rule, top shelf mezcals don't have a worm in the bottle either. But if you do find yourself facing el gusano, fear not. Maguey worms are harmless, considered a delicacy in Mexico, and even sold in restaurants and grocery stores. Salud!

Today, the drinking age in all fifty states is twenty-one because of a federal law that ties compliance to highway funding. However, there was a period from the early 1970s to mid-1980s when thirty states, including Arizona, lowered their drinking age to eighteen or nineteen. The reason was the **TWENTY-SIXTH AMENDMENT**, which lowered the voting age from twenty-one to eighteen. Since this was now the "age of majority" when one is no longer considered a minor, many states adjusted their drinking age limits as well.

In addition to regular DUI charges, Arizona has **"EXTREME DUI"** and "Super Extreme DUI." Extreme DUI is for BAC levels between 0.15% and 0.20% and has a 30-day mandatory prison sentence. Super Extreme DUI is for BAC levels greater than 0.20% and has a mandatory 45-day prison sentence. Nationally, anything more than 0.08% is against the law.

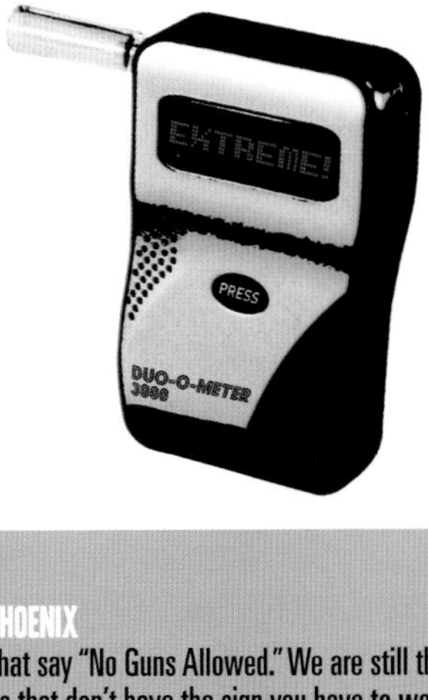

BRANDON CASEY
BARTENDER AT THE GLADLY IN PHOENIX

TIP: "Don't be afraid of the signs that say "No Guns Allowed." We are still the Wild West in our hearts, but it's the bars that don't have the sign you have to worry about. Our city is a the product of an ever migrating nation. If your bartender isn't from where you are, they might not know what drink you are asking for. For instance, Old Fashioneds don't have brandy--sorry Wisconsin. Try something local!"

COLORADO

Nil Sine Numine

(Nothing Without Divine Providence)

"Good people drink good beer," said Hunter S. Thompson, the infamous author of *The Rum Diary* who made his home in Woody Creek, Colorado. With closing in on 200 breweries both big and small, the state has definitely gone gonzo over beer. In 1873, Adolph Coors established what would later become the world's largest brewery in Golden. Jumping forward to 1988, John Hickenlooper established the state's first microbrewery, Wynkoop Brewing, in Denver before becoming governor of the state.

Wynkoop also sponsors the nation's Beerdrinker of the Year, an enthusiast and ambassador of beer who is awarded a lifetime of free beer at the brewery, along with a $250 tab at their local watering hole. The contest seeks out not those who can drink the most—instead, they look for people who have a deep understanding of beer, how it's made, and its history. Past winners have included 2012's J. Wilson, who subsisted for forty-six days on just water and his own home-brewed bock beer, and 2011's Phil Farrell, who's tipped back pints in all fifty states and every country in Europe.

Denver is also the site of what is possibly the world's largest beer festival, the Great American Beer Festival (GABF). The GABF serves more than 2,000 different beers from every state in the union to 49,000 thirsty beer drinkers. In 2013, tickets to the GABF sold out in twenty minutes. Coors Field in Denver is also home to the country's first in-stadium brewery, the Sandlot. While it is indeed owned by MillerCoors, Blue Moon and other small specialty beers are what is brewed here. Though they brew year-round, the Sandlot is only open during baseball season, and all of their beers have baseball names (Blue Moon was originally called Belly Slide Belgian Wit). With all that beery bounty, one would think that Colorado is a progressive state when it comes to selling suds. Sadly, that's not the case when it comes to grocery and convenience store sales, where beer sold must not contain more than 3.2% ABW. Look for higher ABW and craft beer at independent liquor stores.

Though Colorado has the highest mean altitude in the country, and its capitol of Denver sits at over 5,000 feet, it's an old wives' tale that the effects of alcohol increase at high altitudes. While alcohol is no more potent, altitude does affect the human body. The newly arrived may feel fatigue and sluggishness. Indeed, some of the side effects of altitude sickness mimic those of a hangover, so blame the headaches and nausea on being in the Mile High City, not on bending back the old elbow.

CA$H FOR CANS

The recyclable aluminum can was introduced by **COORS BREWING** of Golden, Colorado, in 1959. Coors began a recycling program soon after called "Cash for Cans," offering a penny for each can or bottle returned for recycling. In 1965, Coors collected 13 million cans.

Denver is home to **MODERN DRUNKARD MAGAZINE.**

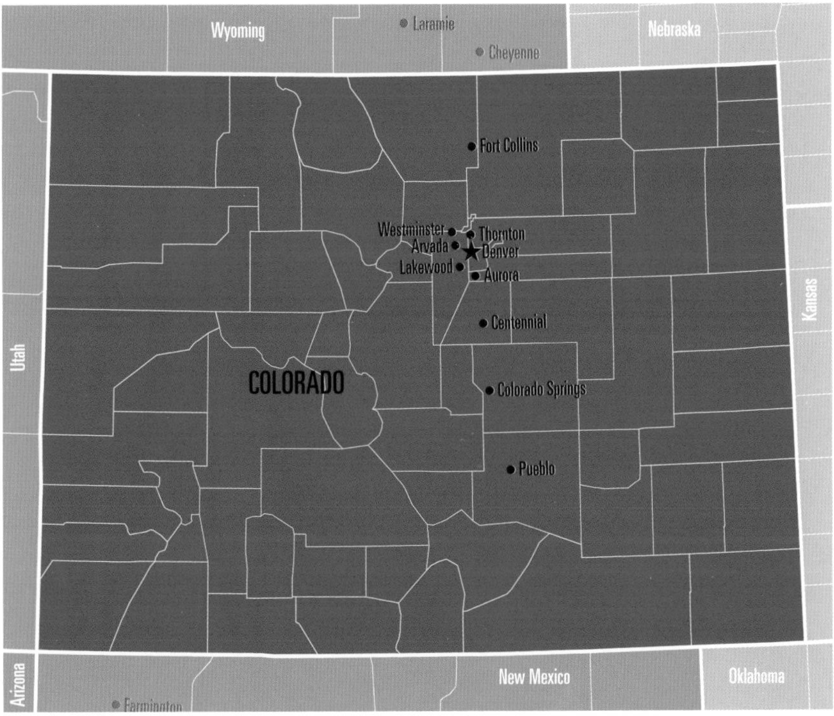

COLORADO

WHAT'LL IT BE?

Colorado has two sets of laws related to alcohol, the liquor code and the beer code. The liquor code regulates liquor, wine, cider, and all beer greater than 3.2% ABW (about 4% ABV), all of which are only available from licensed liquor stores. Liquor store hours are generous, but there are no package sales on Christmas. The beer code concerns all fermented malt beverages 3.2% or less. Beverages covered by the beer code, which must be labeled 3.2% beer or ale, are more readily available and can be found in licensed grocery stores, convenience stores, and pharmacies, including Christmas. Alcohol is available for on-premise consumption seven days a week between 7:00 a.m. and 2:00 a.m. the following day.

Although Colorado state law allows counties and municipalities to limit sales of liquor, none currently do.

QUICK REFERENCE

WHAT YOU CAN DO

- Purchase package liquor, wine, or strong beer from a licensed liquor store between 8:00 a.m. and midnight seven days a week.
- Purchase 3.2% beer at a grocery store, convenience store, or pharmacy between 5:00 a.m. and midnight.
- Order a drink at a bar or restaurant between 7:00 a.m. and 2:00 a.m. seven days a week.
- Fill a growler at a brewery.

WHAT YOU CAN'T DO

- Bring your own bottle of wine to a restaurant.
- Beg for alcohol.
- Smoke in bars and restaurants.
- Purchase package alcohol over 3.2% on Christmas.
- Order a drink at a bar or restaurant between 2:00 a.m. and 7:00 a.m.
- Purchase 3.2% beer for off-premise consumption between midnight and 5:00 a.m.
- Purchase liquor, wine, or strong beer between midnight and 8:00 a.m.

Source: Colorado Department of Revenue, Liquor and Tobacco Enforcement Division

CHAIN STORES are only allowed to hold one liquor license (to sell beer, wine, and liquor), which means that only one of their locations in the state is able to provide one-stop shopping. Some chain pharmacies and grocery stores with a pharmacy take advantage of a Prohibition-era loophole that allows pharmacies to sell liquor, although they are subject to the one-store rule as well.

Gonzo journalist **HUNTER S. THOMPSON** lived in Woody Creek, Colorado. His neighbor, George Stranahan, was the founder of Flying Dog Brewpub in nearby Aspen and they formed a close friendship bonding over booze, guns, and politics. The brewery grew and relocated to Maryland, but Thompson introduced his friends at Flying Dog to artist Ralph Steadman, whose iconic style began appearing on their labels in 1996.

It is illegal to beg for drinks in Colorado.

A. MINETTA GOULD
BARTENDER AT THE SQUEAKY BEAN IN DENVER

TIP: "Being the craft beer holy land that Colorado is, one would expect to find their favorite high-end, high-octane beers in every corner store of the state: not true! You need a special trip to the liquor store if you want something a bit more potent. And don't even think about taking that special beer to a city park in Denver: beer above 3.2% ABW carries a hefty fine if found consumed in our parks."

UTAH

MOUNTAIN

Industry

The Beehive State gets its motto from the hard-working Mormons who turned the desert state into a blooming flower. They are celebrated annually on Pioneer Day, but toast them with Postum (the caffeine-free coffee substitute popular in Utah), since the liquor stores are closed. Even if it isn't a holiday, it takes a little elbow grease to find a drink in temperate Utah.

The 2002 Olympics brought some changes to the draconian liquor laws, and efforts were recently redoubled in an attempt to draw in tourists. But there are still hurdles to jump through and curiosities to giggle at when it comes to getting a drink here.

Infamous private clubs are a thing of the past. Now you can get a cocktail at bars and restaurants. Anyone looking younger than thirty-five can expect to be carded using an electronic ID scanner. Getting a drink in a restaurant means ordering food; bars may serve alcohol without food, but bars are a rare thing to find in the state (sometimes only a single bar license is issued in a year). To comply with the law stating that restaurants may not prepare drinks in front of customers, some have opted to erect a partition, jokingly known as a "Zion curtain," to hide the business end of the bar. Cocktails may only be made with 1.5 ounces of the primary spirit, with a maximum total of 2.5 ounces. Only one drink may be served at a time. The law does allow for a side shot, however, provided it is not the same spirit that is in the drink. So you may order a gin & tonic with a side shot of vodka, but not a G & T with a side shot of gin. Drink with a buddy who likes vodka tonics and you can trade your side shots to make your own double. No matter what kind of establishment you're drinking at, all draft beer is limited to 3.2% ABW. Bottled beer can be any strength (look for the words "strong" or "heavy" on the label).

Supermarkets and convenience stores only sell 3.2% beer as well. Strong beer, wine, and spirits are sold at state-controlled liquor stores, as well as independent package stores. Licensed brewpubs, wineries, and distilleries may sell their own wares to go.

Drinking is on the upswing in Utah, with lots of local options awaiting your order. Look for award-winning, 3.2% beer on tap from major micros Uinta, Sasquatch, and Wasatch Brewery, which advertises its Polygamy Porter with the tag line "Why have just one?" Ogden's Own Distillery pokes fun at early Mormon polygamy with its Five Wives Vodka. You won't need magic underwear or a secret password to get into Salt Lake's excellent Prohibition-era lounge Bar-X or the hidden Speakeasy in the Avenues Bistro. Order a cocktail, make a toast, and say a prayer for the continued loosening of Utah's liquor laws.

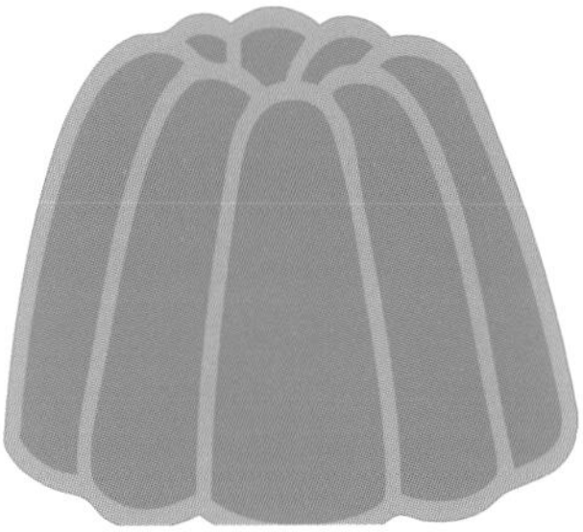

Salt Lake City is the number one consumer of **JELL-O** in the US, which would also make them the number one consumer of non-alcoholic Jell-O shots.

SALT LAKE CITY INTERNATIONAL AIRPORT has lounges with full bar service available from 8:00 a.m. to midnight. The purchase of food is not required in airport lounges.

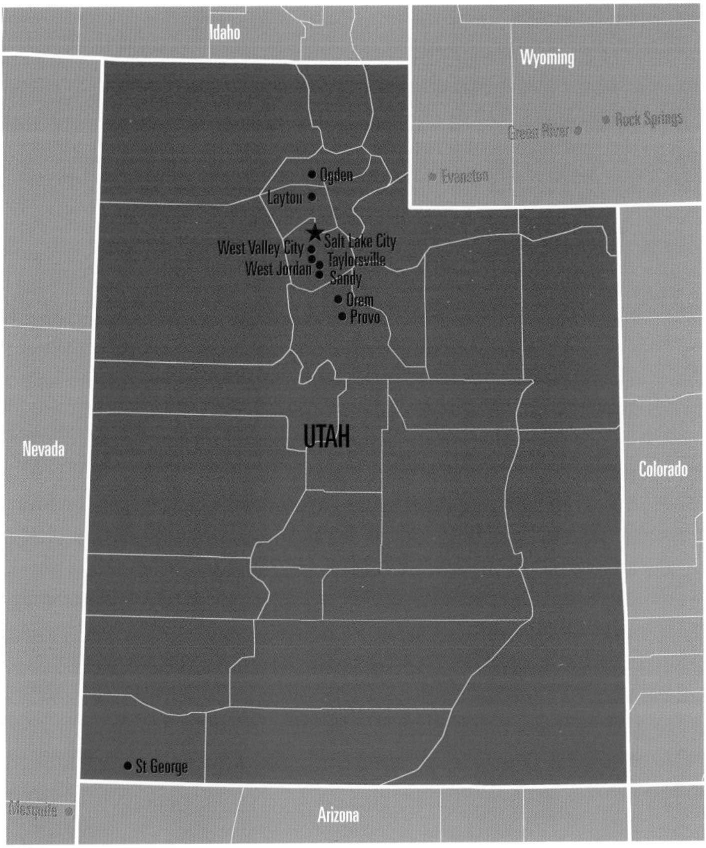

WHAT'LL IT BE?

Utah controls the wholesale and retail sale of liquor, wine, and "strong beer," which is beer higher than 3.2% ABW (or about 4% ABV). Liquor, wine, and strong beer are available from 41 state-run liquor stores and 111 smaller package agencies. There are no set hours of sales, but stores generally don't open before 11:00 a.m. and are closed by 10:00 p.m. Beer under 3.2% ABW is available in grocery and convenience stores. Liquor, wine, and strong beer are available for on-premise consumption with the purchase of food. Utah also has a club license that allows full liquor service without the purchase of food. It's also illegal to bring alcohol into the state, as only the Utah Department of Alcoholic Beverage Control may import and ship alcohol into Utah.

Utah does not allow for a local option. Laws relating to alcohol are consistent statewide.

QUICK REFERENCE

WHAT YOU CAN DO

- Buy package 3.2% beer from grocery stores, convenience stores, and pharmacies.
- Buy package liquor, wine, and strong beer in state-controlled liquor stores and agencies.
- Order a liquor, wine, or strong beer in a restaurant with a full-service liquor license between 11:30 a.m. and midnight with the purchase of food.
- Order 3.2% beer in a restaurant until 1:00 a.m. with the purchase of food.
- Bring your own bottle of wine to a restaurant.
- Take an unfinished bottle of wine from dinner home.
- Fill a growler with 3.2% beer.

WHAT YOU CAN'T DO

- Buy any package alcohol stronger than 3.2% from anywhere other than a business licensed by the state of Utah, including from individuals.
- Buy package liquor, wine, and strong beer on Sundays and the following holidays: Martin Luther King, Jr. Day, Presidents Day, Memorial Day, Independence Day, Pioneer Day, Labor Day, Columbus Day, Veterans Day, Thanksgiving, Christmas Day, and New Year's Day.
- Buy package liquor on a Monday if a holiday falls on a Sunday, or on a Friday if a holiday falls on a Saturday.
- Order liquor, wine, or strong beer after midnight.
- Buy alcohol for off-premise consumption late. There are no set hours of sale, but most stores are closed by 10:00 p.m.
- Order a drink in a restaurant without also ordering food.
- Smoke in bars and restaurants.
- Watch someone prepare your drink.
- Be drunk. It's illegal to be drunk in Utah.

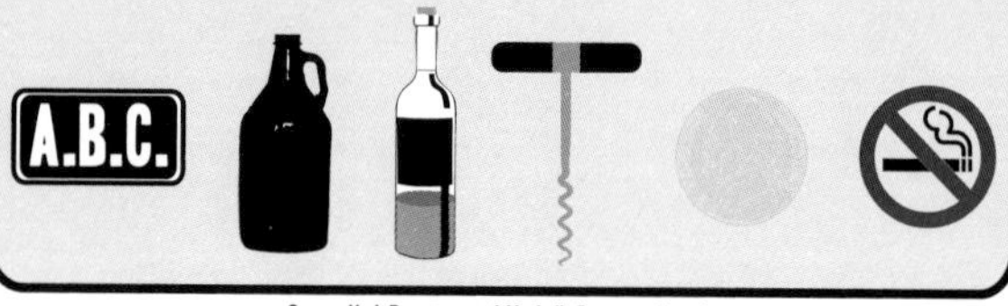

Source: Utah Department of Alcoholic Beverage Control

Ironically, Utah is home to the city of **BACCHUS**, alluding to the Roman god of wine, merry making, and ecstasy. Bacchus, Utah, however, was named after T.E. Bacchus, the founder of an early twentieth-century gunpowder company.

ADVERTISING

Alcohol advertising in Utah cannot imply that drinking will increase a person's health, physical or sexual prowess, athletic ability, social welfare, or their "capacity to enjoy life's activities." Presumably, Utahns are not aware of Dos Equis' Most Interesting Man in the World.

State law prohibits alcohol consumption in a public building, park, or stadium. While most sporting events are alcohol-free, some large stadiums, such as the Jazz's Energy Solution Arena, have **"POCKET PUBS"** that operate as clubs.

CHRIS BARLOW
LEAD DISTILLER AT BEEHIVE DISTILLING IN SALT LAKE CITY

TIP: "Utah is the land of big mountains, big families, and big liquor laws. Despite these challenges, the Beehive State's alcohol industry is booming, although bartenders' mixing skills are often hidden behind a frosted glass wall called the 'Zion Curtain'. Yes, we're a weird little pocket of the Wild West, but the unique craft gin, whiskey, and other libations created here more than make up for our quirks."

WYOMING

The Cowboy State

The frontier spirit is alive and kicking in Wyoming. Ten-gallon hats and boots are rag proper, and whether you're in the middle of nowhere or on your way to everywhere, you'll find a rodeo. "The Daddy of 'em All," the Cheyenne Frontier Days Rodeo, is the world's largest, drawing hundreds of thousands of visitors each year to the state's capitol. Cowboys looking to kick up their boots and quench their thirst head to the Buckin' A Saloon at the north end of the midway.

Fittingly, the country's first saloon opened in Wyoming. Established in 1822 in Brown's Hole, WY, Brown's Saloon catered to the needs of the beaver-hunting fur trappers that first came through the region. The story goes that a poor, lonesome, French-Canadian trapper named the Grand Tetons after the shape of the missus he was missing.

There's a bonanza of interesting bars to belly up to in the state. Visitors to the Buffalo Bill Center of the West in Cody should be sure to have a cold one at the massive bar in the Irma Hotel. The grand hotel's cherry wood bar was a personal gift to Buffalo Bill from Queen Victoria. The Dip in Medicine Bow is home to the world's largest jade stone bar, and it also sports a hand-painted dance floor. In the Old West town of Jackson, the Silver Dollar Saloon has a bar made up of, that's right, silver dollars: 2,036 silver dollars minted in 1921, to be exact. There's even a bar in the Old Faithful Inn (with a view of the geyser, of course). In Wyoming, restaurants must stop serving alcohol when the kitchen closes, but bars, wineries, and microbreweries may continue to pour until closing.

The brewer at the state's first microbrewery, Jackson Hole's Grand Teton Brewing, should be remembered in beer drinkers' prayers. It was Charlie Otto who popularized the contemporary party-to-go jug, the glass beer growler. The term "growler" supposedly comes from the sound of carbon dioxide escaping from the lidded tin pail that beer was carried home in. Growlers can be filled at any of the state's seventeen microbreweries, or at establishments with a special retail permit. Park your growler in the back of the truck to comply with the state's open container laws.

How about a campside boilermaker to go with that beer? The term "boilermaker" (whiskey with a beer back) originated as slang for the men who built and maintained the steam locomotives which crisscrossed the West. Now the hard stuff can be sourced from locally made Wyoming Whiskey. The state's first (and currently only) distillery uses local grain and water from a nearby limestone spring for their bourbon. Remember to follow the cowboy code when drinking in Wyoming: never pass anyone on the trail without saying "Howdy," and always drink your whiskey with your gun hand to show your friendly intentions.

The term **"BOILERMAKER"** (whiskey with a beer back) originated as slang for the men who built and maintained the steam locomotives which criss-crossed the West.

WHISKEY + BEER

BROWN'S SALOON catered to the needs of the beaver-hunting fur trappers that first came through the region.

The **SILVER DOLLAR SALOON** has a bar made up of 2,036 silver dollars.

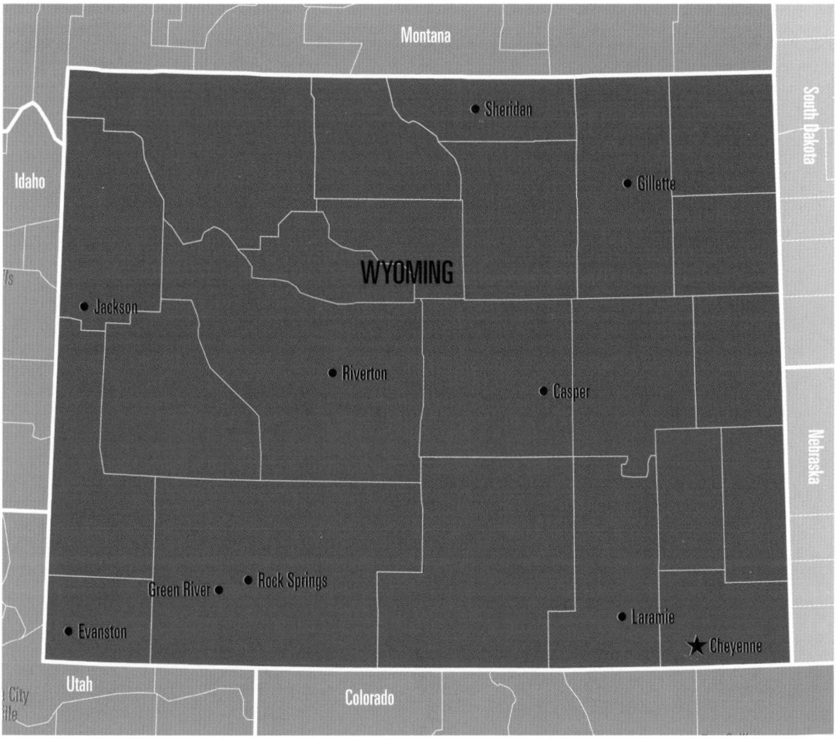

WYOMING

WHAT'LL IT BE?

In Wyoming, a business with a full retail license can sell beer, wine, and liquor for on- and off-premise consumption between 6:00 a.m. and 2:00 a.m. seven days a week. Full retail licenses are not issued to grocery stores, convenience stores, or pharmacies: only liquor stores, bars, and restaurants can sell alcohol. The number of full retail liquor licenses issued in a given area is determined by population. There are also limits on the number of bar and grill licenses, and in some cases, restaurant licenses, so not all establishments will serve alcohol.

Wyoming does allow for local variation. Some municipalities have chosen to restrict Sunday sales.

QUICK REFERENCE

WHAT YOU CAN DO

- Buy package beer, wine, and liquor between 6:00 a.m. and 2:00 a.m. seven days a week from licensed retailers.
- Order a drink in a bar or restaurant between 6:00 a.m. and 2:00 a.m. seven days a week.
- Enjoy happy hour and drink specials.
- Purchase alcohol at a drive-through.
- Bring your own bottle of wine to a restaurant.
- Take an unfinished bottle of wine from dinner home.
- Smoke in bars and restaurants.
- Fill a growler.

WHAT YOU CAN'T DO

- Buy alcohol between 2:00 a.m. and 6:00 a.m.
- Buy beer, wine, or liquor in grocery stores, convenience stores, or pharmacies.
- Smoke in bars and restaurants in Cheyenne, Laramie, or Evanston due to local ordinances.

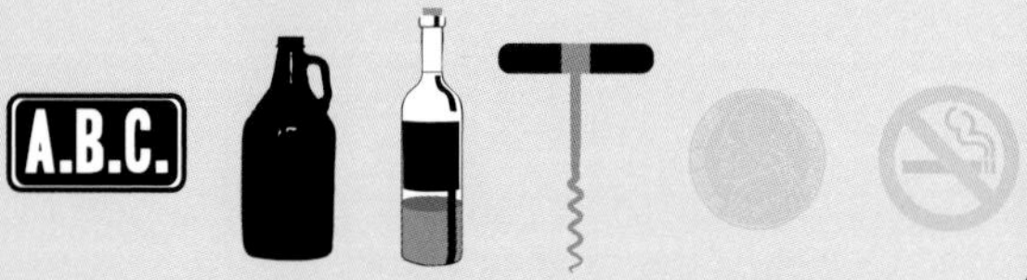

Source: Wyoming Liquor Division

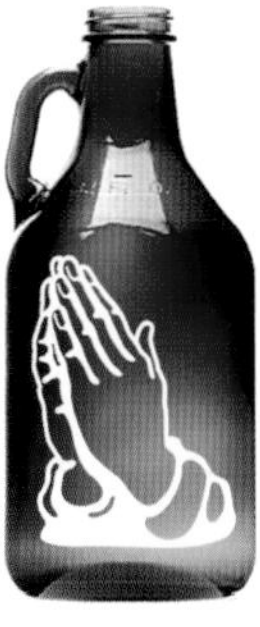

On the first day, **CHARLIE OTTO** gave us growlers.

Until 1942, **THE WONDER BAR AND GRILL** in Casper allowed cowboys to ride their horses right up to the bar and order a round for each of them, then exit through the back alley. Nowadays the horses stay outside.

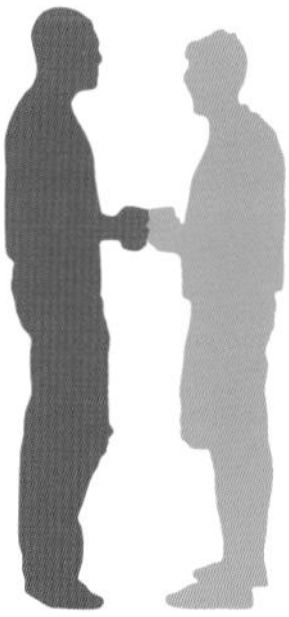

In Wyoming, you can give liquor to your kids. Minors are allowed to drink if their parent or legal guardian is present.

Snake River Brewing hides an **"EASTER KEGG"** each year. The lucky winner who finds it receives a free pint of beer every day for a year.

FYI

Drive-through liquor sales are permitted in Wyoming.

ROCKY RABJOHNS
BREWER/BEER SCIENTIST AT SNAKE RIVER BREWING IN JACKSON HOLE

TIP: "Grab a six-pack of cans or a vodka-grapefruit slushy to-go and head for the river or the mountains! Enjoy libations while rafting, fishing, or in a National Park after an adventure—as long as they aren't in a glass container. Also, while bars can serve until 2:00 a.m., we locals prefer to start early and get to sleep early, so we can be up and ready to play early!"

MONTANA

The Last Best Place

Welcome to Montana! Home of more grizzly bears and beer brewers (per capita) than any other state in the Lower 48!

Lewis and Clark spent more time and traveled more miles exploring the great state of Montana than they did any other. The Corps of Discovery expedition arrived in Montana on the second of June, ending up in the middle of the state at Great Falls nearly two weeks later. The Corps would take nearly a month to portage boats and supplies the eighteen miles around Great Falls. On July 4, 1805, they celebrated the end of this grueling portage, as well as Independence Day, by drinking the remainder of their 120 gallons of alcohol.

Think that was a rager? For many years during the 1970s, Missoula played host to the Aber Day Kegger. Begun in 1972 as a festival of music, mud, and pitcher-sized mugs, the Kegger was an all-you-can-drink western Woodstock. By the time the festival stopped due to pressure from the county and the health department in 1979, the price for a day of music and free beer was just $8 apiece for the 10,000 partiers.

Montana is the fourth-largest state in the union, with a population that is the third least dense. Some roads are so lonely that it's customary to give the two-finger wave to every oncoming vehicle. You may have heard urban-legend-like stories about the free-drinking ways of Montana's highways: the lack of speed limits and a six-pack for a passenger. Sadly, the Wild West days of Montana are technically over. The maximum speed limit in the state is seventy-five. And though you might not be pulled over for a road soda, there is now a $100 fine if you're caught making Coors your co-pilot, even if you do manage to score a perfect ten in the roadside Olympics.

Fortunately, there are still saloons in Big Sky Country. If you want to drink like a local, you can order a red beer (beer with tomato juice), or a Caesar (a Bloody Mary with Clamato). If you like your whiskey with water, order it "ditch," as in, "I'll have a Jack ditch." Take the bartender's warning if he calls you "high centered," because he's about to shut you off.

Montana's reputation as the Wild West's last stand against DRINKING AND DRIVING was the result of a saloon-era attitude towards drinking, a Libertarian streak that rejected government regulation and law enforcement, and a sense that in the middle of nowhere you could simply do things that you couldn't in other parts of the country. Over the years, judges, lawmakers, and even Miss Montana have all been issued DUIs. That "wide-open" culture is slowly changing; open containers are no longer allowed and multiple DUIs are no longer tolerated the way they once were.

LEWIS AND CLARK'S Corps of Discovery had such a grueling portage around Great Falls that when they were finished they celebrated by drinking the remainder of their 120 gallons of alcohol.

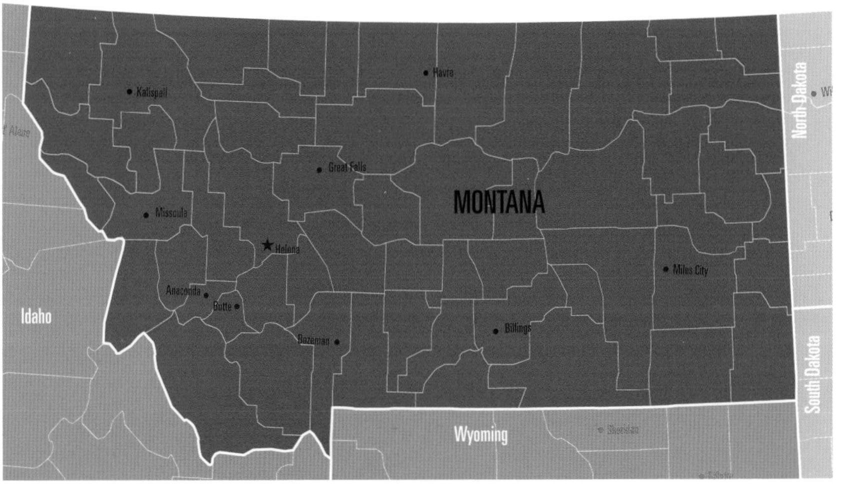

MONTANA

WHAT'LL IT BE?

Montana regulates the sale of beverages over 16% ABV. Package liquor and wine over 16% ABV (such as port, sherry, and other fortified wines) are available from the 96 state-run liquor stores throughout the state. These stores are required to be open at least six hours a day Tuesday through Saturday, but are closed on Sundays, Mondays in some locations, and federal holidays. Beer and wine that are 16% ABV and under are available from licensed grocery stores, convenience stores, and pharmacies. Alcohol is available for on-premise purchase between 8:00 a.m. and 2:00 a.m. seven days a week. There is a mandatory one-day jail sentence for DUI violations.

Montana does not allow for a local option. Laws relating to alcohol are consistent statewide. Local agency liquor stores in a market area may petition to open on Mondays, but this is subject to state rather than local approval.

QUICK REFERENCE

WHAT YOU CAN DO

- Purchase package liquor and wine over 16% ABV from state-run liquor stores between 8:30 a.m. and 2:00 a.m. Tuesday through Saturday. State-run liquor stores are open Mondays in some locations.
- Order a drink at a bar or restaurant between 8:00 a.m. and 2:00 a.m. seven days a week.
- Enjoy happy hour specials.
- Bring your own bottle of wine to a restaurant.
- Fill a growler at a brewery, grocery store, bar, or restaurant.

WHAT YOU CAN'T DO

- Order more than three pints of beer per day in a single brewpub.
- Smoke in bars and restaurants. Montana has a statewide smoking ban for all enclosed spaces.
- Purchase package liquor and wine between 2:00 a.m. and 8:30 a.m. or on Sundays, federal holidays, and Mondays in some locations.
- Order a drink at a bar or restaurant between 2:00 a.m. and 8:00 a.m.

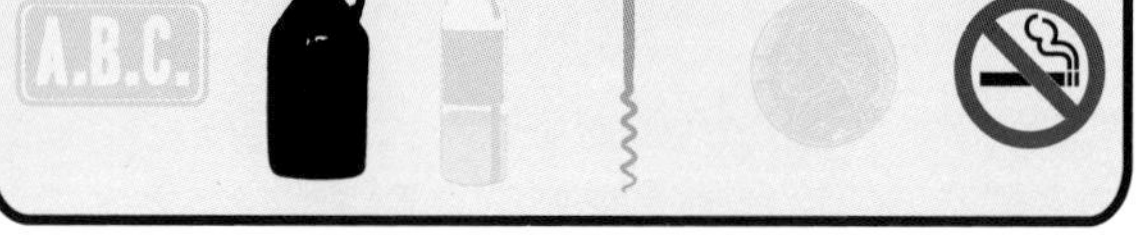

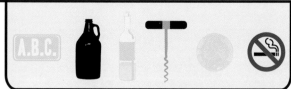

Source: Montana Department of Revenue, Liquor Control

An abundance of wheat combined with isolated homesteads turned many Montana women into bootleggers during Prohibition, opening "home speaks" and roadhouses to supplement their family income. The most famous of them all was **JOSEPHINE DOODY**, the Bootleg Lady of Glacier Park. Men working the Great Northern Railway would toot the train's whistle to indicate how many gallons of moonshine they needed, which she would then deliver by boat across the Middle Fork of the Flathead River.

Despite a growing craft beer industry, Montana law keeps microbreweries in check. The amount of beer they can brew (10,000 barrels annually) is exceptionally low compared to national averages, and brewery taprooms **CAN ONLY SERVE 48 OUNCES OF BEER**, or three pints, per person per day between the hours of 10:00 a.m. and 8:00 p.m. For consumers, this means simply less locally-brewed beer.

Montana has more beers and bears!

PAUL MORUP
SALES AT ÜBERBREW IN BILLINGS

TIP: "Montana is rapidly becoming a state famous for its homemade alcohol. Its largest town, Billings, houses six breweries and two distilleries. Most of our sample rooms are downtown and are within walking distance of each other. So, rent a room, pound the pavement, and don't be surprised if you see children running amidst the pints. Some parts of the Wild West still remain untamed."

IDAHO

Esto Perpetua
(Let It Be Perpetual)

There are at least two things that everyone knows about Idaho: its shape and potatoes. Idaho looks like the teacher's pet, holding an arm skyward as if to say, "Pick ME, Pick ME!" Here's to-day's geography lesson: Idaho is one of the lucky states in America that straddles two time zones. To intelligent imbibers, this means that it's possible to tackle two last calls in two hours. The resort town of Riggins is in MST, but once you cross the bridge over the Salmon River, you're in PST. Travel just twenty minutes north to the town of White Bird to get one for the road. Remember that in Idaho, barflies have thirty minutes after closing time to finish their drinks. And buy your bartender a round while you're at it, because a shift drink for them can occur during service.

Idaho is trout streams and ski slopes. It's also the birthplace of Picabo Street, Napoleon Dynamite, Sacagawea, Deep Throat, and Larry Craig. But the main thing that Idaho is famous for is potatoes. Forget tater tots, think tater shots! Potatoes are just premature vodka, after all. There are bushels of vodka brands in the Gem State, including Glacier Idaho Potato Vodka, 44 North, Revolution, Koenig, Blue Ice, Teton Glacier, and the aspirationally named Uber Tuber.

The Spud State is also home to possibly the nation's first distillery restaurant, Bardenay in Boise ("boy-see" is the local pronunciation). But Idaho is a control state, which means that in order for Bardenay to make cocktails with the spirits it distills, it needs to sell the spirits to the state and then buy them back again. Curiously, "bardenay" was what sailors used to call a cocktail. Perhaps you won't see seamen sipping cocktails in Idaho, but the formula seems to have worked for the restaurant. It now has three locations and produces fine spirits including vodka, gin, and rum.

The words of Ernest Hemingway, who lived out the last years of his life in Ketchum, can help in the search for your own private Idaho: "Always do sober what you said you'd do drunk. That will teach you to keep your mouth shut."

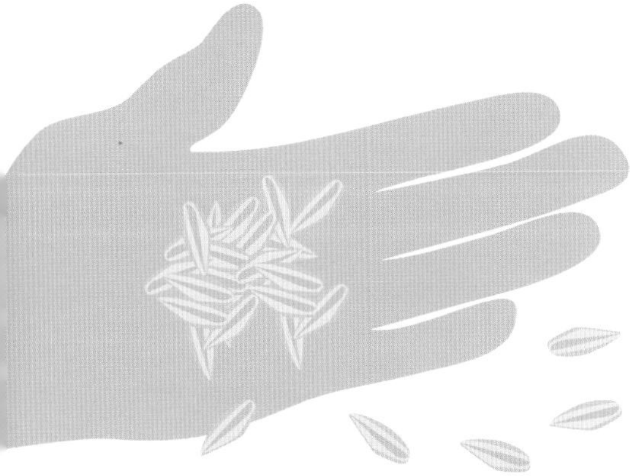

Idaho is the top producer of BARLEY in America. It's primarily grown on irrigated land, making it less weather-dependent, and it's almost always under contract for malt, making it a very stable crop.

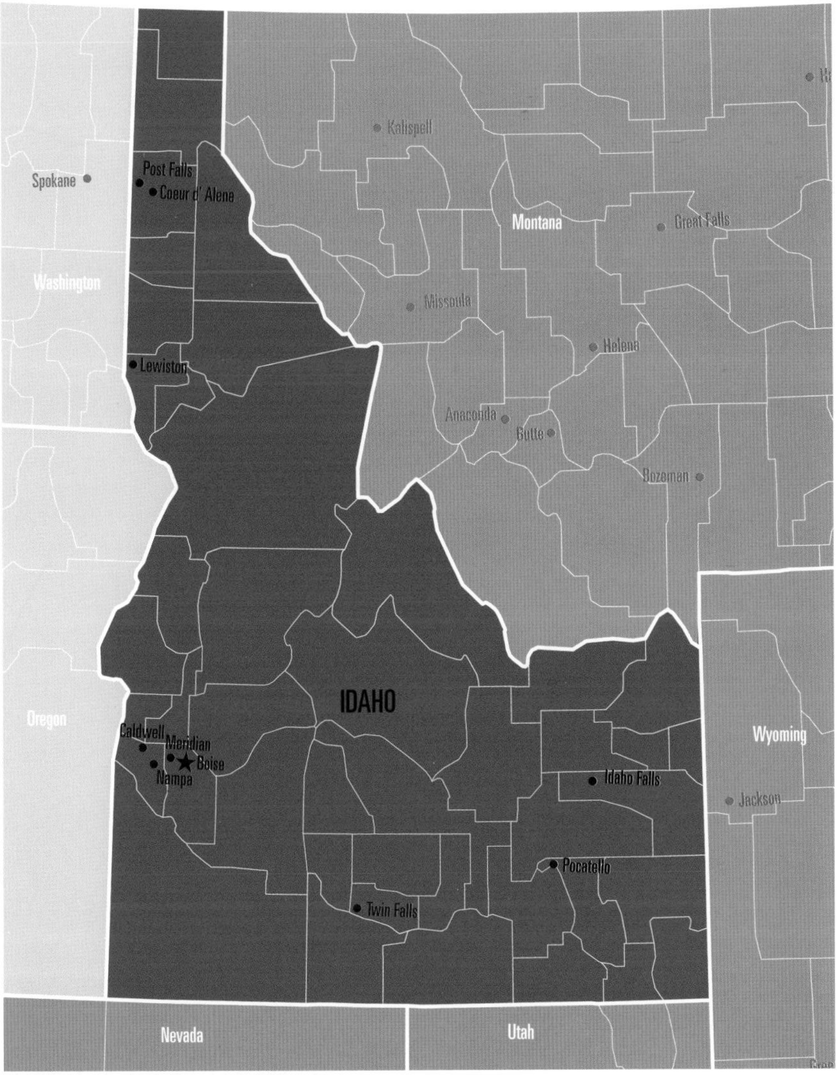

IDAHO

WHAT'LL IT BE?

Idaho is a control state for beverages over 6% ABV, which are available either through the 66 state-run liquor stores or through over 100 contracting retailers, which can include grocery stores and convenience stores. Although the state does not set hours for package sales of liquor, wine, and beer over 6% ABV, both state-run and contracting liquor stores are not generally open before 10:00 a.m. and after 9:00 p.m. Monday through Saturday. Package beer under 6% ABV is widely available in grocery stores, convenience stores, and pharmacies between 6:00 a.m. and 1:00 a.m. On-premise sales are allowed between 10:00 a.m. and 1:00 a.m. Monday through Saturday. Some municipalities may extend these hours to 2:00 a.m.

Idaho state law allows for local variation. Local governments set sale hours and can allow Sunday sales. If a county does choose to allow Sunday sales, Christmas sales are still prohibited, even if Christmas falls on a Sunday.

QUICK REFERENCE

WHAT YOU CAN DO

- Purchase package beer between 6:00 a.m. and 2:00 a.m. seven days a week from grocery stores, convenience stores, and pharmacies
- Purchase package alcohol over 6% at a licensed liquor store.
- Order a drink at a bar between 10:00 a.m. and 1:00 a.m. Monday through Saturday. Some municipalities may extend these hours to 2:00 a.m. or allow Sunday sales.
- Enjoy happy hour drinks and specials.
- Bring your own bottle of wine to a restaurant.
- Fill a growler at a brewery, grocery store, or convenience store, including some gas stations.

WHAT YOU CAN'T DO

- Purchase package wine and liquor on Sundays, Thanksgiving, Christmas, or Memorial Day.
- Smoke in restaurants and some bars, including all bars in Boise.
- Order a drink at a bar or restaurant between 2:00 a.m. and 10:00 a.m.
- Purchase package beer between 2:00 a.m. and 6:00 a.m.

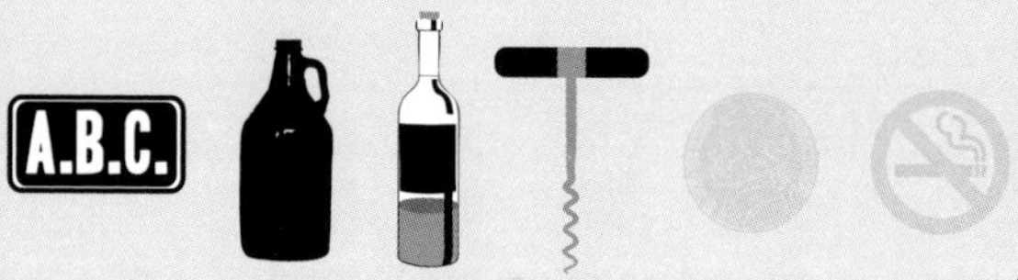

Source: Idaho State Liquor Division

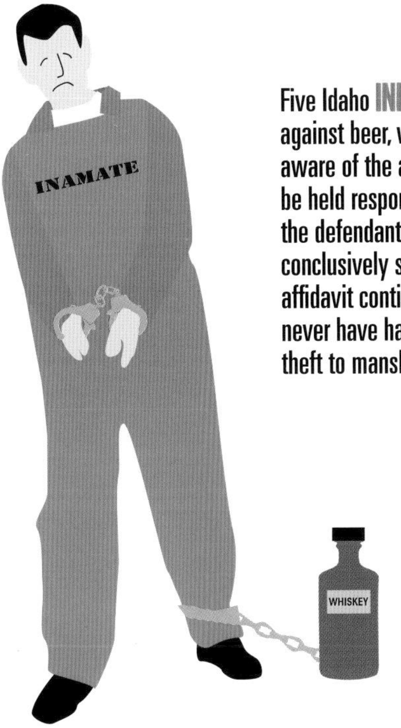

Five Idaho **INMATES** recently filed a billion-dollar lawsuit against beer, wine, and liquor companies claiming they were unaware of the addictive nature of alcohol and that they shouldn't be held responsible for their crimes. One affidavit claimed "if the defendants . . . had a warning label on their products... I can conclusively state that I would not have drank the products." The affidavit continued, "if I was not an alcoholic, the shooting would never have happened." The inmates' crimes range from grand theft to manslaughter.

FYI

Pasteurization, the process of applying heat to kill microbes that cause spoilage, was applied to beer and wine long before it was applied to milk.

In the nineteenth century, Idaho was **BEERVANA** for locally-produced beer. As German immigrants flocked to the gold fields, brewers followed, setting up breweries in remote locations to provide lagers to thirsty miners. But by the 1870s, the invention of pasteurization allowed major breweries like Pabst and Schlitz to ship their products via rail to western markets. Increased competition coupled with Prohibition virtually destroyed the Idaho brewing industry, and by 1960 there was not a single commercially-brewed beer in the state. Today, however, there are nineteen craft breweries in the state and more on the way.

MICHAEL BOWERS
BARTENDER AT THE MODERN IN BOISE

TIP: "Though no bastion of progressive drinking laws, things have improved in Idaho over the last decade. Up until a few years ago, bars couldn't serve liquor on election days until the polls closed, port and sherry couldn't be sold in wine shops, and liquor stores were closed on Sundays. The state run liquor dispensary has a surprisingly well-stocked warehouse, but what's actually on the shelves in smaller town liquor stores can be disappointing."

NEVADA

The Silver State

Nevada earned its nickname after the Comstock Lode, one of America's most significant mining discoveries, was unearthed there in 1859. Thousands of prospectors followed, along with a handful of journalists, including Mark Twain (who started out as a prospector) and the California gold rush chronicler William J. Forbes. The hard-drinking Forbes was barely making ends meet as a newsman, so he threw it all in to open a saloon. "Of twenty men," Forbes said, "nineteen patronize the saloon and one the newspaper. I'm going with the crowd."

That miles-long line of cars and trucks in the desert is for Burning Man, a once-a-year, week-long "city" of 50,000 in Black Rock City. Held over Labor Day, The Burn appears to be a pretty safe place to cut loose. In fact, more people are treated for literal burns at Burning Man than are treated for drug or alcohol problems. This is a festival of self-reliance, and there are no sales or bartering at the Burn, so BYOB and share. Pack in, drink up, and MOOP out!

Reno is great place to visit in December for their Santa Pub Crawl. Purchase a commemorative cup (with the proceeds going to charity) and receive discounted drinks all night long. More than 10,000 participate each year, many of them dressed as Santa, and they all congregate at midnight to sing carols under the Reno Arch, which bears the words "The Biggest Little City in the World."

Despite its reputation of "anything goes," Nevada is far from being the most liberal drinking state in the country. Sure, you can drink 24/7 anywhere in Las Vegas and can carry a cocktail outside on the Strip and on Fremont Street, but the state itself does have a dry town (Panaca, pop. 963), a limit on high-proof alcohol (a maximum of 80%), and was one of the first states to make alcohol vaporizers illegal. You can get married at a drive-through in Las Vegas, but you may not buy alcohol that way.

Three days in Vegas is all the time you'll need to go on a proper bender. Things you'll need: determination, analgesics, energy drinks, and a good pair of sunglasses. The place in Vegas to begin, end, or sustain a bender is the dirty, divey, Double Down Saloon. Their motto is simply "Shut up and drink" and they have no last call (it's open 24/7). And by all means, if you order the AssJuice—an evil pinkish-brown brew with a suspect recipe—be sure to order a chaser and tack on the twenty-dollar Puke Insurance.

There's no shame in admitting that you're a mere mortal when it comes to consuming the quantity of alcohol that a Vegas vacation prompts. There's a high cost to low living. But only in Vegas can you recover like a boss with the ultimate hangover cure from Hangover Heaven. These medical professionals serve up an IV known as a "banana bag," named after the coloring in B vitamins. It's filled with hydrating fluids and vitamins, minerals, and medicines guaranteed to calm the most tenacious morning trembles. In the end, the only way to make sure that what happens in Vegas stays in Vegas is to party until you can't remember.

FLAIR BARTENDING, in which the performance of making a cocktail is as important as the final product, is taught at the Las Vegas Flair Academy. Here some of the "top professional flair bartending performers in the world" show students how to juggle, balance, toss, spin, twirl, bump, pour, and ignite liquor before serving it. Two-day classes are enough to get novices started and advanced classes are available as well.

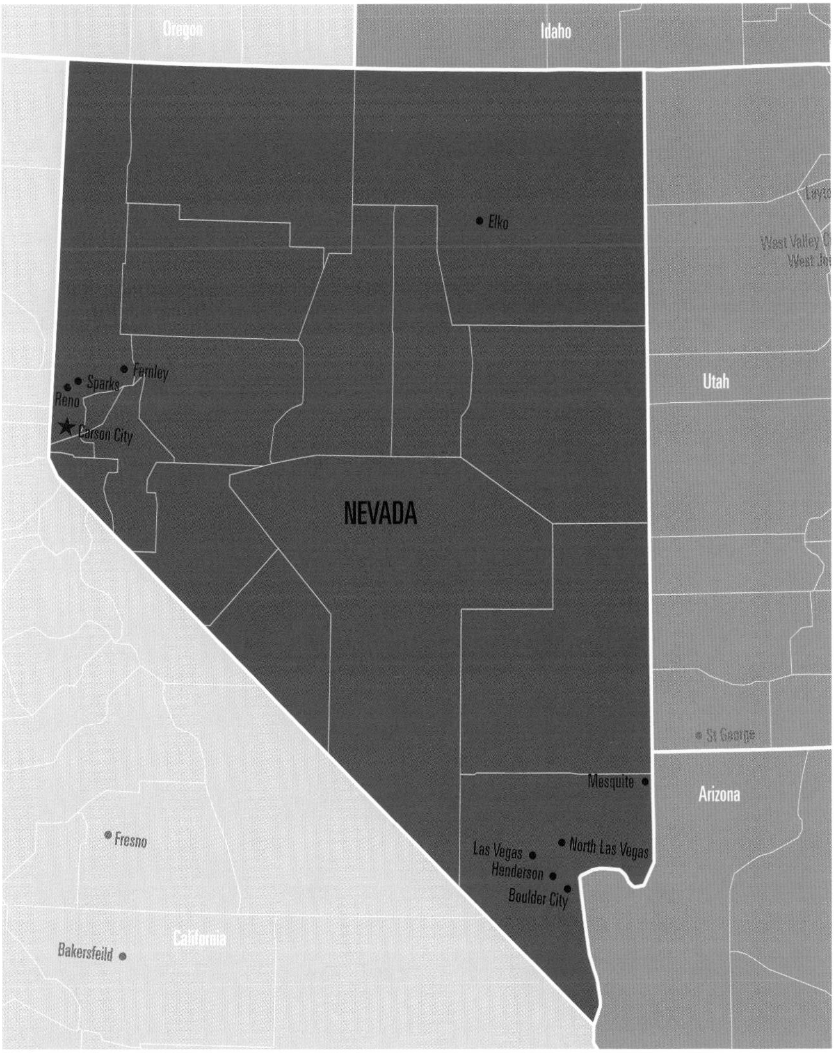

NEVADA

WHAT'LL IT BE?

Beer, wine, and liquor are widely available from a variety of licensed businesses twenty-four hours a day, every day of the year, including holidays. Alcohol is sold in liquor stores, grocery stores, convenience stores, pharmacies, and other businesses. The regulation of alcohol for on- and off-premise consumption is left to each of Nevada's sixteen counties, but they are nearly uniform in their permissiveness.

Nevada does allow for local variation, but counties are prohibited from passing any ordinance that would make drunkenness a public offence. The Mormon community of Panaca in southern Nevada is the only dry town in the state.

QUICK REFERENCE

WHAT YOU CAN DO

- Buy package beer, wine, and liquor in grocery stores, convenience stores, and gas stations, twenty-four hours a day, every day of the year.
- Order a drink in bars and restaurants twenty-four hours a day, every day of the year.
- Enjoy happy hour and drink specials.
- Fill a growler at a brewpub or grocery store.
- Take an open container out on the Vegas Strip.

WHAT YOU CAN'T DO

- Purchase or consume vaporized alcohol.
- Purchase alcohol more than 80% ABV or 160 proof.
- Ride an amusement ride while under the influence of alcohol.
- Use a skateboard park while under the influence.
- Enter a "recreation area" under the influence. These are defined as trailheads and bodies of water.
- Bring your own bottle of wine to a restaurant. State law leaves it to county and municipal governments to decide.
- Take an unfinished bottle of wine from dinner home, but this can vary from county to county.
- Fill a growler at a brewery.

Source: Nevada Alcohol Beverage Control

Before there was Las Vegas, there was **VIRGINIA CITY**. Located about thirty minutes south of present-day Reno, this silver-mining boomtown at the base of the Comstock Lode was Nevada's original Sin City. It boasted one hundred saloons at its peak, one for every thirty-two residents. Mark Twain, who documented the spectacle as a cub reporter, described it as "the 'livest' town, for its age and population, that America had ever produced." Today the city hosts more than two million tourists annually, many visiting the Bucket of Blood Saloon—a local favorite since 1876.

The **PIONEER SALOON**, a half hour south of Vegas in Goodsprings, is one-of-a-kind. Featured in many movies, both its interior and exterior walls are made of stamped tin manufactured by Sears and Roebuck. The building is thought to be one of the last of its kind in the country. The bar itself was made by the Brunswick Company in Maine during the 1860s and still boasts the original brass foot rail. Over the years the saloon has hosted miners, cowboys, and sporting gals, but its most famous patron was Clark Gable, who spent three long days in 1942 waiting at the bar for word of his wife Carol Lombard before learning that she had died in a plane crash.

WENDY VERDEL-HODGES
BARTENDER AT FUSION MIXOLOGY BAR IN THE PALAZZO RESORT IN LAS VEGAS
TIP: "Some things to know about drinking in Las Vegas. Yes, you can drink while walking down the street. Also, at most casino bars with gaming you will receive complimentary cocktails. Just ask your bartender for the rules as they vary from property to property. However, you can't just walk up to the bar and get free drinks. If you are gambling on the floor, it is the cocktail server who will bring you a complimentary cocktail."

CALIFORNIA

Eureka! (I Have Found It!)

Galileo said, "Wine is sunlight, held together by water." It's no wonder then that 90% of the wine produced in America is grown in the Golden State, earning winemakers over $1.5 billion. Napa produces just about 4% of the state's vino, and wine grapes are grown in most of the counties in California. Statewide, wineries draw nearly as many tourists as Disneyland! Check out Paso Robles, the fastest growing wine region in the state, where the film *Sideways* takes place. A stop at the Oxnard Visitor's Center is nicely rewarded at their self-serve Ventura County Wine Trail tasting room. While there, raise a glass and shout "¡Viva la Causa!", toasting Cesar Chavez, who got his start as a farm workers' labor union organizer in Oxnard. The Delano grape field strike and boycott, which he helped organize, lasted five years and ended with a contract for the laborers and Chavez on the cover of *Time*.

Wine not your cup of tea? Craft beer's birthplace is arguably San Francisco's Anchor Brewing, and there are more than 300 other microbreweries to visit along the state's ale trail. Travel north an hour and you'll find yourself on the true left coast of brewing, which means that you're drinking tooth-enamel-melting, hopped-up IPAs. Russian River Brewing's Pliny the Elder IPA ends up on nearly as many "Most Overrated" lists as it does "Best Of" lists. Further south, find Stone Brewing's Arrogant Bastard IPA, which is so hoppy that they don't even disclose the IBUs. Its label plainly says, "You're not worthy." Beer makes up nearly 2% of the GDP of the state. The 709 million gallons of beer that Californians consume can be purchased at any one of 72,000 locations. California Über Alles!

There are dozens of craft distilleries in California, producing every spirit under the sun. The state recently made paid tastings legal—so let the great booze crawl begin! The World Spirits Competition, one of the most well-respected awards in the business, began in the year 2000 in San Francisco, which is no slouch itself when it comes to craft cocktailing. While there, seek out speakeasy Bourbon & Branch; look for the "Anti-Saloon League" sign on the corner of Jones and O'Farrell. Authentic tiki awaits at The Tonga Room and Hurricane Bar in the basement of the Fairmont Hotel. Since 1945, it's been slinging out potent Polynesian potables amidst the thatched tiki tropes of yesteryear, complete with periodic tropical rainstorms. And to take it all in and taste the full bounty of California spirits, beer, wine, and everything else the state has to offer, visit Mohawk Bend in LA, an establishment where every ingredient is locally sourced from California.

When in California, skip the vodka sodas and heed the words of the original California girl, Julia Child, who brought not just French cookery but wine to America's dinner tables. When asked what she attributed her longevity to, she answered with four words to live by: "red meat and gin."

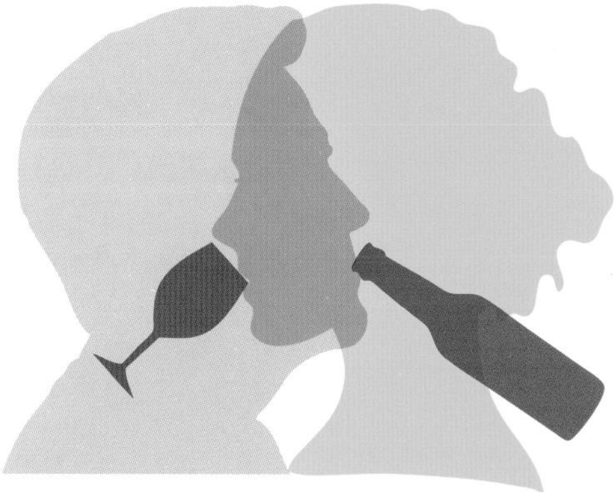

CALIFORNIANS consume over 709 million gallons of beer per year, making it the largest market in the country. Californians also consume the most wine, with almost one in five bottles going down their hatch.

CALIFORNIA

WHAT'LL IT BE?

California liquor licensing is not restrictive. Package liquor, wine, and beer are available for purchase in licensed grocery stores, convenience, stores, pharmacies, and some gas stations. The state allows alcohol sales for on- and off-premise consumption between 6:00 a.m. and 2:00 a.m., every day of the year. Bars and restaurants serving only beer and wine greatly outnumber those with a full bar, because liquor licenses are substantially more expensive than beer and wine licenses. The state also has a thriving wine and craft-beer industry, and tastings are allowed at vineyards, breweries, and distilleries.

California state law allows for local variation, which is usually exercised by limiting retail hours.

QUICK REFERENCE

WHAT YOU CAN DO

- Buy package beer, wine, and liquor at licensed grocery stores, convenience stores, gas stations, and pharmacies between 6:00 a.m. and 2:00 a.m. seven days a week.
- Order a drink in bars and restaurants between 6:00 a.m. and 2:00 a.m. seven days a week.
- Enjoy happy hour specials.
- Get your nickel back from bottle and can deposits.
- Bring your own bottle of wine to a restaurant.
- Fill a growler at a brewery.

WHAT YOU CAN'T DO

- Bring back more than a liter of alcohol duty-free if traveling from Mexico
- Order a pitcher of beer or a bottle of wine if you are dining alone.
- Purchase more than two drinks at a time.
- Smoke in bars and restaurants. California was the first state to implement a smoking ban.
- Buy alcohol for on- or off-premise consumption between 2:00 a.m. and 6:00 a.m.
- Finish a drink in a bar after 2:00 a.m.

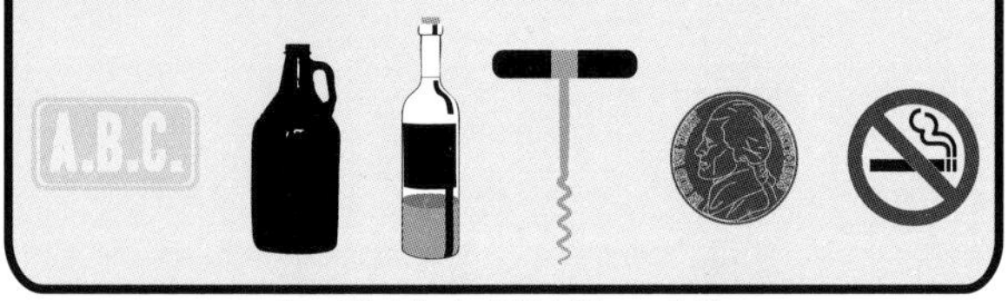

Source: California Department of Alcoholic Beverage Control

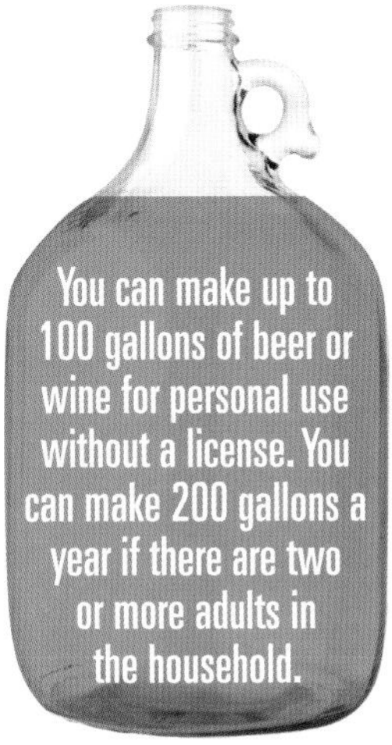
You can make up to 100 gallons of beer or wine for personal use without a license. You can make 200 gallons a year if there are two or more adults in the household.

FYI

If California were a nation, it would be the fourth-largest wine-producing country in the world, behind France, Italy, and Spain.

SAN FRANCISCO
WORLD
SPIRITS
COMPETITION
DOUBLE
GOLD

THE WORLD SPIRITS COMPETITION, one of the most well-respected awards in the business, began in San Francisco.

ERNEST AND JULIO GALLO'S first business venture was shipping grapes back East for people to try their hand at home winemaking. A loophole in the Volstead Act allowed Americans to make small amounts of wine at home during Prohibition. In 1933, when Prohibition was repealed, the brothers began making wine themselves. They never claimed to be experts; everything they knew, they said, came from a winemaking pamphlet they found in the basement of the Modesto Public Library. In a classic American success story, they went on to found what would become the largest family-owned winery in the world and also the largest exporter of California wines. Today, about two-thirds of the wine sold in the US comes from California. The Gallo brand now includes such illustrious labels as Andre, the number one selling sparkling wine in the country, and convenience store stalwart Boone's Farm.

FARRON GONZALES
BARTENDER AT THE ARGYLE HOLLYWOOD IN HOLLYWOOD

TIP: "To drink without breaking the bank, pay attention to the sandwich boards out front of the bars where they display the specials. The terms "happy hour" and "free" are illegal in California regarding the sale of alcohol. But sometimes we offer "buy one, get one" deals, either for free or for a penny, dollar, or coin. There are underground after-hour establishments, but I don't recommend going as they get raided by law enforcement regularly."

OREGON

Alis Volat Propriis
(She Flies with Her Own Wings)

From the snowy peaks of Mount Hood to the crystal blue depths of Crater Lake to the long and craggy Oregon coast, you might have a picture of what Oregon is like before you even visit. You might think of rain and doughnuts, of bikes and food carts, of books and beer. But whatever you think of Oregon, you probably already know that things are different there.

There's a certain sense of deliberate independence in Oregon, which breeds a DIY culture. As a result, a veritable feast of drinking awaits the ambitious imbiber. Meaderies have sprung from backyard hives, and cideries from garages. There is winemaking in the Willamette Valley, a sake maker in the suburbs, and big-time beer brewing in both Bend and the track town of Eugene. Distilleries have opened all over the state, with the core congregating in Portland's inner east side. You've arrived in Oregon, here's hoping you've come thirsty.

Though the Oregon state flower is the Oregon Grape, it may be known best for its Pinot Noir variety. Pinot Noir produces optimal fruit when the grapes slowly struggle to ripen in the Willamette Valley's notoriously fickle weather. That same tenacity is a characteristic of the Willamette region's pioneering winemakers themselves, with the number of wineries growing from just five in the 1960s to more than 400 today. Oregon has some of the strictest appellation of origin laws in the world, so when it says "Willamette Valley" on the label, 100% of the juice comes from that region's grapes.

On the Oregon ale trail, nearly one out of every two pints served in the state is brewed there. There are 137 breweries in the state to whet your whistle, with over 50 in Portland (more than any other city on the planet). It's not known as Beervana for nothing. With dozens of breweries connected by easy-to-use public transportation, Portland makes a great place for car-free brewery crawling. Though every day seems to be a craft beer day here, by state proclamation, July is Oregon craft beer month. In those four short weeks, Oregon craft beer is celebrated around the state, culminating in the Oregon Brewer's Festival, which is held on the last weekend of the month along the grassy banks of the mighty Willamette.

It's the water, the melt off of the snow-capped Mt. Hood, and the drizzly Oregon rains. It's the temperate climate. It's the home-grown hops and grain and grapes. It's all of those indigenous components, plus one that is sometimes imported: the people. Because once you start thinking like a local and drinking like a local, it's not too long before you start making like a local. Some say it's not the place, it's the people. But there comes a time—about the time when you throw away your umbrella and pull up your hood—when the place makes the person. Not everyone can tell you that they are from Oregon, but many can say that they are an Oregonian.

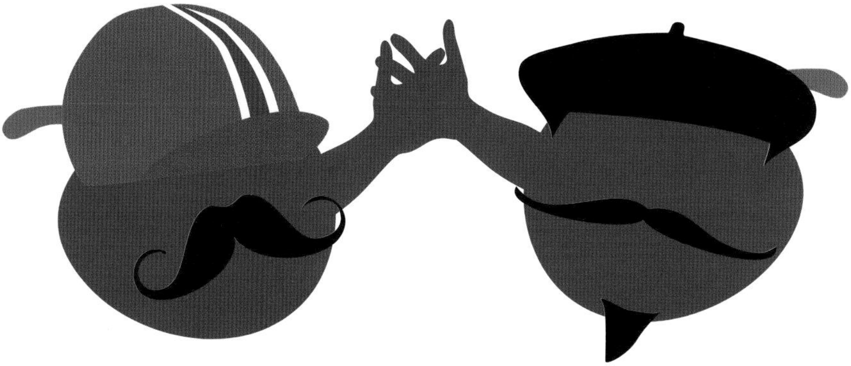

THE WILLAMETTE VALLEY and **BURGUNDY, FRANCE**, lie on the same latitude and have similar climates. This explains why Willamette Valley winemakers also grow the same types of grapes commonly associated with Burgundy: Pinot Gris, Pinot Noir, and Chardonnay.

FYI

In 1971, Oregon enacted the nation's first bottle bill. Oregonians recycle over a billion beverage containers annually.

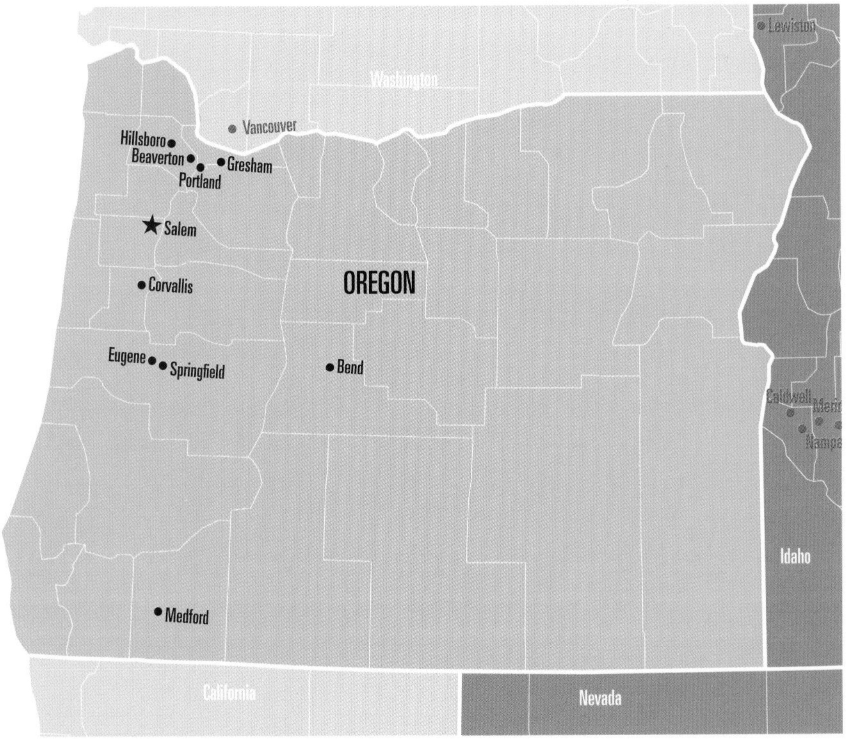

OREGON

WHAT'LL IT BE?

Oregon is a control state for liquor. Liquor stores are privately owned, but they are licensed by the Oregon Liquor Control Commission to act as sales agents on the state's behalf. Oregon does not set hours of operation and allows liquor sales seven days a week, every day of the year. Most stores close by 8:00 p.m., and not all stores choose to open on Sundays. Package beer and wine are readily available in grocery stores, convenience stores, and pharmacies. Oregon does not have a sales tax, which includes alcohol. Alcohol is available for on-premise consumption between 7:00 a.m. and 2:30 a.m. seven days a week, every day of the year. As in California, it is more common to find beer and wine service rather than a full bar at restaurants.

Oregon does not allow for a local option. Laws relating to alcohol are consistent statewide.

QUICK REFERENCE

WHAT YOU CAN DO

- Buy beer, wine, and liquor seven days a week, every day of the year, depending on retailer hours.
- Buy package beer and wine in grocery stores, convenience stores, and pharmacies.
- Buy package liquor only in state-authorized liquor stores.
- Order a drink at bars, restaurants, and even food carts between 7:00 a.m. and 2:30 a.m. seven days a week.
- Bring your own bottle of wine to a restaurant.
- Take an unfinished bottle of wine from dinner home.
- Fill a growler with beer or wine.
- Get your nickel back from bottle and can deposits.
- Enjoy happy hour and drink specials.

WHAT YOU CAN'T DO

- Buy package alcohol after 2:30 a.m.
- Buy package liquor anywhere other than a state-licensed liquor store.
- Order a drink in a bar or restaurant after 2:30 a.m.
- Smoke in bars and restaurants.
- Use a beer bong in a bar.
- Pour alcohol directly into someone's mouth.
- Play games meant to encourage drinking, such as Beer Pong, in a bar.
- Get a payday loan in a bar.
- Waterski or surf while drunk.

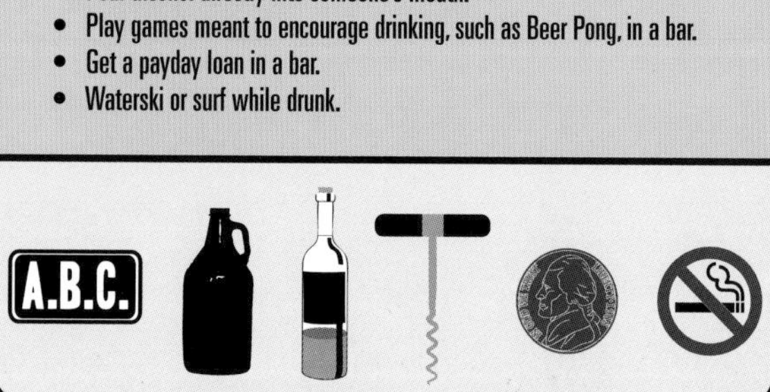

Source: Oregon Liquor Control Commission

If the seeds of the craft beer movement were sown in Oregon soil, then they were certainly watered regularly at **PORTLAND'S HORSE BRASS TAVERN** by legendary publican **DON YOUNGER.** In the early 1980s many of Portland's first craft brewers met at the Horse Brass to let their ideas ferment. Younger's steady encouragement of Oregon brewers allowed him to found Oregon Craft Beer Month, held annually in July. At last count, the total economic impact of the beer industry in Oregon was $2.83 billion and employed 29,000 people. Cheers, Don!

Any place that serves beer, wine, or cider on tap can sell it to go. **GROWLERS** can be filled in taprooms and bottle shops, and even grocery stores, convenience stores, and liquor stores have begun to offer draft beer in bulk. Oregon's craft beer culture benefits because breweries can offer unique varieties on tap and not be burdened with the expense of bottling. Consumers benefit because they can enjoy more varieties of craft beer at home.

Full bars in Oregon must offer at least **FIVE DIFFERENT MEALS** to their patrons after 5:00 p.m. Three of the five meals must be entrees prepared or cooked on the premises beyond reheating pre-cooked frozen food. Bars must also provide seating for at least thirty diners. Counter seats and bar stools don't count.

BRANDON WISE
BARTENDER AT IMPERIAL IN PORTLAND

TIP: "In Oregon, an establishment must offer a substantial food menu to serve booze. Naturally, this has given way to an overwhelming number of fantastic restaurant bars and dive bars serving top-notch cuisine. It's hard to go wrong in a state that has emphasized the importance of a balanced approach to food and drink so much as to have it written into law."

WASHINGTON

Al-ki
(Chinook for "Hope for the Future")

Often beset by rains of biblical proportions, Washingtonians brighten their days with a liberal application of liquid sunshine. Everyone knows "It's the Water" that makes Washington's legendary Olympia beer so delicious. And iconic Rainier beer, brewed since 1884, was so well known for its "Mountain Fresh Taste" that many people believed an urban legend that the snowy peak visible from Seattle was named after the beer. Both brands are now owned by Pabst. The Evergreen State is the largest hop producer in the nation, and beer options abound for the noble northwesterner. In Seattle, seek out uber craft bar Brouwer's, the 160-tap Taphouse Grill, and the Pine Box (housed, fittingly, in the former chapel of a mortuary).

Where to go for wine in Washington? No state other than California produces more. You'll find a wide range of varieties in the state, with fantastic vintages coming from the Columbia Valley and Walla Walla in Central Washington, with more than half of the state's output coming from the Yakima Valley. The Yakima Valley is also the source of 75% of the nation's hop acreage and produces 77% of the nation's hop crop.

In the time since Washington voted to eliminate the three-tier liquor system (producer, distributor, retailer) in 2011, it has been viewed as somewhat of a test case for privatization by the country's other control states. Alcohol is available in nearly ten times as many retail outlets as it was before privatization. But in an effort not to lose too much revenue from the divestiture, taxes and fees have made most alcohol prices increase. This liquor sticker shock isn't evident until the consumer gets to the cash register, as the increase comes in added-on taxes, including a whopping 20.5% liquor sales tax (the largest in the country). Booze can often be had at a bargain by crossing the border. There is no sales tax on alcohol in Oregon, and Idaho alcohol taxes are lower.

Though the weather may drive Washingtonians to drink, it also serves to lubricate the creative class. UW alum Tom Robbins wrote his children's book *B is for Beer* here, Tacoma-born Gary Larson famously drew cows drinking martinis when people weren't watching, and Seattlite Jimi Hendrix wailed against the businessmen who drank his wine. You don't even need the experiments of the Emerald City's own Bill Nye the Science Guy to prove these words are true: "Technically, alcohol IS a solution."

Washington is the top producer of apples in the country, contributing 42% of the nation's total crop. **CIDER** continues to be one of the fastest-growing segments of the beverage market and six states now celebrate National Cider Week: Washington, Oregon, California, Michigan, New York, and Virginia. In 2014, twenty-seven cideries from the region competed in the Pacific Northwest Cidery Awards.

In 1963, Seattleite Jim Whittaker became the first American to reach the summit of Mt. Everest, and with him was a supply of **RAINIER BEER**. Rainier was one of the expedition's sponsors.

FYI

Washington allows self-service beer taps and self-service wine dispensers.

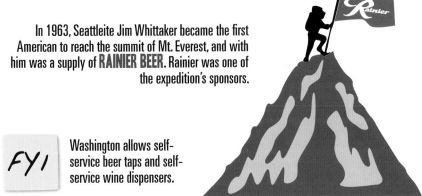

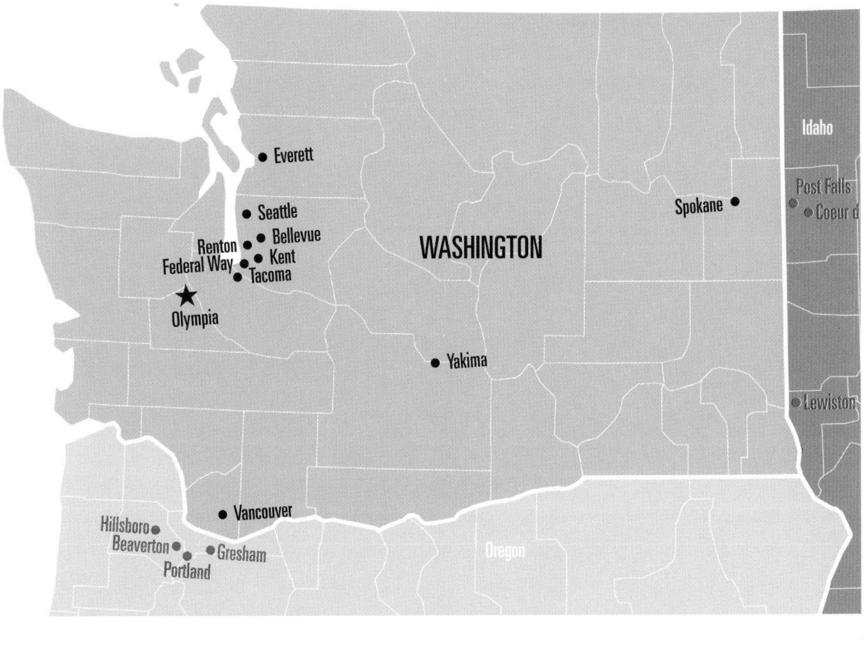

WASHINGTON

WHAT'LL IT BE?

Washington liquor licensing is not restrictive. Package beer, wine, and liquor are available for purchase between 6:00 a.m. and 2:00 a.m. at licensed grocery stores, convenience stores, and pharmacies, much like in California. Hours for on-premise purchases are the same, but all drinks must be consumed while seated. Alcohol is available for purchase every day of the year.

Although Washington state law does allow for local variation, it seldom occurs.

QUICK REFERENCE

WHAT YOU CAN DO

- Buy package beer, wine, and liquor at licensed grocery stores, convenience stores, and pharmacies between 6:00 a.m. and 2:00 a.m. seven days a week.
- Order a drink in bars and restaurants between 6:00 a.m. and 2:00 a.m. seven days a week.
- Enjoy happy hour specials.
- Bring your own bottle of wine to a restaurant.
- Fill a growler with beer or cider, generally at bottle shops, but also at some breweries and grocery stores.

WHAT YOU CAN'T DO

- Smoke in bars and restaurants. Washington has a statewide smoking ban for workplaces.
- Buy alcohol between 2:00 a.m. and 6:00 a.m.
- Purchase wine in growlers.
- Purchase beer at a farmers market.
- Buy people drinks or give away booze on Election Day if you are the candidate.

Source: Washington State Liquor Control Board

Washington's Yakima Valley contains about 75% of the nation's total HOP acreage and produces 77% of the nation's hop crop. The desert-like conditions coupled with abundant irrigation create an ideal environment for growing hops. The Yakima Valley is one of the most important hop-growing regions in the world, producing such aromatic varieties as Cascade, Willamette, and Mount Hood, as well as alpha varieties like Columbus, Tomahawk, and Zeus.

FYI

Hops are a traditional remedy for insomnia, because they possess natural sedative and muscle-relaxing qualities. Sleep pillows are made by stuffing them with hops.

When Washington voters made the recreational use of MARIJUANA legal in 2012, the Washington State Liquor Control Board became the regulatory agency. The WSLCB is responsible for issuing producer, processor, and retailer licenses; collecting excise taxes; establishing rules and procedures for labeling marijuana and marijuana-infused products; and determining the number of retail outlets. Despite privatizing liquor sales in 2011 and no longer controlling the sale of spirits, changing the name of the Washington State Liquor Control Board is described by the agency as being a "low priority."

ANDY MCCLELLAN
BAR MANAGER AT WESTWARD IN SEATTLE

TIP: "Seattle, Washington, is a mecca for locally-made booze. With so many breweries, distilleries and wineries in the greater Seattle area, you could literally drink your way around every neighborhood in the city. Drinking locally is what makes Seattle and the Pacific Northwest one of the best imbibing destinations in the country."

ALASKA

North to the Future

The fact about drinking seems to be this: nature provided one fruit. . . the grape, whose juice made a pleasant, healthful beverage, exhilarating when used in excess. . .
—William Henry Seward

Secretary of State William Henry Seward was an oenophile and, as fate would have it, an Arctic-phile to boot. Seward was so dedicated to the idea of expanding America into Alaska that he lobbied Congress exhaustively for the purchase of the region. Over a series of wine-soaked diplomacy dinners with key members of Congress (which would lay waste to Seward's cellar) he proved successful. Alaska was admitted to the Union in 1867.

Dropping anchor down in Anchorage? It's the home of a watering hole called Seward's Folly (the state's old nickname), as well as Chilkoot Charlie's. 'Koot's started out as a small timber building with sawdust floors and is now an Anchorage drinking institution. It has expanded over the years to ten bars (eleven in the summer).

In the land of the midnight sun, the very north of Alaska, the sun rises in June and doesn't set for ninety days. But if you're interested in viewing the Northern Lights, time your visit to occur near the equinoxes or during dark nights. Outside of Fairbanks, the Chena Hot Springs Resort is a good vantage point for viewing the aurora borealis. As an added bonus, the nation's only year-round ice museum, the Aurora Ice Museum, is located nearby—which is worth mentioning because, hello, ICE BAR.

Alaska's state capital was originally named by (and after) Richard Harris, one of two prospectors who founded the town around a gold mine. His prospecting partner was the jealous Joe Juneau, who reportedly persuaded the rest of the miners to name the town after him by buying them drinks all night long. The joint where this supposedly took place still stands, the over 100-year-old Red Dog Saloon. Ring the large bell at the Red Dog if you want to buy the house a round. Sadly, it no longer comes with naming rights. Juneau's Alaskan Brewing built its business on an old recipe last brewed during the Yukon Gold Rush, which they simply named Alaskan Amber. Alaskan was opened in 1986, the first brewery to open in Juneau after Prohibition. Juneau is so very remote that everything that goes into making their beer, except for water, is transported by boat or by plane. They produce about 11,000 gallons of beer a day.

Here are some tips to keep you from looking like a "cheechako" (greenhorn): when it comes to alcohol in Alaska, the more densely populated an area, the more liberal its drinking laws. Some rural communities and reservations have outlawed even the possession of alcohol. Remember, one for each hand: you will not be served more than two drinks at a time in Alaska. In many regions, showing proof of age is mandatory. A first drunk driving offense is a guaranteed three days in jail. Finally, it is illegal to wake bears for photographic purposes, and when in Fairbanks, please don't feed the moose beer.

As rural villages attempt to combat the damages of alcoholism, life in Alaska's bush is not much different that it was during Prohibition. Local option laws allow concerned citizens to prohibit or limit the sale, importation, and possession of alcohol. **BOOTLEGGERS** make large profits and risk serious penalties by smuggling alcohol into dry or damp communities. On the resulting black market, alcohol sells for up to fifteen times its price in a wet community, with all of the money going into an underground economy.

PLEASE DON'T FEED THE MOOSE BEER!

ALASKA

WHAT'LL IT BE?

Alcohol laws in Alaska are strict. Liquor licenses are issued based on population quotas, so most communities outside of Anchorage, Fairbanks, and Juneau have limited availability both for on- and off-premise purchases. Package beer, wine, and liquor can be sold between 8:00 a.m. and 5:00 a.m. the following day, seven days a week, although most stores close earlier. Licensed liquor stores are not permitted to sell groceries, but mixers, juices, and snacks are available. On-premise sales at bars and restaurants are allowed during those same hours. Alcohol is not for sale on Election Day until after the polls close, although cities may choose to remain exempt from this law. There is a mandatory three-day jail sentence for DUI violations.

Alaska's local option allows communities to control and limit the availability of alcohol. As a rule, the most populated areas and those accessible by road are wet. In the bush, villages can either be "dry" or "damp." Damp communities limit the amount of alcohol carried into the community. The state enforces limits on alcohol purchased by mail from package stores. Luggage can be inspected when you enter a damp community. Bootlegging is a serious offense in Alaska and should not be treated lightly. Travelers headed into the bush should refer to the local ordinances. Currently, there are thirty-four communities that ban the sale, importation, and possession of alcohol; forty-three that ban the sale and importation of alcohol; and nineteen that ban only the sale of alcohol.

QUICK REFERENCE

WHAT YOU CAN DO

- Buy package beer, wine, and liquor at a licensed liquor store between 8:00 a.m. and 5:00 a.m. the following day, seven days a week.
- Order a drink in bars and restaurants between 8:00 a.m. and 5:00 a.m. the following day, seven days a week.
- Bring your own bottle of wine to a restaurant that has a wine license.
- Fill a growler.

WHAT YOU CAN'T DO

- Buy alcohol between 5:00 a.m. and 8:00 a.m.
- Play drinking games in a bar or win alcohol as a prize.
- Buy alcohol in powdered form.
- Be drunk in a bar.

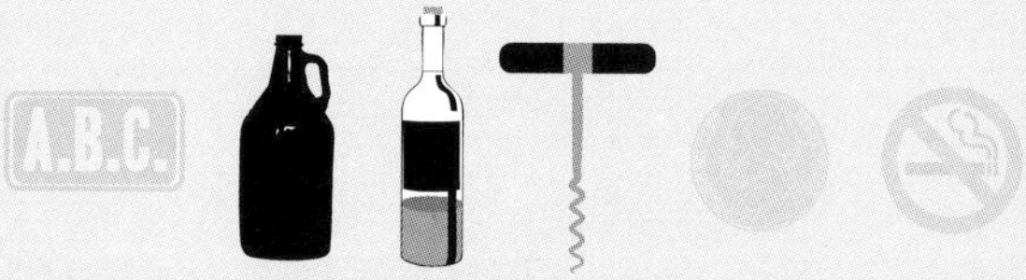

Source: Alaska Alcoholic Beverage Control Board

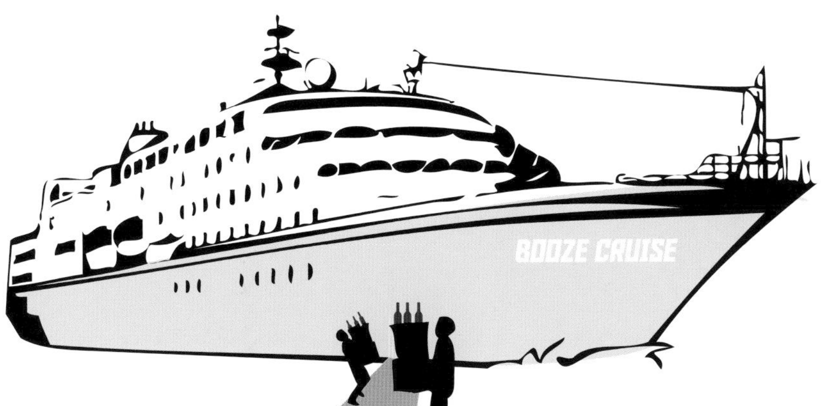

CRUISE LINES have their own regulations regarding on-shore purchases of alcohol and what is allowed to come back on to the boat. As these vary between independent businesses, it's best to inquire what their policy is.

The world's largest ice bar was unveiled at the 2011 BP WORLD ICE ART CHAMPIONSHIP in Fairbanks. It was 209 feet long and featured a towering ice luge at the center. An ice luge is an ice sculpture with a narrow channel for liquor to be poured down and into a waiting glass or mouth.

Alaska has the highest ratio of males to females in the United States. Look for (or watch out for) LADIES NIGHTS in the bars.

GEOFF LARSON
CO-FOUNDER, ALASKAN BREWING CO. IN JUNEAU

TIP: "We wanted to tie our brewery to Juneau's rich brewing heritage that existed before Prohibition. Our Amber Ale is an interpretation of a 1907 recipe discovered in local historical documents, and our Alaskan Smoked Porter uses smoky malts also used at the time. We want people to taste Alaska when they taste our beer - and that's not just in the glacier-fed water, but the history and adventures of the people who live and brew here."

Ua Mau ke Ea o ka ʻĀina i ka Pono

(The Life of the Land is Perpetuated in Righteousness)

HAWAII

Hanging loose in Hawaii? The island gods are smiling down on you, my friend, because drinking in this state is as laid back as its people.

When the Hawaiian Islands were discovered by Captain Cook, the natives drank only three things: water, coconut milk, and an intoxicating brew called "awa" or "kava." Kava was used for many things: in rituals, as medicine, and to relax and calm the nerves.

It may have been that spacey island feeling that legendary entrepreneur Don the Beachcomber tried to capture when he created tiki culture in mainland, USA. He was not as lucky in love as he was in libations, and lost ownership of his namesake establishments in a divorce, but stayed on as a consultant. The Beachcomber then set sail for the white sands of Waikiki, bringing his Chichis and Mai Tais to the Islands where everyone thinks they originated. Tiki bars are not as popular as they once were, but the inquisitive drinker can still go on a sippin' safari. Of the ubiquitous Mai Tai, it's been said, "It takes five minutes to drink and another two hours to get the smile off of your face."

One thing that you might be tempted to do is to drink on the beach. While it is illegal, discrete drinkers abound, tempting fates and fines that go as high as $1,000. If you're afraid of the fines, just head into the bar! You'll find bars on the islands with a "cabaret" license that can serve until 4:00 a.m. Two laws will help you pace yourself: only one drink per person at a time (though a shot is not considered a drink), and pitcher drinks must be shared by at least two people. All bets are off on the water, where all-you-can-drink booze cruises abound. Toast the island gods in Hawaiian by saying "Huli Pau!"

Famous Hawaiians include Duke Kahanamoku, who held the Olympic 100-meter freestyle swimming record for almost twenty years, and Don Ho, who sang the song "Tiny Bubbles" nearly every night of his forty-year career. Interestingly, Duke opened a tiki lounge in Waikiki's International Market Place, which was also home to fellow tiki pioneers Don the Beachcomber's and Trader Vic's back in the '60s. It was at Duke Kahanomoku's, with its slogan "Suck 'em up!" (which made it onto everything from swizzle sticks to Hawaiian shirts), that Don Ho was discovered and brought to national attention. He even recorded a live album at Duke's. The title? "Suck 'em up," of course.

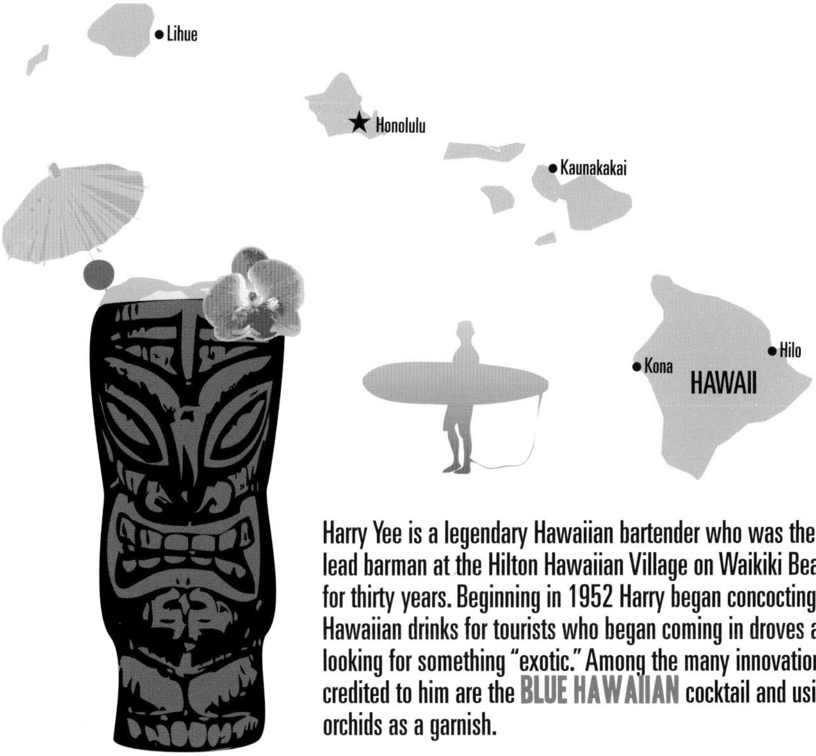

Harry Yee is a legendary Hawaiian bartender who was the lead barman at the Hilton Hawaiian Village on Waikiki Beach for thirty years. Beginning in 1952 Harry began concocting Hawaiian drinks for tourists who began coming in droves and looking for something "exotic." Among the many innovations credited to him are the **BLUE HAWAIIAN** cocktail and using orchids as a garnish.

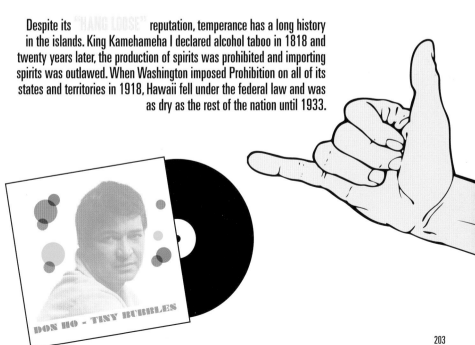

Despite its "HANG LOOSE" reputation, temperance has a long history in the islands. King Kamehameha I declared alcohol taboo in 1818 and twenty years later, the production of spirits was prohibited and importing spirits was outlawed. When Washington imposed Prohibition on all of its states and territories in 1918, Hawaii fell under the federal law and was as dry as the rest of the nation until 1933.

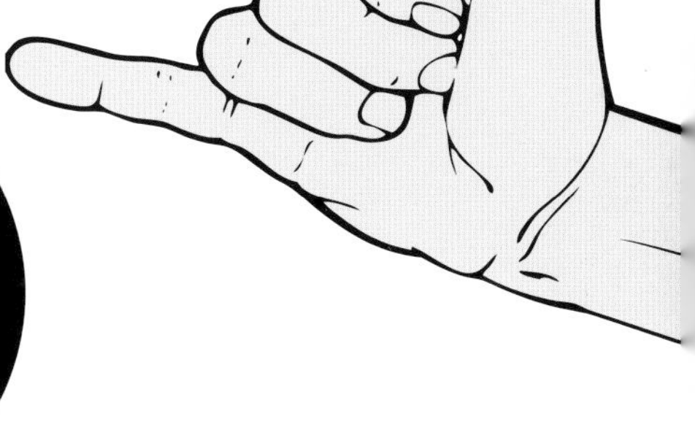

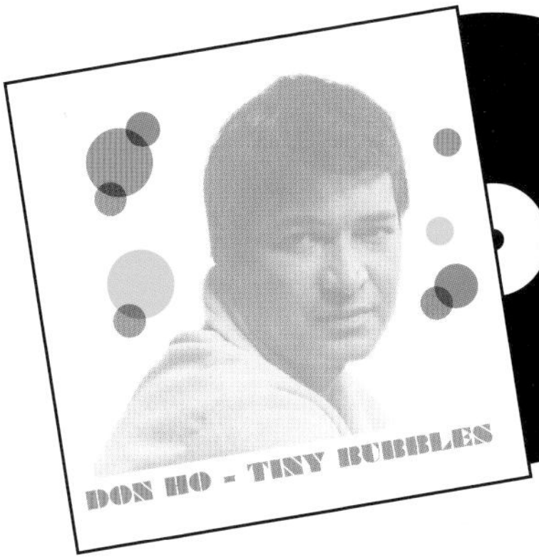

WHAT'LL IT BE?

Hawaii's liquor laws are permissive and tourist-friendly. Bars and restaurants are open until 2:00 a.m., and with a cabaret license, venues can stay open until 4:00 a.m. Package beer, wine, and liquor are available for purchase in grocery stores, convenience stores, and pharmacies until 11:00 p.m. (midnight in Honolulu County) every day of the year. Buyers should expect to be carded for all purchases.

Liquor laws are set by the counties, but there are no significant variations between the counties' laws. Honolulu County allows longer hours for alcohol sales than the other islands.

QUICK REFERENCE

WHAT YOU CAN DO

- Purchase package beer, wine, and liquor between 6:00 a.m. and 11:00 p.m. seven days a week in most grocery stores, convenience stores, and pharmacies, and up to midnight in Honolulu County.
- Order a drink in bars and restaurants between 6:00 a.m. and 2:00 a.m., or until 4:00 a.m. if the establishment has a cabaret license.
- Get your nickel back from bottle and can deposits.
- Enjoy happy hour specials.
- Bring your own bottle of wine to a restaurant.
- Fill your growler at a brewery.

WHAT YOU CAN'T DO

- Smoke in bars and restaurants, including all open-air patios. Hawaii has a statewide smoking ban for workplaces.
- Drink on the beach.
- Order a drink at a bar or restaurant between 2:00 a.m. and 6:00 a.m. (excepting cabarets).
- Purchase package beer, wine, or liquor between 11:00 pm or midnight and 6:00 a.m.

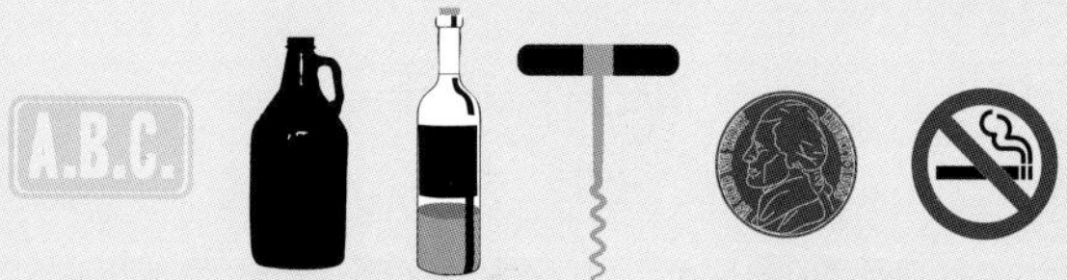

Sources: Hawaii County Department of Liquor Control, Honolulu Liquor Commission, Maui County Department of Liquor Control, Kauai County Department of Liquor Control

Hawaii has two official languages, English and Hawaiian. A third language, Pidgin, is commonly spoken by locals and best not attempted by visitors. Originally, Pidgin was a way for those who spoke many different languages to communicate. Today, Pidgin is a sort of island slang that separates the locals from the tourists.

Below is a list of Hawaiian and Pidgin words that are relevant to your interests, if your interests are drinking.

HAWAIIAN WORDS

'Ae — Yes
'A'ole — No
Kala mai ia'u — Excuse me
Mahalo — Thank you
'A'ole pilikia — You're welcome / No problem
E Komo Mai — Welcome! Enter!
Malihini — Newcomer, visitor
Haole — A foreigner (slang: Caucasian)
Aloha 'auinala — Good afternoon
Aloha ahiahi — Good evening
Aloha 'oe — Farewell to you
'Ono — Delicious or tasty
Pau — Finished, all done
Hana hou — Encore, do it again
Kala — Money
Manuahi — Free
Maika'i — Excellent
Laule'a — Peaceful, happy
Lolo — Feeble minded, numb
Hehena — Raving mad, possessed, lunatic
Maha'oi — Insolent, rude, brazen
Hina — To fall; topple over from an upright position
Inu — Drink
Kini — Aluminum can
Lama pa'ipa'i — Cocktail
Wai — Water
Pupu — Snacks or appetizers

PIDGIN WORDS

Brah — Brother
Broke da mouth — Very delicious
Buckaloose — Break loose; go out of control
Choke — A lot of
Da kine — The most multi-functional word in Pidgin; literally "the kind"
Grind — Eat
Grinds — Food
Lua — Toilet (in Hawaiian lua means 'hole')
Make ass — Make a fool of one's self
Mento — Mental; insane
Mo Betta — Better
Moke — Tough local man
Pakalolo — Marijuana
Pau hana — After work drinks
Shaka — Right on!
Shishi — Urinate
Stink eye — Dirty look
Throw out — Vomit
Tita — Tough local woman

DAVE NEWMAN
OWNER AND BARTENDER AT PINT & JIGGER IN HONOLULU

TIP: "If you really want to experience Hawaii and the local drinking scene you need to ask a local. Make sure to get out of Waikiki because the best spots are away from the tourist areas and there are a few bars that serve until 4:00 a.m. Also, lots of places serve kava, which isn't alcoholic but does have mild sedative and anesthetic qualities. Worth checking out while you are here."

SOURCES

All laws and statutes were verified with the agency of each state that is responsible for alcohol licensing and regulation. The official name of each state's specific division is listed as a source beneath the state's Quick Reference chart. All diligence was made to ensure that what is listed in *The Field Guide to Drinking in America* was accurate and current at the time of press. Corporate histories were verified with the respective company's website. Statistics and rankings were reported by reputable news organizations and attributed to credible sources.

In addition, the following books were helpful in providing reliable histories and sorting fact from fiction, particularly when it comes to a subject as inherently fuzzy as the history of alcohol and drinking in America.

Allured, Janet and Michael S. Martin. *Louisiana Legacies: Readings in the History of the Pelican State.* Chichester, West Sussex, UK: Wiley & Sons, Inc., 2013.

Bauer, Bryce. *Gentleman Bootleggers: The True Story of Templeton Rye, Prohibition, and a Small Town in Cahoots.* Chicago: Chicago Review Press, 2014.

Blue, Anthony Dias. *The Complete Book of Spirits: A Guide to their History, Production, and Enjoyment.* New York: HarperCollins, 2004.

Carson, Gerald. *The Social History of Bourbon.* Lexington: The University Press of Kentucky, 2010.

Chapelle, Francis H. *Wellsprings: A Natural History of Bottled Spring Waters.* Piscataway, NJ: Rutgers University Press, 2005.

Curtis, Wayne. *And a Bottle of Rum: A History of the New World in Ten Cocktails.* New York: Three Rivers Press, 2006.

Davis, Elaine. *Minnesota 13: Stearns County's Wet Wild Prohibition Days.* Elaine Davis Publisher, 2007.

Downey, Christopher Byrd. *Stede Bonnet: Charleston's Gentleman Pirate.* Charleston, SC: The History Press, 2012.

Goins, Charles Robert and Danney Goble. *Historical Atlas of Oklahoma.* Norman, OK: University of Oklahoma Press, 2006.

Grimes, William. *Straight Up or On the Rocks: A Cultural History of American Drink.* New York: Simon & Schuster, 1993.

Haigh, Ted. *Vintage Spirits and Forgotten Cocktails.* Beverly, MA: Quarry Books, 2009.

Ling, Sally. *Run the Rum In: South Florida During Prohibition.* Charleston, South Carolina: The History Press, 2007.

Mishev, Dina. *Wyoming Curiosities.* Guilford, CT: The Globe Pequot Press, 2007.

Mowry, David P. *Listening to the Rumrunners: Radio Intelligence During Prohibition, second edition.* National Security Agency: Center for Cryptologic History, 2014.

Okrent, Daniel. *Last Call: The Rise and Fall of Prohibition.* New York: Scribner, 2010.

Peck, Garrett. *Prohibition in D.C: How Dry We Weren't.* Charleston, SC: The History Press, 2011.

Pollan, Michael. *The Botany of Desire: A Plant's-Eye View of the World.* New York: Random House, 2001.

Raines, Robert K. *Hot Springs: From Capone to Costello.* Charleston, SC: Arcadia Publishing, 2013.

Sakoda, Kent and Jeff Siegel. *Pidgin Grammar: An Introduction to the Creole Language of Hawaii.* Honolulu, HI: Bess Press, 2003.

Salinger, Sharon V. *Taverns and Drinking in Early America.* Baltimore, MD: The Johns Hopkins University Press, 2002.

Slaughter, Thomas P. *The Whiskey Rebellion: Frontier Epilogue to the American Revolution.* New York: Oxford University Press, 1986.

Smith, Gregg. *Beer In America: The Early Years—1587-1840.* Boulder, CO: Brewers Publications, 1998.

Veach, Michael. *Kentucky Bourbon Whiskey: An American Heritage.* Lexington: University Press of Kentucky, 2013.

Wells, Ken. *Travels with Barley: A Journey Through Beer Culture in America.* New York: Free Press, 2004.

Wondrich, David. *Imbibe.* New York: Penguin, 2007.

INDEX

THIS BOOK WOULDN'T BE POSSIBLE WITHOUT THE EFFORTS AND INSPIRATION OF THE FOLLOWING INDIVIDUALS AND ORGANIZATIONS. SALUD!

Rachel Bell, Carol Burgess, Meaghan Corwin, Alan Dubinsky, Cheryl Frey, Jeff Ganong, Cole Gerst, Greg Griffiths, Selena Bell Heise, Ryan Heise, Per Henningsgaard, Lisa Hill, Brenton Salo, Dennis Stovall, Matt Wagner, Amanda Winterroth, Prost! (for providing a photo shoot location), U.S. Bartender's Guild - National Office and Local Chapters, and Ooligan Press.

Photo Credits:
Author Photo - Brenton Salo
Alaska brewer, Jeff Larson pictured with partner March Larson - photo by Alaskan Brewing
Kentucky bartender Jacquelyn Zykan - photo byJesse Hendrix
Idaho bartender Michael Bowers - photo by Guy Hand
Maine distiller Ned Wight - photo by Tim Fisher
Maryland bartender Brendan Dorr - photo by B&O Brasserie
New Jersey bartender Shane Markley - photo by Kristen Kichline
Pennsylvania bartender Tim Kweeder - photo by Chloe Berk
Tennessee bartender Matt Tocco- photo by to Andrea Behrends
Utah distiller Chris Barlow - photo by Erik Ostling
Vermont bartender Jeff Baker - photo by Paul Sarne
Washington D.C bartender Glendon Hartley - photo by Christopher Prosser

NIKI GANONG is a food and drink writer from Portland, Oregon. She is a frequent traveler, contributor to epicurean publications, and beer judge. This is her first book.

Future Editions of

the FIELD GUIDE *to Drinking in* AMERICA

Want to provide feedback, offer interesting historical anecdotes, submit a correction, or share regional drinking customs for a future edition of the book?

Visit thefieldguidetodrinking.com/contact to contribute.

Our goal is to be the best source of information for tippling travelers available.

FIELD NOTES

FIELD NOTES

JUN 24 2016